Silver Burdett & Ginn

SCIENCE

GEORGE G. MALLINSON
Distinguished Professor
of Science Education
Western Michigan University

JACQUELINE B. MALLINSON
Associate Professor of Science
Western Michigan University

CATHERINE VALENTINO
Former Director of Instruction
North Kingstown School Department
North Kingstown, Rhode Island

WILLIAM L. SMALLWOOD
Head, Science Department
The Community School
Sun Valley, Idaho

SILVER BURDETT & GINN
MORRISTOWN, NJ • NEEDHAM, MA
Atlanta, GA • Cincinnati, OH • Dallas, TX • Menlo Park, CA • Northfield, IL

THE SILVER BURDETT & GINN ELEMENTARY SCIENCE PROGRAM

Pupil Books Levels 1–6
Teacher Editions Levels K–6

 ISBN 0-382-14826-6

Silver Burdett & Ginn

SCIENCE

Contents

The Adventure of Science .... A

Unit One
Learning About Our Plant and Animal World

1

CHAPTER 1   Animals That Live Together   2
CHAPTER 2   The World of Plants   24
CHAPTER 3   Food Chains and Food Webs   46
CHAPTER 4   How Living Things Survive   64

Science in Careers   86
People in Science   87
Developing Skills   88

Unit Two
Learning About Matter and Energy

90

CHAPTER 5   Measuring Matter   92
CHAPTER 6   Energy and Machines 112
CHAPTER 7   Heat Energy 132
CHAPTER 8   Electricity and Magnetism 150

Science in Careers 168
People in Science 169
Developing Skills 170

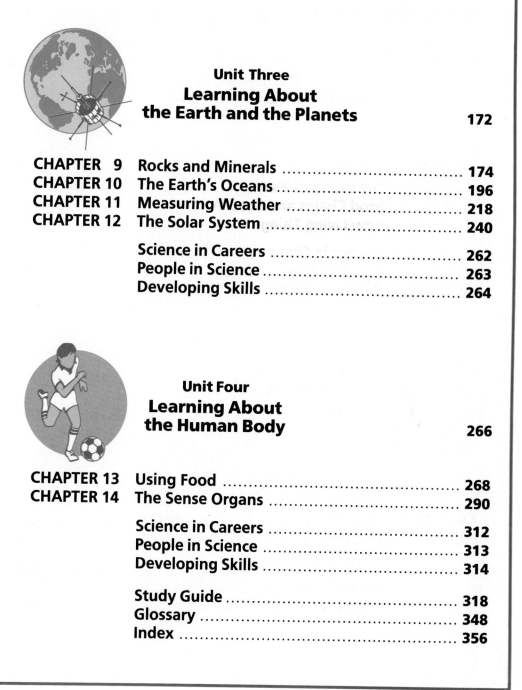

Unit Three
Learning About the Earth and the Planets
172

CHAPTER 9	Rocks and Minerals	174
CHAPTER 10	The Earth's Oceans	196
CHAPTER 11	Measuring Weather	218
CHAPTER 12	The Solar System	240
	Science in Careers	262
	People in Science	263
	Developing Skills	264

Unit Four
Learning About the Human Body
266

CHAPTER 13	Using Food	268
CHAPTER 14	The Sense Organs	290
	Science in Careers	312
	People in Science	313
	Developing Skills	314
	Study Guide	318
	Glossary	348
	Index	356

The Adventure of Science

What Is Science?

Science is a way to ask and to answer questions about the world. It is a way that you can learn more about the world.

Did you ever wonder why rainbows appear in the sky? Scientists know that there are reasons why things like this happen. To find these reasons, scientists make observations. Then they gather information, test their ideas, and draw conclusions.

The science questions you ask may be put into four groups.

1. Questions about living things
2. Questions about matter and energy
3. Questions about the earth and space
4. Questions about your body

There is one group of questions for each area of science. Look at the pictures. Find a picture for each area of science.

Not all questions are science questions. Science questions must be answered with facts. Other questions can be answered by giving an opinion. For example, suppose you were asked to name the most beautiful color in the rainbow. Your answer to this question would be an opinion. There is no way to gather facts about this kind of question. Now look at the pictures again. Ask a science question about each picture.

What Will You Learn in Science?

In science you will learn many things about the world. You will learn to think about things. You will learn to solve problems. You will discover many ways to find the facts that answer science questions. One way is to do an experiment. The students in the picture are doing an experiment. What questions do you think this experiment will answer?

All science questions cannot be answered by doing experiments. Sometimes scientists answer questions by gathering information from many places. Then they study the information and draw conclusions from it. In science you will learn how to gather information and how to draw conclusions from it.

C

How Is Science Important in Your Life?

Why do some birds migrate? What causes hailstones to form? Studying science helps you to answer questions like these. Without science many things that happen around you would be a mystery.

Every day there are many kinds of problems for you to solve. What is an easy way to move a heavy object? How can you stop a bicycle from squeaking? Studying science helps you to solve problems like these.

D

How Can You Solve a Science Mystery?

How do scientists solve problems? Scientists are like detectives who solve mysteries. Scientists begin by making observations. Then they search for information. Scientists always keep an open mind as they search. This means that they listen to the ideas that others have. Scientists continue to work this way until they can solve the problem.

Now you can try to solve a science mystery. Use a cup to make a water detector. To do this, you may change the cup in any way that will help you discover the presence of water. After you leave school, your teacher may or may not put three drops of water into your cup. Your problem will be to determine if water was put into your cup.

Problem Solving in Space

Have you ever wondered what it would be like to live on a space station? What would you eat? How would you sleep? Could you take a shower in space? Thanks to scientists, you may one day find out the answers to these questions. You may live and work on an orbiting space station. You may even travel to the moon or to Mars.

What questions did scientists have to answer before the first astronaut rode a rocket into space? What problems did they have to solve before people could live and work in space?

Scientists have observed astronauts in space. These scientists study body changes. They use instruments that send the information back to Earth. They use television cameras to keep records of each space trip. This information has helped scientists solve problems in space travel.

The first astronauts said that while they were in space, their suits were too tight. Scientists knew that the suits were measured and sewn to fit each astronaut. They also knew that the suits had fit before the flight. What did scientists have to know to solve this problem? What do you think caused the suits to become tight?

Soon astronauts could spend longer periods of time in space. Then scientists had new problems to solve. Living in space for weeks or months is different from orbiting the earth for a few days. What new problems might astronauts have on a longer mission?

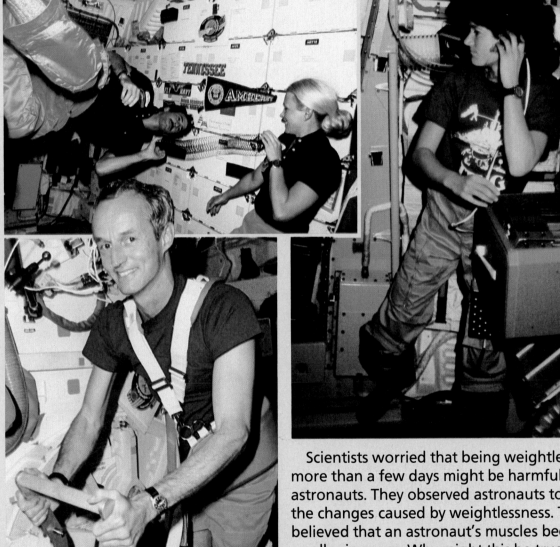

Scientists worried that being weightless for more than a few days might be harmful to astronauts. They observed astronauts to discover the changes caused by weightlessness. They believed that an astronaut's muscles became smaller in space. Why might this be true? How do you think scientists tested this idea? What do you think they did to solve this problem?

Weightlessness caused other problems for astronauts. How could they sleep without bumping into things? How could their food be kept on a plate?

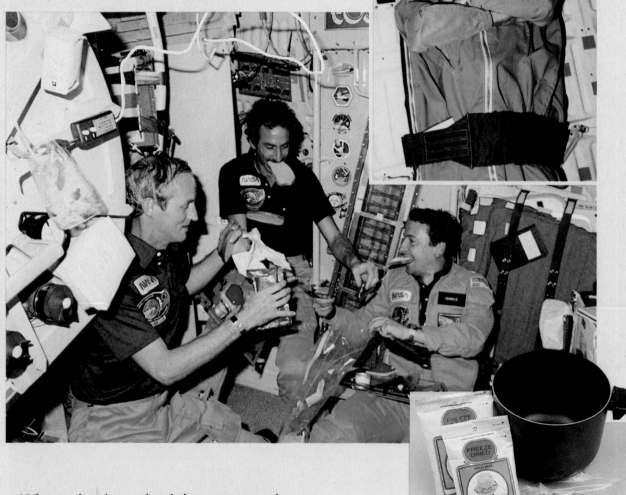

When scientists solved the astronauts' problems in space, they helped everyone. Look at the pictures. Each one shows an object or technology meant for use in space. What problems do you think each one solved for astronauts? How do other people use these things?

When people begin to travel to the moon and the planets there will be new problems to solve. Scientists are already trying to solve some of these problems. The drawing shows a Lunar Pogo Stick. It was designed by two scientists— Howard Seifert and Marshall Kaplan.

The Lunar Pogo Stick can leap about 60 meters high. Then it lands about 300 meters away. It can change direction and lift off again. It uses compressed air for fuel. What problems do you think the Lunar Pogo Stick may solve? What are some of its advantages and disadvantages? Can you think of some other new and better ways to travel on the surface of the moon or planets?

UNIT ONE

Learning About Our Plant and Animal World

Chapter 1–Animals That Live Together   Red kangaroos live in groups called mobs. In this chapter you will learn why other animals live in groups.

Chapter 3–Food Chains and Food Webs   Pelicans are birds that always live close to water. This is because they eat fish. In this chapter you will learn that all animals must have food to give them energy.

Chapter 2–The World of Plants
Did you know that some plants are not green? A bracket fungus is a kind of nongreen plant. Plants like this often live in places that are dark and damp.

Chapter 4–How Living Things Survive Spiders trap insects in webs. In this chapter you will learn what other animals do to get their food.

CHAPTER 1
Animals That Live Together

Splash! A giant animal breaks through the water right next to you. You are on a "whale watch." The whale comes close to the edge of the boat. You can see that the whale is over nine meters long. It turns over on its side. It gently waves its flipper. Then it disappears below the water again.

Soon you spot six or seven other whales nearby. These whales live and travel together in a group. The group is called a herd. Living in a herd helps the whales find food. It also helps to protect them from enemies.

Scientists think that whales use sounds to send messages to others in their group. Some sounds probably help keep the group together. Other sounds help to warn members of the herd that danger is present. Whale sounds carry a long way under water. Some scientists think whales can hear these sounds hundreds or even thousands of kilometers away!

Some whales also use sounds to locate objects. A whale makes short bursts of sound. This sound bounces off any solid object. The sound returns to the whale. Then the animal knows how far away the object is. The whale also knows in what direction to look for the object. This helps the whale find its way in the ocean. It may help the animal to avoid shallow water near the shore.

Living in a herd can help whales survive. Whales have been seen helping other whales in their group. For example, a whale may try to rescue an injured whale by pushing it away from danger. Or one or more whales may help another whale that is in trouble.

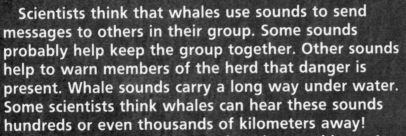

Sometimes a group of whales swims up on the beach. If they remain on the beach, they will die. When a whale is out of the water, its body can overheat.

In the pictures you can see a herd of whales. These whales beached themselves in Massachusetts. People are trying to help the whales. What do you think they are trying to do? Scientists try to understand why groups of whales swim up

2b

Imagine that you are a scientist working on the problem of whale beachings. You work on a team with other scientists. What would you need to know to decide why whales act this way?

Make a list of questions that you must answer in order to solve the problem. Then pick the three most important questions on the list. Compare your questions with those of your classmates. Do you see some of your questions on other lists? What are some things you think a scientist could do to help the beached whales?

on the beach. They study the whales and form possible reasons for the whales' actions.

Whales live together in groups in special ways. In this chapter you will learn how other animals live in groups.

3

An Animal Town

How do prairie dogs live together?

Some animals, such as bears and tigers, spend part of their lives living alone. But many animals live in groups with other animals of their own kind. Many fish live in schools. Many deer live in herds. Many birds live in flocks. Schools, herds, and flocks are kinds of animal populations (pop yə-lā'shənz). An **animal population** is a group of the same kind of animal living in an area.

White-tailed prairie dog

Black-tailed prairie dog

Another kind of animal population is a **prairie** (prãr′ē) **dog town**. Thousands of prairie dogs may live together in a single prairie dog town.

Look at the picture of the prairie dog. A prairie dog is not a dog at all. It is closely related to a squirrel. It is called a dog because of the barking sound it can make. Prairie dogs live in the grasslands of the western part of North America.

When you look at a prairie dog town, all you can see are holes. If you look at the picture on page 6, you can see why. Most of a prairie dog town is below the ground. The prairie dogs live in small "rooms" that are connected by tunnels.

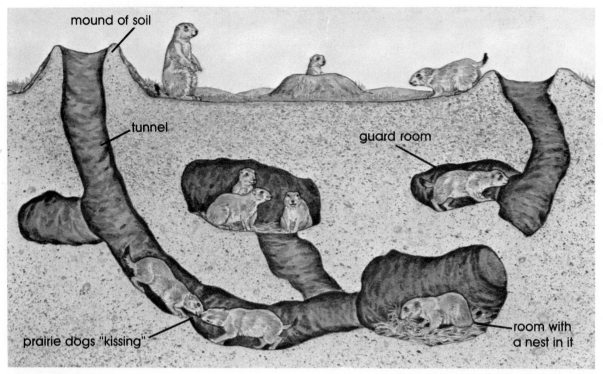

mound of soil

tunnel

guard room

prairie dogs "kissing"

room with a nest in it

Prairie dog town

There is a mound of soil around the hole at the top of a tunnel. The tunnel often leads to a room containing the nest. Along the tunnel, other rooms might be used for storing food or for sleeping. One of these rooms is called the guard room. This room is found near the top of the tunnel. When in danger, a prairie dog can move quickly into the guard room to hide.

A prairie dog town is made up of many small family groups. Each family group contains one adult male. It also contains one to four adult females and several young prairie dogs.

Prairie dogs can tell members of their family group apart from other prairie dogs. They do this by "kissing." Prairie dogs "kiss" by moving slowly toward one another while showing their teeth. They touch their front teeth together. If they do not know each other, one prairie dog will chase the other one away.

A prairie dog is just one type of animal that lives in groups. In what ways is a prairie dog town like a town of people?

For Lesson Questions, turn to page 320.

Prairie dogs kissing

Activity

How many different kinds of birds can be observed in your neighborhood?

Materials plastic bottle / scissors / string / food for birds

Procedure

A. Make a bird feeder out of a clean, empty plastic bottle. With help from an adult, cut two large openings in the sides of the bottle. Tie string around the neck of the bottle and hang the feeder from a tree branch or clothesline.

B. Place food in the bottom of the feeder. Use birdseed, breadcrumbs, bits of fruit, or sunflower seeds. Refill the feeder when it is empty.

C. At the same time of day for five days, watch your feeder for 10 minutes. Keep a record of the kinds of birds and the number of each kind you see.

1. What kind of bird came to your feeder most often?
2. What kind of bird came the fewest number of times?
3. What kind of food did the birds seem to like best?

Results

1. How many different kinds of birds were observed by the members of your class?
2. What total number of birds did your whole class see?

Conclusion

How did the use of the bird feeder help you to find out which birds live in your neighborhood?

Insect Colonies

What is life like inside an insect colony?

Like many other animals, some kinds of insects live together in groups. A group of insects that live together is called an **insect colony** (kol'ə nē). Ants and termites live in insect colonies. Insect colonies are types of animal populations.

Hornet nest

Ant nest

Honeybees and hornets are other kinds of insects that live in colonies. Honeybee colonies can be found in nests called hives. Honeybees build their hives above the ground. A hive may contain thousands of bees.

There are three types of bees in a honeybee colony. These types of bees are called the queen, the worker, and the drone (drōn). Each type of bee has a different job to do in the hive.

TYPES OF HONEYBEES

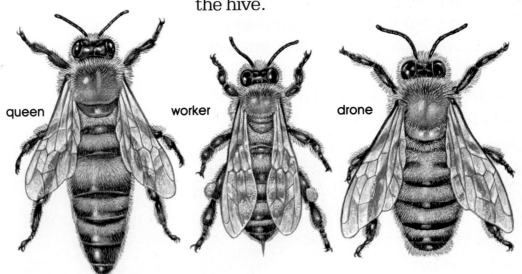

queen   worker   drone

Finding Out

SKILL: Inferring

How are the ants in an ant colony different from one another?

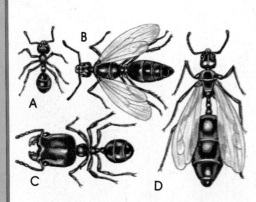

A
B
C
D

Another kind of insect colony is an ant colony. There are different types of ants in an ant colony. Each type of ant does a different job.

You can often tell an ant's job simply by looking at it. The queen is usually the largest ant in a colony. Male ants must be able to fly to mate with the queen. Workers care for the young in the colony. Soldiers protect the colony.

Look at the harvester (här'və stər) ants shown here. What is the job of each of these ants?

The **queen** is the bee that lays all the eggs in the colony. Most of the time there is only one queen in a colony. Every colony must have a queen.

Workers are female bees that do most of the jobs in the colony. Young workers help build the hive, make and store honey, and care for the young. They also care for the queen. Older workers search for food outside the hive. Most of the bees in a colony are workers.

Drones are the only male bees in a honey-bee colony. Drones mate with the queen bee. Workers force the drones out of the hive once they are no longer needed.

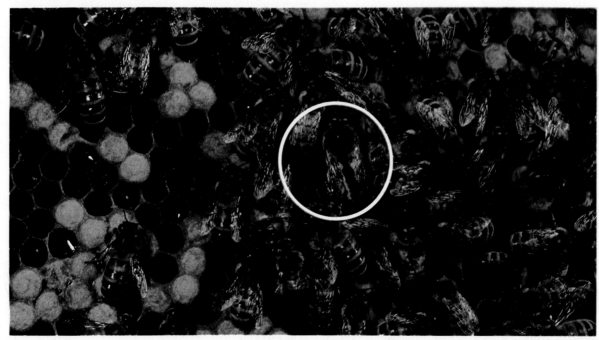

Workers surrounding queen bee

Did you know that honeybees can help people? Some people set up beehives in wooden boxes. These people are called beekeepers. Beekeepers collect honey from the hives. They also collect wax made by the bees. This beeswax is used to make candles, crayons, and lipstick.

Do You Know?

Many scientists believe that honeybees can "tell" each other where to find food. Bees do this by dancing.

When a honeybee finds food, the bee returns to the hive. Once in the hive, the bee dances in a special pattern. If the food is within 9 meters of the hive, the bee dances in a circle. This is called a round dance. With greater distance, the dance is done in a sickle shape. If the food is 90 meters or more from the hive, the bee dances in a figure eight. This is called a waggle dance. The speed of this dance shows the distance to the food. The slower the honeybee dances, the farther away the food is.

Honeybees do the waggle dance at a certain angle to the sun. The angle tells the other bees in what direction to fly to find the food.

Worker bees then watch all the movements of the dance. By doing so, they can find the exact spot where the food is.

waggle dance

round dance

For Lesson Questions, turn to page 320.

Schools of Fish

Why do some fish swim in schools?

Fish are other animals that can live in groups. A group of the same kind of fish is called a **school.** A school is another kind of animal population. Look at the schools shown here.

Schools of fish can be found in ponds, lakes, and oceans. Some schools, like schools of tuna, may contain less than 20 fish. Others, like schools of herring, may contain millions of fish.

Hussar fish

Moorish idols

Only about one out of every five kinds of fish swims in a school. Some fish only swim in schools when they are young. Other kinds of fish live in schools all their lives. Some schools only form during the day. These schools break up at night when the fish feed. Some fish, like salmon, leave the school during mating season.

Why do fish swim in schools? One reason could be for protection. Herring are a type of fish that are protected by swimming in schools. One fish in a school of herring might swim away from something dangerous. This signals the rest of the school to swim away, too. In this way herring are safer swimming in a school than they are swimming alone.

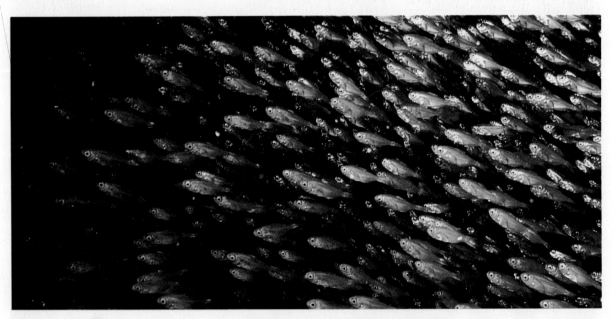

Glassy sweepers

▲ Have you ever wondered where flocks of migrating birds go? To find out, scientists put numbered bands on the legs of certain kinds of birds. Tagging does not hurt birds in any way.

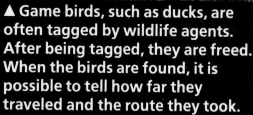

▲ Game birds, such as ducks, are often tagged by wildlife agents. After being tagged, they are freed. When the birds are found, it is possible to tell how far they traveled and the route they took.

▶ Sometimes, electronic tags are put on birds. These tags give off signals that are picked up by tracking devices. How can this information be used to help birds?

Swimming in schools helps some fish to find food. Tuna are one example of this type of fish. Tuna swimming in a school have a better chance of finding food than does a tuna that swims alone. A school of tuna can find food in a large area easier than a single fish can.

As you can see, in some ways it is helpful for fish to swim in schools. Can you think of any way that swimming in a school could be harmful?

For Lesson Questions, turn to page 320.

Animal Herds

How do animal herds differ?

Cattle

Killer whales

Elk

Not long ago, cowboys like this one were common throughout the West. These cowboys spent much of their time rounding up cattle. They gathered the cattle into large herds. The cowboys could move the herds great distances.

Cattle are just one kind of animal that can live in herds. Zebras, elephants, elk, and even whales also live in herds. A **herd** is another kind of animal population.

Burchell's zebras

African elephants

There are many kinds of animal herds. Some herds, like herds of cattle, are formed by people. Other herds, like herds of caribou (kar'ə bü), only form at certain times of the year.

Caribou can be found in parts of Alaska, northern Europe, and northern Asia. Caribou feed on small plants. In late summer these plants become harder to find. Many small groups of caribou join together to form large herds. Some of these herds are made of thousands of caribou. The herds travel to warmer places for the winter. They return the following summer when food is plentiful again.

Barren ground caribou

For Lesson Questions, turn to page 320.

Activity

How can living in a group be a problem for some animals?

Materials   16 file cards / 16 dried kernels of corn

Procedure

A. Pheasants are wild birds that usually feed on seeds. Your file cards stand for a group of pheasants that live close to each other. Write the word *pheasant* on each of the file cards. The kernels of corn will be food for the pheasants.

B. Put 4 pheasant cards in front of you. Divide the kernels of corn equally among the pheasants.
   1. How many kernels of corn does each pheasant get to eat?

C. Suppose 4 more pheasants join the group. Put 4 more cards in front of you. The group now has 8 members. Divide the kernels of corn equally among the pheasants.
   2. How many kernels of corn does each pheasant get to eat now?

D. Put the remaining 8 cards in front of you. The group of pheasants has increased to have 16 members. Now divide the kernels of corn equally among the pheasants.
   3. How many kernels of corn does each pheasant get to eat this time?

Conclusion

1. From what you have learned here, what is one problem a large group of animals might have?

2. Do you think animals in a large group share food equally? Give reasons for your answer.

Other Animals That Live Together

How does a parasite affect its host?

So far you have read about animals of the same kind that live together in groups. Can you think of two different kinds of animals that live together?

Have you ever heard of insects called fleas? Some types of fleas live on dogs. Fleas suck blood from a dog's body. They depend on the dog for their food. This can be harmful to the dog. Some fleas even carry diseases that can make dogs very sick.

A **parasite** (par′əsīt) is a harmful organism that lives on or in another organism and gets food from it. Fleas are parasites. The organism that the parasite lives on or in is called the **host.** A dog is a flea's host.

Springer spaniel

Female and male dog fleas

19

Some different kinds of animals live together without harming one another. Look at the fish attached to this shark. This fish is called a remora (rem′ər ə). Remoras and sharks are another example of two different animals that live together. But unlike fleas and dogs, remoras and sharks do not harm one another. Remoras eat scraps of food left by sharks. Remoras depend on sharks for this food, but they are not parasites. Remoras do not harm sharks. Some other examples of different kinds of animals that live together are shown on page 21.

For Lesson Questions, turn to page 320.

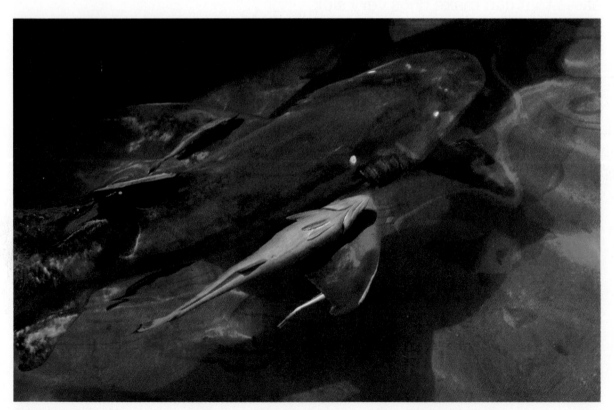

Remoras on shark

A cleaner shrimp gets food by removing parasites living on the shell of this snail.

Birds called oxpeckers get their food by eating harmful insects that live on zebras.

A clownfish is protected by a sea anemone. In return, it attracts food for the sea anemone.

Ideas to Remember

▶ A group of the same kind of animal living in an area is called an animal population.

▶ Prairie dogs live in prairie dog towns.

▶ A honeybee colony lives in a hive. A honeybee colony includes a queen, many female workers, and some drones.

▶ A group of the same kind of fish that swim together is called a school.

▶ Many deer, zebras, caribou, and elephants live in herds.

▶ Parasites are harmful organisms that live on or in other organisms.

▶ Some different kinds of animals that live together help one another.

Reviewing the Chapter

SCIENCE WORDS

A. Use these terms to answer the questions.

animal population worker host school
prairie dog town parasite queen herd
insect colony caribou drone herring

1. I am a living thing that a parasite depends on. What am I?
2. I am an animal that lives in a herd that only forms at certain times of the year. What am I?
3. I am a group of the same kind of fish. What am I?
4. I am a group of insects that live together. What am I?
5. I am a group of zebras, elk, cows, or whales. What am I?
6. I am a group of the same kind of animal that lives in underground rooms that are connected by tunnels. What am I?
7. I am the bee that lays all the eggs in a honeybee colony. What am I?
8. I am a living thing that lives on another living thing and gets food from it. What am I?
9. I am a male honeybee. What am I?
10. I am one of the female bees that does most jobs in a honeybee colony. What am I?

UNDERSTANDING IDEAS

A. Identify each of these groups of animals.

1   2   3

B. Copy the following groups of terms. Cross out the term that does not belong in each group. Then describe what the remaining terms have in common.

1. school, elk, pack, herd, troop
2. hive, worker, drone, soil, queen
3. tunnel, "kissing," grasslands, underground, pond
4. caribou, zebras, tuna, whales, elephants
5. honeybees, fleas, dogs, remoras, sharks

USING IDEAS

A honeybee is just one type of insect that lives in a colony. Use a reference book to find out about other insects that live in colonies, such as ants or termites. Make a chart to show what jobs each member of the insect colony does.

THINKING LIKE A SCIENTIST

You may be able to answer some of these questions just by thinking about them. To answer other questions you may have to do some research.

1. Some animals that do not live together year-round are often found hunting together. Wolves, hyenas, and even lions hunt together. One disadvantage of hunting together is having to share the food. What hypothesis would explain why these animals continue to hunt together?
2. Scientists draw conclusions about animals based on the size and shape of the animals. Name several animals that burrow underground. What body shape do these animals have? How is this shape helpful for burrowing? What problems would a giraffe or a hippopotamus have as a burrowing animal? What conclusions could a scientist draw about burrowing animals?

CHAPTER 2
The World of Plants

Plants grow almost everywhere. Most plants grow in soil. But did you know that some plants grow on animals? Look at the polar bears. Have you ever seen a green polar bear? The thought of green polar bears might seem strange, but they do exist. These animals are not born green. They take on a greenish tone due to the growth of tiny plants in their fur. These plants are called algae (al'jē).

Polar bears are an unusual home for algae. Most algae are found floating in ocean water. They also grow on the sides of a fish tank or on wet rocks along a lake or stream.

In the past, scientists thought that the algae lived on the surface of the polar bear's fur. But in recent years they have looked more closely. They put hairs from a green bear under a microscope. They were quite surprised at what they saw. The photograph shows what the scientists saw.

You have learned about
a strange place in which some
plants grow—the fur of animals.
But fur is not the only unusual
place in which plants can grow.
Plants can also grow in a household sponge.

It is very simple to make a sponge garden.
You will need one or more sponges, seeds, a shallow
dish, and some water. You may want to use sponges
that are in the shapes of animals. Or, with the help of
an adult, use scissors to cut your sponge into the
shape of an animal. It would be helpful to
first trace the outline of the animal onto
the dry sponge.

Begin your sponge garden by soaking
your sponge in water. Place the wet sponge
in the dish. Sprinkle seeds over the sponge. Be
sure some of the seeds are in the holes of the
sponge. You may wish to use just one kind of seed
or a few kinds. Grass seed or other small seeds, such as
those from garden plants, may be used.

Place your seeded sponge where it will get sunlight.
Check the sponge each day to make sure
it stays wet. *Do not let the sponge
dry out.* Observe the small
shoots as they grow.

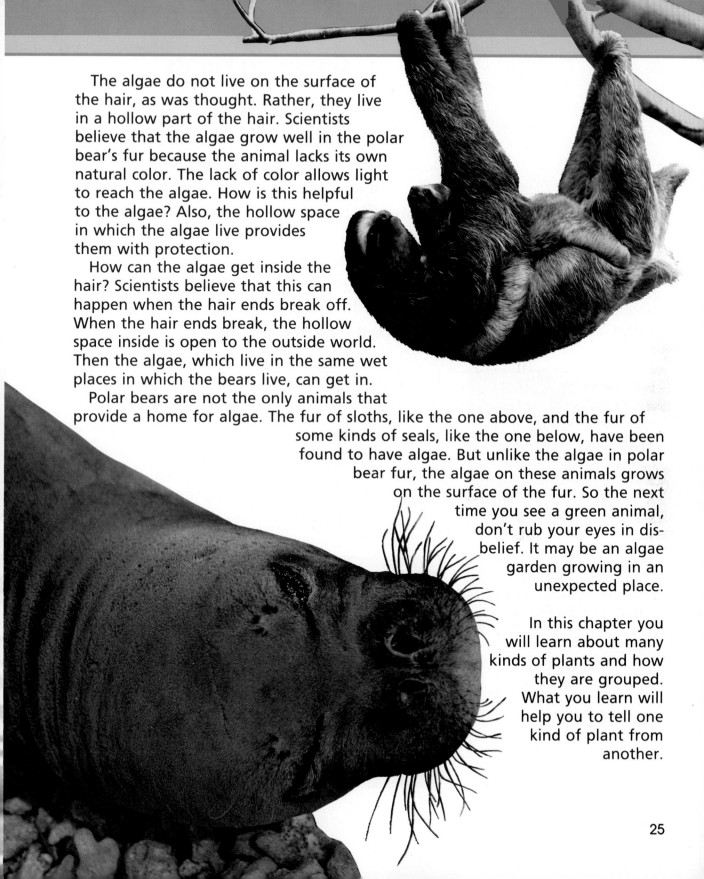

The algae do not live on the surface of the hair, as was thought. Rather, they live in a hollow part of the hair. Scientists believe that the algae grow well in the polar bear's fur because the animal lacks its own natural color. The lack of color allows light to reach the algae. How is this helpful to the algae? Also, the hollow space in which the algae live provides them with protection.

How can the algae get inside the hair? Scientists believe that this can happen when the hair ends break off. When the hair ends break, the hollow space inside is open to the outside world. Then the algae, which live in the same wet places in which the bears live, can get in.

Polar bears are not the only animals that provide a home for algae. The fur of sloths, like the one above, and the fur of some kinds of seals, like the one below, have been found to have algae. But unlike the algae in polar bear fur, the algae on these animals grows on the surface of the fur. So the next time you see a green animal, don't rub your eyes in disbelief. It may be an algae garden growing in an unexpected place.

In this chapter you will learn about many kinds of plants and how they are grouped. What you learn will help you to tell one kind of plant from another.

Grouping Plants

What are some ways you can group plants?

Can you name any of the plants on these pages? How do you know the names? Maybe one plant has flowers you have seen before. Or maybe it has leaves that are different from other plants. There are over 350,000 kinds of plants in the world. So to name any one plant, you must tell how that plant is different from all the others.

Imagine a library that has 350,000 books. What if all the books were scattered around the library? You would have a hard time finding a certain book in such a library. To make it easier to find a certain book, librarians classify (klas′ə fī), or group, their books. Books are classified by subject in a library. Librarians put all the history books together. They do the same with other books, too.

Scientists classify living things. Look at the plants on these pages. Try to classify them.

How did you classify the plants? Did you classify them by their size? By their color? Did you classify them by the shape of their leaves? Why did you classify the plants the way you did?

Some scientists classify plants by the way they reproduce (rē prə düs'), or make new plants. Some plants reproduce with seeds. Other plants do not. Scientists put all the seed plants in one group. Trees and all plants that have flowers are in this group. Scientists put all the plants that do not have seeds in a second group. This group includes ferns, mosses, fungi (fun'jī), and algae (al'jē). As you will see, classification (klas ə fə-kā'shən) helps you to identify plants.

For Lesson Questions, turn to page 322.

How can you identify a leaf?

Procedure

A. Scientists use classification keys to help them to identify plants and animals. Look at the classification key below. This key will help you to identify the leaves pictured here.

B. Look at leaf *U*.
   1. Describe the leaf.

C. Look at the key. Decide which statement—1a or 1b–best describes leaf *U*. Follow the directions at the end of the statement you choose. Keep reading pairs of statements and following directions until you find the name of your leaf.
   2. What is the name of leaf *U*?

D. Repeat steps **B** and **C** with the other leaves.
   3. What are the names of the other leaves?

Conclusion
Did the classification key help you to identify the leaves? Explain how.

CLASSIFICATION KEY

1a If the leaf is broad and flat, go to 2a.

1b If the leaf is needle-shaped, go to 5a.

2a If the leaf is not made up of many smaller leaves, called leaflets, go to 3a.

2b If the leaf is made up of leaflets, it is a locust (lō′kəst).

3a If the leaf is more round than it is long, go to 4a.

3b If the leaf is longer than it is round, it is an oak.

4a If the leaf has pointed edges, it is a maple.

4b If the leaf is fan-shaped, it is a ginkgo (ging′kō).

5a If the needles are short and flat, it is a hemlock.

5b If the needles are long and thin, it is a red pine.

Flowering Seed Plants

How can you classify flowering plants?

As you can see in this classification table, seed plants make up one group of plants. The table also shows that there are two groups of seed plants. One of these groups is made up of seed plants that have cones. You will learn more about this group of seed plants in the next lesson. The second group of seed plants is made up of seed plants that have flowers. More than half of all plants are included in this group.

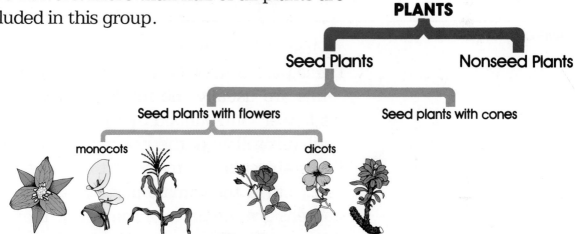

PLANTS

Seed Plants — Nonseed Plants

Seed plants with flowers — Seed plants with cones

monocots — dicots

When you think of a plant that has a flower, what do you think of? Do you think of a small plant that grows in a garden, like a rose or a daisy? Do you think of a plant with brightly colored parts? Well, not all flowering plants are small. In fact, many types of trees are flowering plants. And not all flowers have bright colors. Some flowers, like those on some grasses, have little color.

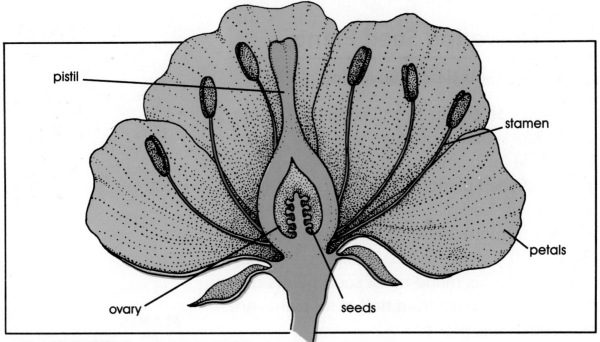

PARTS OF A FLOWER

Most flowers have the same basic parts. These parts can be seen in the drawing. The petals are usually the most colorful part of the flower. Surrounded by the petals are the pistil (pis′təl) and the stamens (stā′mənz). The stamen is the male part of the flower. The pistil is the female part. The pistil and stamens are the parts of the flower that produce seeds. The seeds develop inside the base of the pistil. This part is called the ovary (o′vər ē).

Flowering seed plants can be divided into two groups. One group is made up of plants called monocots (mon′ə kots). **Monocots** are plants whose seeds have one section. The second group is made up of plants called dicots (dī′kots). **Dicots** are plants whose seeds have two sections.

Have you ever eaten a peanut? The part of a peanut that you eat is a seed. As you can see in the picture, a peanut splits into two sections. So a peanut plant is a dicot.

Have you ever eaten corn? A single piece of corn is called a kernel (ker'nəl). A kernel is a seed. A kernel does not have two parts. So a corn plant is a monocot.

Look at these seeds. Which seeds come from plants that are monocots? Which seeds come from plants that are dicots? How can you tell?

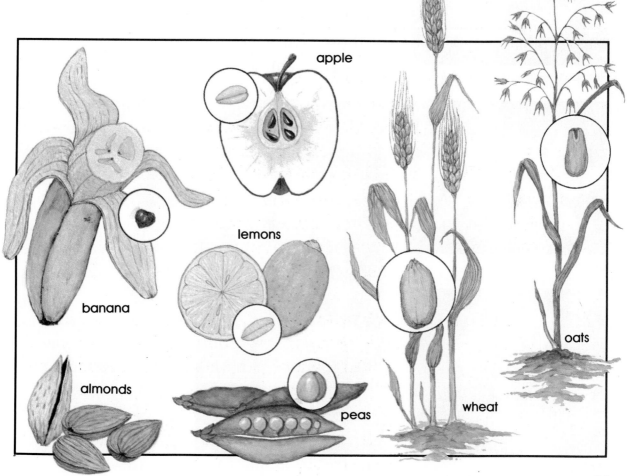

apple

banana

lemons

almonds

peas

wheat

oats

Tulips

Hibiscus

Day lilies

Violets

Looking at seeds is just one way you can classify monocots and dicots. Another way is by counting flower petals. Monocots have petals in groups of three. Dicots have petals in groups of four or five.

Count the number of petals on a tulip. It has six petals. Six is two groups of three. So a tulip is a monocot. Count the petals on this hibiscus (hə bis′kəs). It has five petals. A dicot may have five petals. So a hibiscus is a dicot.

Now look at the other plants. How many petals does each of the flowers have? Which of these plants are monocots? Which are dicots? How can you tell?

Trillium

Wood anemone

For Lesson Questions, turn to page 322.

Cone-Bearing Seed Plants

How can you identify cone-bearing plants?

Look at the classification table now. It shows some of the many types of seed plants that have cones. These plants include pines, firs, hemlocks, spruces, cedars (sē'dərs), and larches. These plants are often called **conifers** (kō'nə fərs).

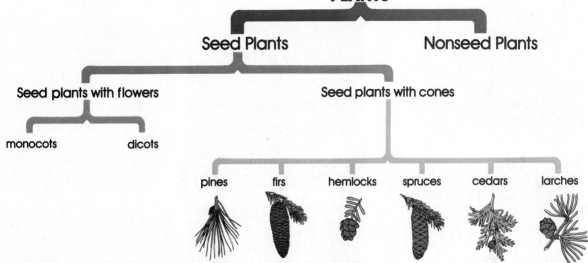

Conifers are like flowering plants in that they both use seeds to reproduce. However, conifers are different from flowering plants in several ways. For one thing, flowering plants produce seeds in flowers, while conifers produce seeds in cones. The seeds of flowering plants are protected by an ovary. The seeds of conifers are protected by the scales of the cone. Most flowering plants have broad leaves. Conifers either have needle-shaped leaves or scalelike leaves.

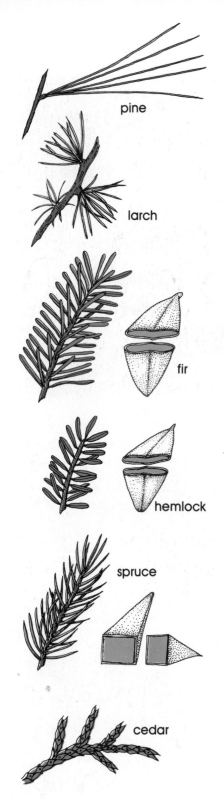

pine

larch

fir

hemlock

spruce

cedar

One way you can classify conifers is by looking at their needles. Only pines and larches have needles that grow in clusters, or groups. A larch loses its needles each autumn, while a pine does not. Firs and hemlocks have flat needles. Hemlock needles are usually shorter than fir needles. Spruces have needles that have four sides. Cedars have scalelike needles.

Look at these needles. Which of them came from a white cedar tree? Which came from an eastern hemlock? Which came from a white pine? Which came from a blue spruce? How did you identify each plant?

The cones of most conifers are brown and scaly. But the cones of some conifers do not look like cones at all. They look more like berries. One conifer that has this type of cone is the juniper (jü'nə pər). The berrylike cones of junipers vary in color from blue to red.

Junipers can be found growing throughout North America. Some types of junipers are trees, while others are shrubs. The needles of most kinds of junipers are shaped like scales. Juniper trees produce oils that are used to make some medicines and perfumes.

swamp pine   red pine   jack pine

mountain pine

Let's say that you have identified a tree as being a pine tree. How can you tell what kind of pine tree it is? One way is by studying the cones of the tree.

Look at these cones. They all come from different types of pine trees. As you can see, the cones are different from one another. Describe each pine cone. How is each cone different from the other pine cones?

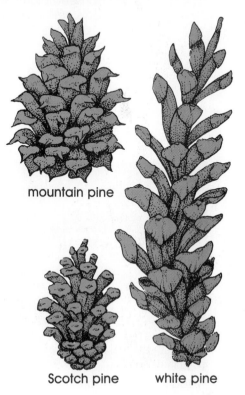

Scotch pine   white pine

For Lesson Questions, turn to page 322.

Nonseed Plants

What are four types of nonseed plants?

As you can see in this classification table, there are many groups of nonseed plants. One of these groups is made up of plants that have roots, stems, and leaves. Plants in this group do not have flowers. **Ferns** make up this group.

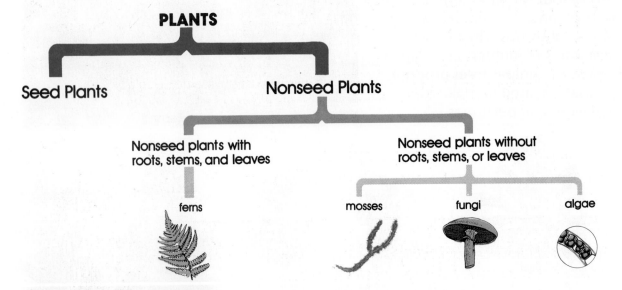

Since they do not have seeds, how do ferns reproduce? Like other nonseed plants, ferns reproduce with **spores.** These spores can be found on the underside of the leaves at certain times of the year. As you can see in the picture, these spores look like dark spots. Since ferns have leaves like seed plants, these spots can be used to help tell ferns from seed plants.

Wood ferns with spores

Moss spore pods

Haircap moss

Carpet of moss

A second group of nonseed plants consists of plants that do not have true roots, stems, or leaves. This group includes **mosses, fungi,** and **algae.** These plants are sometimes called lower plants.

Mosses can be found in many damp places around the world. They grow on rocks, on trees, and in the soil. Like ferns, mosses use spores to reproduce. But unlike the spores on ferns, spores in mosses form in special structures called pods. You can see some pods in the moss shown here.

Look at these different types of mosses. How are these mosses different from ferns? How are they different from one another? How are they alike?

Finding Out

How can you observe the action of yeast?

Yeast is often used in making bread. The yeast is mixed with the dough. Then the dough is set in a warm place. The yeast produces bubbles of gas that are trapped in the dough. This makes the dough rise. The dough is then baked.

You can observe the action of yeast. Put some grains of dry yeast into a small bottle. Your teacher will give you some warm sugar water to pour into the bottle. Stir the mixture. Place the bottle in a warm place. Wait a few minutes. What do you see happening inside the bottle? Put some grains of dry yeast into another small bottle. Add some plain warm water and stir the mixture. Place this bottle in a warm place and wait a few minutes. Can you observe the action of yeast in this bottle?

Mold on orange

Slime mold

A second group of lower plants consists of fungi. Fungi are different from all other plants because fungi cannot make their own food. Fungi must get their food from living or dead plants and animals.

There are many types of fungi. One type is called a slime mold. Slime molds have no definite shape. They are able to move from one place to another. Yeasts are fungi that are too small to be seen without a microscope. Fungi called rusts, smuts, and rots grow on other plants and harm them. Molds that grow on food are still other types of fungi.

You might be most familiar with fungi called mushrooms. There are many kinds of mushrooms. Several kinds are shown here. How are these kinds of mushrooms different from each other?

Shaggymane mushroom

Flycap mushroom

Intricate morel

Activity

How do preservatives affect the growth of bread mold?

Materials 2 jars with lids / water / ½ slice of bread with preservatives in it / ½ slice of bread without preservatives in it / paper / crayon / hand lens / tape

Procedure

A. Gently wipe the bread that contains preservatives (pri zër′və tivz) across the top of your desk or on the floor. Sprinkle a few drops of water on the bread and put it in a jar. Cover the jar and label it *WITH PRESERVATIVES.* Do the same with the bread that does not contain preservatives. Label this jar *WITHOUT PRESERVATIVES.*

B. Store both jars in a warm, dark place.

C. Make a chart like the one shown here.

D. After 3 days, examine both jars. Make a drawing in the chart to show what the mold on each piece of bread looks like.

   1. Do the pieces of bread look alike? If not, how are they different?

E. Return the jars to the warm, dark place.

F. After 4 more days, repeat step **D.**

   2. What does the mold in each jar look like now?

G. Use a hand lens to examine the mold in each jar.

   3. Describe what you see in each jar.

Conclusion

What differences did you notice between the bread with preservatives in it and the bread without preservatives in it?

PICTURES OF BREAD MOLDS		
Type of bread	After 3 days	After 7 days
Bread with preservatives		
Bread without preservatives		

A third group of lower plants consists of algae. Algae are the simplest of all food-producing plants. Algae can be grouped by color.

One type of algae is made up of blue-green algae. Blue-green algae can only be seen under a microscope. They grow in both fresh water and in salt water.

Green algae are a second type of algae. There are many types of green algae. Some types grow to lengths of 1 meter (mē'tər). Other types can only be seen with a microscope. The green scum that grows on the surface of a pond is a type of green algae.

Red algae and brown algae are two other types of algae. Most types of red algae and brown algae are found in salt water. Plants that people call seaweed are often one of these types of algae. Some types of brown algae can grow to lengths of 600 meters.

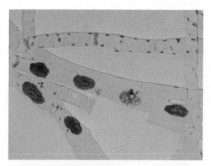
Blue-green algae

Green algae

Brown algae (kelp)

Red algae

41

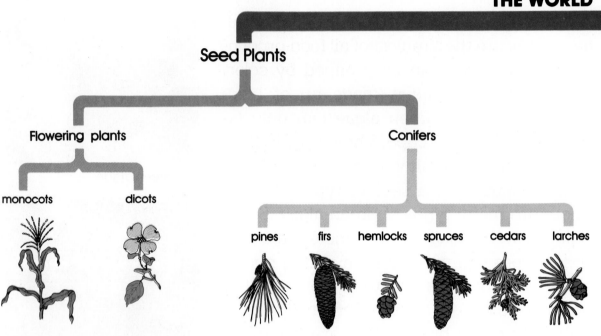

Seed Plants

Flowering plants

monocots   dicots

Conifers

pines   firs   hemlocks   spruces   cedars   larches

In this chapter you have learned about one way that scientists classify plants. You have learned how seed plants are different from nonseed plants. As you learned about different plants, you saw several sections of a classification table.

Look at the completed classification table. It shows how all plants are grouped. How are conifers and flowering plants similar? How are algae and mosses similar? How are monocots different from fungi? How are algae different from ferns?

For Lesson Questions, turn to page 322.

OF PLANTS

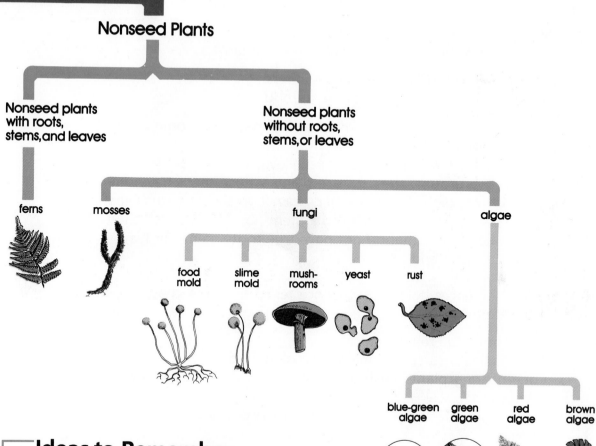

Nonseed Plants

Nonseed plants with roots, stems, and leaves

Nonseed plants without roots, stems, or leaves

ferns

mosses

fungi

food mold

slime mold

mush-rooms

yeast

rust

algae

blue-green algae

green algae

red algae

brown algae

Ideas to Remember

► Two groups of plants are those that use seeds to reproduce and those that do not.

► Two groups of seed plants are those that have flowers and those that have cones. Two groups of flowering plants are monocots and dicots.

► Ferns, mosses, fungi, and algae are nonseed plants.

Reviewing the Chapter

SCIENCE WORDS

A. Use all the terms below to complete the sentences.

monocots	mosses	algae	conifers
ferns	fungi	dicots	reproduce

Some scientists classify plants by the way they __1__. Some plants form seeds while other plants do not. There are two groups of seed plants–flowering plants and __2__. Flowering plants can be divided into two groups. The __3__ are plants whose seeds have one section. Flowering plants whose seeds have two sections are called __4__. Nonseed plants that have roots, stems, and leaves are called __5__. Nonseed plants that do not have true roots, stems, or leaves include __6__, __7__, and __8__.

B. Copy the sentences below. Use science terms from the chapter to complete the sentences.

1. Ferns form _____ to reproduce.
2. Plants called _____ cannot make their own food.
3. Cone-bearing plants, such as pines, firs, and hemlocks, are often called _____.
4. In mosses, spores form in special structures called _____.

UNDERSTANDING IDEAS

A. Make a chart like the one shown. Give four examples of plants found in each plant group.

Plant group	Examples of plants
fungi	
conifers	
algae	
flowering plants	

B. Tell whether each of the following is a monocot or a dicot.

C. In complete sentences, tell how conifers are similar to flowering plants and how they are different. Use examples of each kind of plant.

USING IDEAS

Look around for different kinds of plants. Keep a record of the plants you find. Include the date and place where you find each plant, as well as a sketch of the plant. Use reference books to help you identify some of the plants.

THINKING LIKE A SCIENTIST

You may be able to answer these questions just by thinking about them. To answer other questions, you may have to do some research.

1. Scientists are constantly searching for signs of plant life on other planets. They predict that nonseed plants are more likely to be found than plants with seeds. Why do you think this hypothesis is a logical one?

2. Imagine that you are a scientist exploring a deep, damp cave for signs of plant life. List some plants that you might expect to find. Where do you think they might be growing?

CHAPTER 3
Food Chains
and
Food Webs

What's black and white and spends three fourths of its time eating? The answer is the giant panda of western China. These animals are well loved by people all over the world. But sadly, most people cannot see pandas at their local zoo.

Today, less than 20 giant pandas are in zoos outside of China. This is because pandas are very rare. It is feared that there may be less than 1,000 wild pandas alive today.

Why are there so few pandas? Like all animals, pandas depend on other living things for food. But unlike most other animals, pandas eat just one kind of food. Eating just one kind of food is one of the main reasons that pandas are in danger. In the wild, a panda's diet is made up of bamboo. A panda can eat as many as 3,400 stalks of bamboo a day! Why is a diet of bamboo putting the panda in danger? The answer lies in the life cycle of the bamboo plant.

Most kinds of bamboo flower once in 40 to 100 years. All bamboo plants of the same kind flower at the same time. The problem is that after they bloom, all the adult plants die. The adult plants are the ones the pandas eat. It takes several years for new adult plants to grow. In that time, hundreds of pandas may starve to death.

In the past, pandas could move to other places when the bamboo died out. But people have

You have learned what happens to pandas when a major part of their diet disappears. The loss of just one kind of plant means the death of many pandas. But unlike pandas, people eat many different kinds of plants. Think about all the plants that are a part of your diet.

Make a list of every plant that is a part of your diet. Your list should include all the grains, fruits, and vegetables that you eat. Don't forget that juices you drink come from plants. Put all the plants in your list in order, starting with those you eat most often. You may wish to ask a friend or a family member to also make a list such as this.

Now look at your list and another person's list, if it is available. About how many different kinds of plants are a part of a human's diet? Think about the diet of the panda. Explain why it is better to have many different kinds of plants in your diet instead of just one kind.

cleared many of these places of bamboo and used the land for farming. Now the pandas live in small areas that are far from each other.

In 1975 all of one kind of bamboo died out. More than 150 giant pandas starved as a result. In 1983 all of another kind of bamboo died out. But this time the pandas were helped by people. Scientists from China and from a group called the World Wildlife Fund moved as many pandas as they could. They brought the pandas to an area where bamboo of a third kind grew.

This action saved many panda lives.
No one could be sure if some pandas had been left behind in the area where the bamboo had died out. So fresh bamboo was brought into this area from time to time. Efforts such as these make the future for pandas a bright one.

Food is one of the basic needs of all living things. In this chapter you will learn about some of the ways in which living things depend on one another for food.

light energy

Living Things Need Energy

How do living things get energy?

Have you ever tried to work or play when you have not had enough to eat? You get tired easily when you have not eaten enough food. You need food to give you energy.

All living things need energy. Living things need energy to move and grow. Living things die if they do not get enough energy.

How do green plants get energy? Like other living things, they get energy from food. But unlike other living things, green plants are able to produce, or make, their own food. To do this the plants need water and carbon dioxide from the air. Plants then use energy from sunlight to make food. Plants use some of the food they make to live and grow. Food that is not used is stored in their roots, stems, and leaves. Because green plants produce their own food, they are often called **producers** (prə dü′serz).

carbon dioxide

food made in leaves

water

HOW PLANTS MAKE FOOD

Deer mouse

Green plants get energy from the food they produce. But how do animals get energy? All animals must consume, or eat, food to get energy. Since animals consume food, they are often called **consumers** (kən-sü'mərz). Some animals, like this mouse, eat parts of green plants. These animals get energy right from the green plants. Some animals, like this hawk, eat other animals. They get energy from the animals they eat. But what if a hawk eats a mouse? The mouse got *its* energy from green plants. By eating a mouse, a hawk gets energy that once came from green plants. In fact, all animals depend on energy that comes from green plants.

Hawk

For Lesson Questions, turn to page 324.

49

Animals and Their Food

What are herbivores, carnivores, and omnivores?

At the beginning of this chapter, you read about a hummingbird. Hummingbirds eat sweet liquids made by flowers. You also read about a hawk that eats mice. Mice eat seeds and insects. As you can see, different animals eat different kinds of foods. Some animals eat only plants. Some animals eat only other animals. Still other animals eat both plants and animals.

An animal that eats only plants is called a **herbivore** (hėr′bə vôr). Herbivores may eat roots, leaves, stems, fruits, flowers, or seeds. Deer, rabbits, elephants, cows, and many insects are herbivores. So are elk, squirrels, bison, and prairie dogs. Some herbivores are shown in these pictures. What kind of plant is each herbivore eating?

Holstein cow

Bull elk

Eastern chipmunk

Monarch butterfly

Cheetah

Short-tailed weasel

Bobcat

Eagle owl

Some animals only eat other animals. An animal that only eats other animals is called a **carnivore** (kär′nə vôr). A wolf is a carnivore. A wolf eats rabbits, mice, and deer. Most sharks are also carnivores. These sharks eat fish. A weasel is a carnivore that eats mice. Anteaters, snakes, and owls are also carnivores. Look at the pictures of the carnivores. What kind of animal is each of these carnivores eating?

How do carnivores get their food? Some carnivores must hunt and catch other animals. A carnivore that hunts other animals for food is called a **predator** (pred′ə tər). The animal that a predator hunts is called a **prey** (prā). This eagle is a predator. The animal that the eagle has caught is a prey. Which of the animals in the pictures on page 51 are predators? Which animals are prey?

SKILLS: Observing, Classifying, Communicating

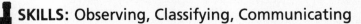

Finding Out

What kinds of animals live outside your home and school?

Look around outside your home and school. See how many different kinds of animals are there. Make a list of all the animals you see. Use a reference book to find out what each animal eats. Label each of the animals on your list as either a herbivore, a carnivore, or an omnivore. To which group do most of the animals you saw belong?

Puffins are not very fierce-looking predators. These birds feed mainly on small fish. To catch its prey, a puffin first swims on the surface of the water. When fish are spotted, the puffin dives underwater and chases after them. The puffin uses its wings like oars. The bird swims so fast that it appears to fly underwater. A puffin can catch several fish in one dive. The bird then holds them in its beak and continues to catch more fish.

Some animals eat both plants and other animals. These animals are called **omnivores** (om'nə vôrz). A bear is a good example of an omnivore. Bears eat berries and other fruits. Bears also catch and eat small animals, such as fish. Some types of mice are omnivores. So are some types of birds and turtles. Some omnivores are shown on these pages.

For Lesson Questions, turn to page 324.

53

Food Chains

How does a food chain show that energy moves from one living thing to another?

You know that living things need food for energy. You also know that green plants use energy from sunlight to produce food. Plants use some food for energy. They store extra food in their roots, stems, and leaves.

But how is the food stored in plants used by animals? Imagine a grasshopper on a blade of grass. The grasshopper munches on the grass. By eating the grass the grasshopper takes in food that was stored in the grass. It uses some of the food for energy. And it stores extra food in its body. Then a frog may eat the grasshopper. The frog uses some of the food for energy. Extra food is stored in the frog's body. Later the frog may be eaten by a smallmouth bass. Now the fish has food for energy and extra food to store in its body.

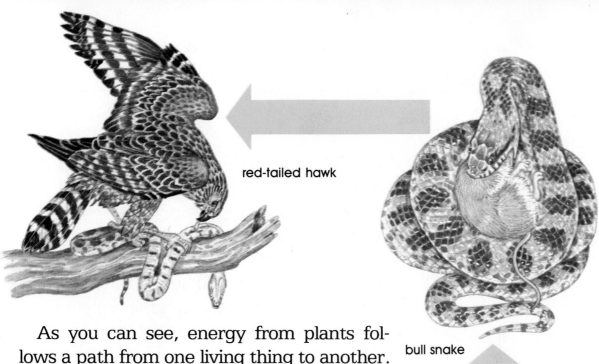
red-tailed hawk

bull snake

deer mouse

seeds

As you can see, energy from plants follows a path from one living thing to another. A path like this is called a food chain. A **food chain** is the path by which energy passes from one living thing to another. A food chain links together living things that depend on one another.

A food chain always begins with a green plant, a producer. It continues with an animal—a consumer—that eats the green plant. This consumer is often a herbivore. Another consumer may eat the herbivore. The second consumer may be either a carnivore or an omnivore. Other consumers may also be either carnivores or omnivores.

One food chain is made of seeds, mice, snakes, and hawks. In this food chain a deer mouse eats seeds. Bull snakes eat deer mice. Red-tailed hawks eat bull snakes. As you see, this food chain leads from seeds to mice to snakes to hawks.

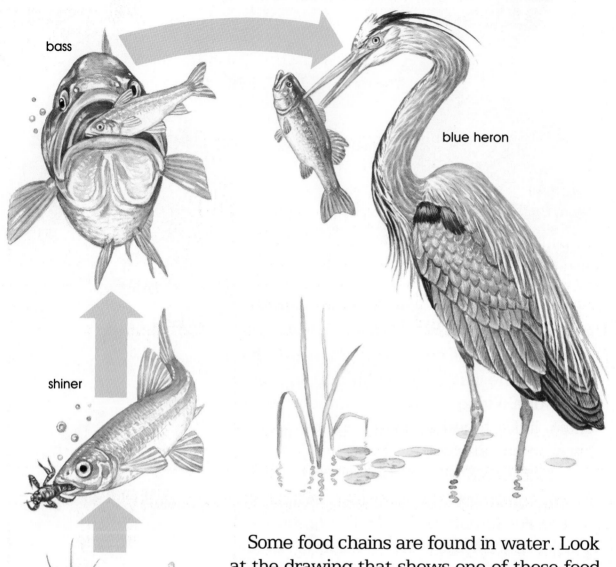

bass

blue heron

shiner

mayfly nymph

Some food chains are found in water. Look at the drawing that shows one of these food chains. Mayfly nymphs (nimfs) eat tiny water plants. The mayfly nymphs are eaten by small fish called shiners. The shiners are eaten by larger fish called bass. The bass are eaten by birds called blue herons. This food chain begins with tiny plants that use energy from sunlight. It leads to mayfly nymphs to shiners to bass, and ends with blue herons.

For Lesson Questions, turn to page 324.

How do food-chain members affect each other?

Materials 2 sheets of drawing paper / scissors / glue

Procedure
A. Draw a large triangle, a rectangle, a circle, and a square on a sheet of drawing paper. All four shapes should fit on one sheet. Cut out each shape. Write the word *carnivore* on the triangle. Write the word *herbivore* on the square. Write the word *producer* on the circle. Write the words *large carnivore* on the rectangle.

B. Place the four paper shapes on a sheet of drawing paper in an order that forms a food chain. Draw arrows to show what each of the members eats.

C. Pretend that a disease has killed the herbivores in your chain. Remove the square.
   1. What happens to the carnivores in the food chain?
   2. How are the producers affected by this change?

D. Look back in this chapter and find plants and animals that might fit this chain. Label each cutout with an animal's name. Glue each shape to your paper to show a food chain.

Conclusion
1. How do the members of a food chain depend on each other?
2. What happens to the food chain when any one member is removed?

Food Webs

How are food chains and food webs related?

In a food chain, energy moves from one living thing to another. But most living things eat more than one kind of food. For example, you have learned that hawks eat snakes. Hawks also eat mice and rabbits. Mice might eat seeds, nuts, and insects. Rabbits might eat many different kinds of plants. So you can see that it is possible for food chains to overlap. Food chains that overlap form a **food web**.

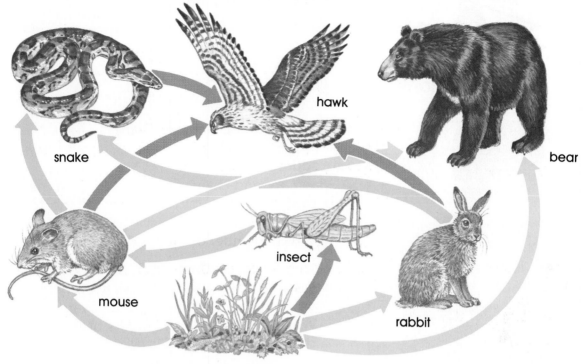

snake

hawk

bear

mouse

insect

rabbit

green plants

As you know, plants and animals live close to one another. All the plants and animals in an area make up a **community** (kə myü′nə-tē). A food web shows how all the animals in a community get their energy.

A food web can be thought of as being like a spider web. All the threads of a spider web are connected to each other. All the living things in a food web are also connected to each other.

Study the drawing of the food web. Look at the hawk. As you can see, hawks eat snakes, mice, and rabbits in this food web. Look at the mouse. Mice eat insects and green plants in this food web. What do bears eat in this food web?

For Lesson Questions, turn to page 324.

Activity

How are food webs formed from food chains?

Materials food-chain card / yarn

Procedure

A. Hang a food-chain card around your neck. This card tells you which member of the food chain you stand for.

1. Which member of the food chain are you?

B. Find the other members of your food chain. Connect your food chain by having everyone in your group hold on to a long piece of yarn.

2. What are the other members of your food chain?

C. Keep your food chain connected by the piece of yarn. Then find other food chains that have been formed by your classmates. Look for a member of another food chain that you can feed on. With your free hand, hold a new piece of yarn between you and this other member.

3. What did you form?

D. Pretend that a flood has destroyed the producers in your food web. All producers should let go of their yarn and sit down.

4. What do you think might happen to the other members of your food web?

Conclusion

1. How are food webs formed from food chains?

2. How does every member of a food web depend on producers?

3. What happens to the other members of a food web when one group of members dies off?

Ideas to Remember

▶ Living things need energy to live. They get energy from food.

▶ An animal that eats only plants is called a herbivore.

▶ An animal that eats other animals is called a carnivore.

▶ An animal that eats both plants and animals is called an omnivore.

▶ A food chain shows how energy passes from one living thing to another.

▶ Food webs are formed from food chains that overlap.

Reviewing the Chapter

A. Write the letter of the term that best matches the definition. Not all the terms will be used.

1. An animal that eats only plants
2. An animal that a predator hunts
3. A green plant
4. An animal that eats both plants and animals
5. Something that shows how all the animals in a community get their energy
6. Something that is needed by all living things
7. An animal that eats only other animals
8. An animal that hunts other animals for food
9. The path by which energy passes from one living thing to another
10. All the plants and animals in an area

a. predator
b. food chain
c. consumer
d. prey
e. community
f. herbivore
g. energy
h. producer
i. food web
j. carnivore
k. omnivore

UNDERSTANDING IDEAS

A. Show a food chain made up of each of the following groups.

1. lettuce, rabbit, wolf
2. grasshopper, frog, grass, bass
3. mouse, sunflower seed, weasel

B. Look at the picture of the food web on page 59. Write down three food chains that you can see in the picture. Explain what is happening in each food chain.

C. Copy the following groups of living things. All but one living thing in each group get their energy in the same way. Cross out this one living thing in each group. Describe what the remaining living things have in common.

1. apple tree, mouse, clover, grass
2. deer, wolf, rabbit, squirrel
3. wolf, anteater, elk, hawk
4. bear, turtle, weasel

USING IDEAS

Venus's-flytraps and pitcher plants are two plants that eat insects. Use a reference book to find out about these unusual plants. How do they capture their food? How do they get energy from the food once they have captured it?

THINKING LIKE A SCIENTIST

You may be able to answer some of these questions just by thinking about them. To answer other questions you may have to do some research.

1. Some animals, like seed-eating birds, eat many times during the day. Other animals, like some snakes, may eat only once a week. How can you explain the difference in the eating habits of these animals?
2. Why should people be very cautious about introducing new kinds of animals into a food chain?
3. Weather conditions such as floods, droughts, and extreme hot or cold temperatures can affect animals in many ways. Sometimes the weather can affect a food web. Give an example of a problem that might be caused by the weather.
4. Study the picture of the hummingbird on page 46. Why do you think the legs and feet of a hummingbird are so small and undeveloped compared with those of other birds?

CHAPTER 4
How Living Things Survive

How did you feel when you saw the baby animals on these pages? Did you think, "Aren't they cute?" Scientists think cuteness may help babies survive. Many young animals need parents to care for them. A young animal has certain features that show it is a baby.

A young cheetah has a large round head, big eyes, and a soft furry body. Scientists think these things show the adults that it is a baby. Some baby animals have spots or other marks.

▲ Raccoons   ▲ Flickers

Baby swans are brown. What color are adult swans?

Some baby animals are born blind and without fur or feathers. They are helpless and must depend on their parents for food. These baby birds, called flickers, open their mouths to be fed. Can you find any other animals here that are born without fur or feathers?

◀ **Cheetahs**　　　　　　▼ **Swans**

▲ Opossums

▼ Mule deer

Baby animals also show they are babies by the way they act. Have you noticed puppies playing with each other? Some puppies nip at one another or at adult dogs. An adult dog would not let another adult dog do this.

Why does a baby opossum or monkey cling to its mother's fur? The mother carries the baby with her and protects it from danger. Some baby animals cry and

▲ **Asiatic elephants**

make other noises when they are left alone. This helps to make sure that their parents take care of them.

Sometimes, baby animals must learn skills from their parents. These skills help the babies survive. Mother bears teach the young animals to hunt. Baby opossums learn to "play dead" when they are in danger. Many baby animals watch their mothers to learn what to do. Learning from their mothers helps the young animals stay alive and grow to be adults. What do human babies need to learn from their parents?

◀ **Orangutans**

▲ **Kit foxes**

64c

Adult animals have body parts and activities that help them to survive, too. In this chapter you will learn more about how animals survive. You will also find out some ways in which plants survive.

▲ White-footed mice

▲ Koalas

▲ Emperor penguins

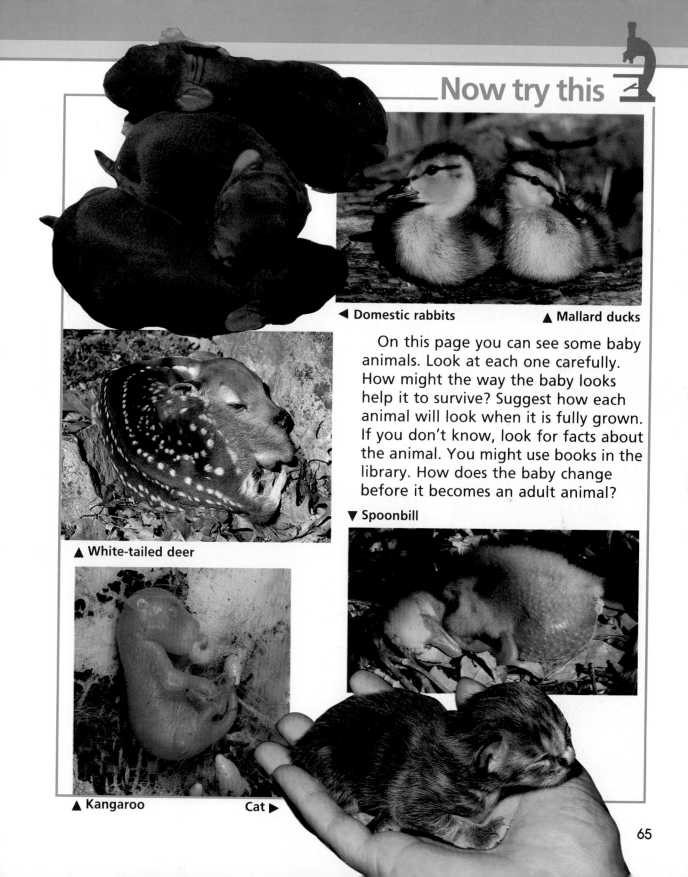

◀ **Domestic rabbits**   ▲ **Mallard ducks**

On this page you can see some baby animals. Look at each one carefully. How might the way the baby looks help it to survive? Suggest how each animal will look when it is fully grown. If you don't know, look for facts about the animal. You might use books in the library. How does the baby change before it becomes an adult animal?

▼ **Spoonbill**

▲ **White-tailed deer**

▲ **Kangaroo**   **Cat** ▶

Why Living Things Are Different

What things help living things to survive?

Stop and think about how living things are different from one another. Each kind of living thing has certain body parts that make it different from other kinds of living things. The body of an eagle is covered with feathers. The body of a fish is covered with scales. Pine trees have cones, while apple trees have flowers. Living things also have their own way of doing certain things. Robins build their nests out of twigs. Honeybees build part of their hives out of beeswax. How are the living things in the pictures different from one another?

Leopard

Dolphin

Moth

Apples

Black bar soldierfish

Some of the body parts or activities of a living thing help it to survive (sər vīv'), or stay alive. A body part or an activity that helps a living thing to survive is called an **adaptation** (ad ap tā'shən). Feathers, scales, and flowers are adaptations. Activities such as building a nest are also adaptations.

Compare the feathers of the bird with the scales of the fish. How might feathers help a bird to survive? How might scales help a fish to survive? Could a fish survive with feathers? Could a bird survive with scales?

Blue jay

For Lesson Questions, turn to page 326.

Trees Change with the Seasons

Why do some trees change each season?

Have you ever noticed how some trees change during the year? A maple tree is one kind of tree that changes with each season. A maple tree is bare during the winter. But if you look closely, you can find tiny buds on the tree. These buds begin to grow in the spring. They slowly open up to become broad green leaves. During the summer a maple tree is covered with green leaves. Late in the summer some of the green leaves turn bright red or orange. By autumn the whole tree is covered with brightly colored leaves. As winter approaches, all the leaves fall off the tree. The pictures show how the same tree changes with each season.

Norway maple—winter

Norway maple—spring

The changes that take place in a maple tree are a type of adaptation. How do these changes help the tree to survive? Maple trees are like most other types of green plants. Maple trees take in water from the ground through their roots. They lose water through their leaves.

If maple trees kept their leaves during the winter, they would lose water through their leaves. But in most places where maple trees grow, water in the ground freezes during the winter. So the maple trees would not be able to replace the water they lost. Without water, the trees would soon die.

By losing their leaves during the winter, maple trees do not lose much water. This helps them to survive the winter. So the act of losing leaves is an adaptation.

Norway maple—summer

Norway maple—autumn

If maple trees must lose their leaves to survive the winter, then why do pine trees keep most of their needles? Needles are actually long thin leaves. But needles are different from the broad leaves found on maple trees. Trees that have needles lose very little water through their needles. So pine trees do not have to lose all of their needles to survive during the winter. Since needles help pine trees to survive, they are an adaptation of pine trees. What are some other adaptations of pine trees?

For Lesson Questions, turn to page 326.

Ponderosa pines—winter

Ponderosa pines—summer

Plant Adaptations

What adaptations help plants to get sunlight and water?

Green plants need certain things to survive. One of these things is sunlight. Green plants grow toward light. But many times tall plants, such as trees, keep sunlight from reaching smaller plants. These smaller plants must have adaptations to help them get the sunlight they need.

Some small plants are able to climb to get sunlight. Different plants climb in different ways. Bean plants can climb by twisting their stems around larger plants. Rose plants can climb by hooking their thorns into larger plants. Ivy uses special roots to climb buildings. Cucumbers and peas can use structures called tendrils (ten′drəls) to climb larger plants. **Tendrils** are thin coiled structures that help plants to climb. Which of these climbing adaptations do you think is the best? Why?

Ivy

Pole bean

Grape tendril

Another way small plants can get the sunlight they need is by growing on other plants. Plants that grow on other plants are common in jungles. Orchids (ôr′kids) and Spanish moss are two plants that have this adaptation. Spanish moss grows in many places in the southern United States. What problems might this adaptation cause?

Spanish moss

Orchids

SKILLS: Observing, Inferring

Finding Out

How do plants react to sunlight?

Place a small potted plant on a windowsill that gets sun. Give the plant water when it needs it. After a week, turn the plant around so that the part of the plant that faced the sun is now facing in the opposite direction. Wait another week. Has the plant changed in any way? Describe the changes you see. How do you think this adaptation might help plants to survive?

A second thing plants need to survive is water. Getting water is not a problem for most plants. But it is a big problem for plants that grow in deserts.

A creosote (krē'ə sōt) bush is a desert plant that gives off chemicals from its roots. These chemicals kill any plants growing nearby. The creosote bush can then get water that would have been taken by the other plants.

Cactus plants have adaptations that help them to get and to store water. The roots of cactus plants cover a large area. They do not grow very deep into the ground. This helps cactus plants to take in as much water as possible when it rains.

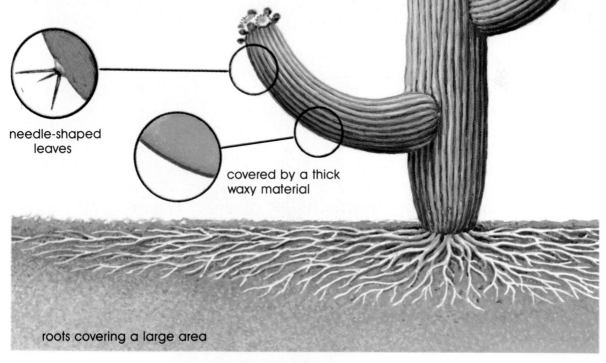

needle-shaped leaves

covered by a thick waxy material

roots covering a large area

ADAPTATIONS THAT HELP CACTUS PLANTS GET AND SAVE WATER

Prickly pear cactus

Cactus plants are able to store large amounts of water in their stems. They do not lose much water from their stems or leaves. Their stems are covered with a thick waxy material. Their "leaves" are spines. Like pine trees with their needles, cactus plants lose very little water through their spines. Why don't cactus plants lose their spines each autumn as maple trees lose their leaves?

For Lesson Questions, turn to page 326.

Do You Know?

Many plants have adaptations that help to keep them from being eaten by animals. Some plants have leaves that are covered with a layer of wax. Other plants produce chemicals that have a bad taste. Cactus plants have stems that are covered with sharp spines. Honey locust trees are covered with thorns. Still other plants contain chemicals that can harm animals. One type of nightshade plant produces bright red berries that are poisonous if eaten. Poison ivy, shown here, is a harmful plant. How does poison ivy affect people?

74

Animal Adaptations

What adaptations help animals get food?

Compare this zebra and giraffe. Zebras and giraffes are often found in the same places. Both zebras and giraffes eat plants. How are zebras and giraffes different? For one thing, giraffes have a much longer neck than zebras do. But if they live in the same places and eat the same things, why do zebras and giraffes look so different?

Giraffes

Burchell's zebra

Like plants, animals have adaptations that make them look different from other animals. And like plant adaptations, animal adaptations help animals to get what they need to survive. A giraffe uses its long neck to reach leaves on trees. A zebra uses its shorter neck to reach grasses.

Pileated woodpecker

Most animals have adaptations that help them to get food. Look at the birds shown here. Each of these birds has a different type of beak. Each kind of beak is an adaptation that helps the bird to get a certain kind of food.

Song sparrow

Little blue heron

Brown pelican

Calliope hummingbird

King vulture

Sparrows (spar′ōs) have short thick beaks that they use to crush seeds. Hummingbirds have long thin beaks that are used to get food that is deep within a flower. Eagles and vultures (vul′chərs) use their hooked beaks to tear meat. Woodpeckers use their long hard beaks to peck into wood to look for insects. Both pelicans (pel′ə kəns) and herons (her′əns) feed on fish. Compare their beaks. A heron spears fish, while a pelican scoops fish.

Rose-breasted grosbeak

Look at the beaks of the grosbeak (grōs′bēk), the duck, and the tern in the pictures. Which of these birds spears fish? Which bird feeds on seeds? Which bird eats plant materials floating in water? For what reasons did you make each choice?

Ruddy duck

Common tern

Science & Technology

▶ You know that bacteria can make you sick. But certain kinds of bacteria have adaptations that are useful. You would not have foods like cheese, yogurt, or buttermilk without bacteria. These foods are made from milk. The bacteria in milk help to change it into other dairy products.

◀ Now there are new uses for bacteria. Scientists have found a way to change some materials inside certain bacteria. These bacteria can be used to make insulin (in′sə lin). Insulin is a medicine used by people with diabetes (dī ə bē′tis). Visit your library and find out about other uses of bacteria.

For Lesson Questions, turn to page 326.

Activity

How does the size of a bird's beak help it to get food?

Materials 2 clothespins / 2 long pieces of an ice-cream stick / 2 short pieces of an ice-cream stick / glue / several short pieces of a plastic straw

Procedure

A. Glue two long pieces of an ice-cream stick to a clothespin, as shown. Glue two short pieces of an ice-cream stick to another clothespin. Let the glue dry. Think of each clothespin as a bird. One bird has a long beak, while the other bird has a short beak.

B. Use the short-beaked bird to pick up a piece of a plastic straw.
   1. What did the short beak do to the straw?

C. Use the long-beaked bird to pick up another piece of straw.
   2. What did the long beak do to the straw?

Results

Compare the two straws after they have been picked up by the two different beaks. Which beak put more force on the straw? How can you tell?

Conclusion

1. Many seed-eating birds crack open their food. Would it be better for these birds to have a short beak or a long beak? Why?

2. Some other birds eat soft foods, like berries. What type of beak would be better for these birds to have? Why?

Winter Adaptations of Animals

What adaptations help animals in the winter?

All animals find it hard to survive during the winter. It is often difficult for animals that eat plants to find food. Some animals can freeze to death in the cold temperatures of winter. All animals must have adaptations to help them survive the winter.

Some animals travel great distances during the winter. This adaptation is called **migration** (mī grā′shən). Whales, wildebeests, and many types of birds migrate.

Wildebeests

Canada geese

Monarch butterflies

Animals often migrate in large groups. Elk migrate in large herds, which may have thousands of animals. Millions of monarch butterflies migrate together.

Different kinds of animals migrate different distances. Robins migrate only as far south as is needed to find food. Other birds, called terns, migrate from the North Pole to the South Pole. This trip is about 35,000 km.

Arctic tern

Activity

How are some animals adapted to travel in snow?

Cottontail rabbit

Varying hare

Materials animal tracks / graph paper / scissors

Procedure

A. From your teacher, get a sheet of paper with the tracks of a varying (vãr'ē ing) hare and a cottontail rabbit on it. A varying hare is about the same size as a cottontail rabbit.

B. Cut out the varying hare tracks. Trace the outline of the tracks on a sheet of graph paper. Count the number of squares that the tracks cover on the graph paper.

    1. About how many squares do the varying hare tracks cover?

C. Repeat step **B** with the cottontail rabbit tracks.

    2. About how many squares do the cottontail rabbit tracks cover?

Results

Compare the numbers of squares that each rabbit's tracks cover on the graph paper. Which rabbit's tracks cover a large area?

Conclusion

1. Some people wear snowshoes to help them walk in deep snow. By wearing snowshoes your feet cover a larger area. This helps to keep you from sinking in the snow. Which animal has feet that would be better for traveling in deep snow— a varying hare or a cottontail rabbit?

2. Which animal would you expect to live farther north?

Some animals that do not migrate spend the winter in hibernation (hī bər nā'shən). **Hibernation** is a long, deep sleep. Squirrels, woodchucks, and chipmunks have this adaptation. Brown bats and birds called swifts also hibernate.

Animals that hibernate store food as fat in their bodies during the autumn. When the weather turns cold, they crawl into a safe place, such as a cave or a deep hole. There they fall into a deep sleep. Some animals wake up many times during the winter. Others do not wake up until spring.

Ground squirrel

For Lesson Questions, turn to page 326.

Ideas to Remember

▶ An adaptation is a body part or an activity that helps a living thing to survive.

▶ Plant adaptations help plants to survive the winter, to get sunlight, and to get and keep water.

▶ Most animals have adaptations that help them to get food.

▶ Migration and hibernation are two adaptations that help animals to survive the winter.

Reviewing the Chapter

SCIENCE WORDS

A. Write the letter of the term that best matches the definition. Not all the terms will be used.

1. A thin coiled structure that helps plants to climb

2. The movement of animals from one place to another during the winter

3. A long, deep sleep

4. A body part or an activity that helps a living thing to survive

a. adaptation
b. beak
c. tendril
d. hibernation
e. migration

UNDERSTANDING IDEAS

A. Write a sentence to tell how each animal below survives the winter.

B. Explain how maple trees are able to survive the winter by losing their leaves. How can pine trees survive the winter without losing all their needles?

84

C. Make a table like the one shown. Using what you learned in the chapter, fill in the empty spaces.

Type of bird	What its beak looks like	What its beak is used for
sparrow	short and thick	
	long and thin	gets food from deep within flower
eagle	hooked	
woodpecker		pecks into wood to get insects
pelican		scoops fish
	long and pointed	spears fish

USING IDEAS

1. A turtle has a hard shell. A snowshoe rabbit's fur turns white during the winter. How do their adaptations help these animals to survive?

2. Make a booklet of bird pictures. Explain how the beak and feet of each bird help it to get food.

THINKING LIKE A SCIENTIST

You may be able to answer this question just by thinking about it, or you may have to do some research.

Elephants have a very interesting and useful adaptation called a trunk. How does the elephant use its trunk? What might happen if elephants did not have trunks?

Science in Careers

People who are interested in working with living things might consider a career in conservation. Conservation is the management, protection, and wise use of natural resources. **Conservationists** are also called *ecologists.* Many careers in conservation require a person to have a college degree.

Forester

A person with an interest in animals might become a **wildlife biologist.** Some wildlife biologists try to determine how many animals are living in a certain area. They also try to find ways to protect the animals from being harmed by people.

People with an interest in plants often look for jobs in forestry. The U.S. Forest Service, the National Park Service, state forest agencies, and logging companies need **foresters.** Foresters study the science of growing trees, fire protection, and disease control.

Wildlife biologist

People in Science

ALDO LEOPOLD
(1887–1948)

Aldo Leopold became interested in nature at an early age. He believed that people should enjoy wilderness areas as places for recreation. But he also believed that the wilderness should be preserved as much as possible. He asked the U.S. Forest Service to preserve a half-million acres of the Gila National Forest in New Mexico as an undisturbed wilderness area. People are able to enjoy this area today because of Aldo Leopold.

Gila National Forest

Developing Skills

The Glossary and Index for this book begin on page 348. The Glossary shows you the meanings of important terms. The Key to Pronunciation at the beginning of the Glossary shows the symbols used in respelling these terms. The Index, which follows the Glossary, shows the pages on which important topics are discussed.

Use the Glossary and Index to answer these questions.

1. On what pages can you find out about kinetic energy?
2. On what pages can you find out about weather?

3. What term is respelled (hī bər-nā′shən)? What does this term mean?

4. On what page could you find out more about this term?

5. What term is respelled (kən sü′mər)? What does this term mean?

6. On what page could you find out more about this term?

7. What is the meaning of the term friction?

8. What is the meaning of the term tissue?

READING A MAP

Different types of maps show different things. This map shows where bison herds could be found in North America at different times. Use the map to answer the following questions.

1. During which year could herds of bison be found in the largest area?
2. Could bison herds be found in Mexico in 1870?

3. When was the last time bison herds could be found east of the Mississippi River?
4. In what countries could bison herds be found in 1906? In what countries could they be found in 1850?
5. Between 1850 and 1900, what happened to the area in which bison herds could be found?

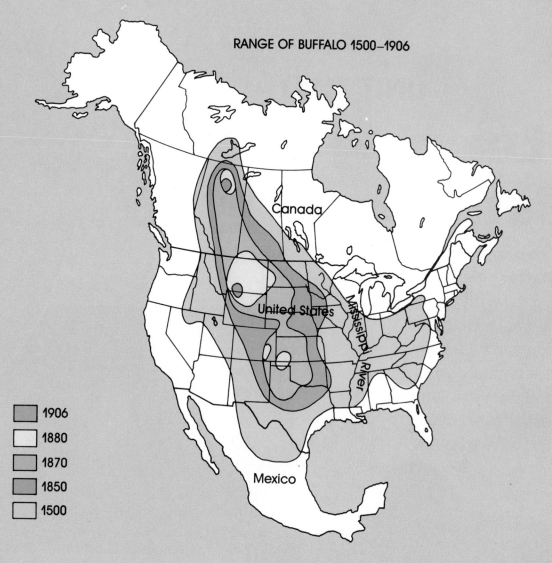

RANGE OF BUFFALO 1500–1906

- 1906
- 1880
- 1870
- 1850
- 1500

Canada

United States

Mississippi River

Mexico

USING THINKING SKILLS

At one time huge bison herds could be found throughout the plains of North America. After years of hunting, all that was left of the bison in the United States was a herd of 20 animals. By protecting this herd, there are now about 50,000 animals in the United States. Think about this as you answer these questions.

1. What, if anything, might happen if all the bison were allowed to die?

2. Should animals be protected? Explain your answer.

UNIT TWO
Learning About Matter and Energy

Chapter 5–Measuring Matter A person learning to swim often holds on to an object that floats in water. In this chapter you will find out why some objects float in water and others do not.

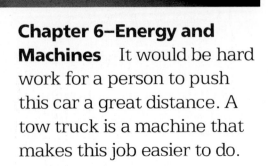

Chapter 6–Energy and Machines It would be hard work for a person to push this car a great distance. A tow truck is a machine that makes this job easier to do.

Chapter 7—Heat Energy
The air inside this balloon is being heated. It is the warm air that causes the balloon to rise. In this chapter you will learn how warm air is different from cool air.

Chapter 8—Electricity and Magnetism This train uses electricity to run. The electricity moves through overhead wires. In this chapter you will learn how electricity is made.

91

CHAPTER 5
Measuring Matter

Chicago is sparkling tonight. The beauty of the skyline takes everyone's breath away. The tour guide walks towards the group and smiles. The tour is about to begin.

"Good evening, ladies and gentlemen. Step this way. We are now standing at the top of the Sears Tower in Chicago. The Sears Tower, 443 meters high, is the tallest building in the world.

"The world's tallest building is just the first stop on our tour. As we travel, we'll see other exciting sights. And we'll learn an interesting fact about each sight. So get your cameras ready, we're on our way!

"Here we see optical fibers. They can carry light as far as 160 kilometers. Optical fibers work in a group or alone. A group of 40 optical fibers would only be as thick as the 'lead' in a pencil. Optical fibers are being used in communications and medicine.

"Quickly, everyone, look up. There's the fastest airliner, the Concorde. On March 2, 1969, the Concorde flew 128 passengers at a speed of 2,333 kilometers per hour. On January 20, 1980, a record was set traveling from New York to London in 2 hours 59 minutes 14 seconds. The average speed of the plane was 1,876.54 kilometers per hour.

"Now we are standing on the deck of a supertanker. This tanker, the *Arco Fairbanks*, cruises at 16 knots per hour and has a crew of 27 people. It can carry 132,000 metric tons of cargo. This is equal to the weight of 20,000 elephants! The supertanker is 42 meters wide and 270 meters long. That is as long as three football fields.

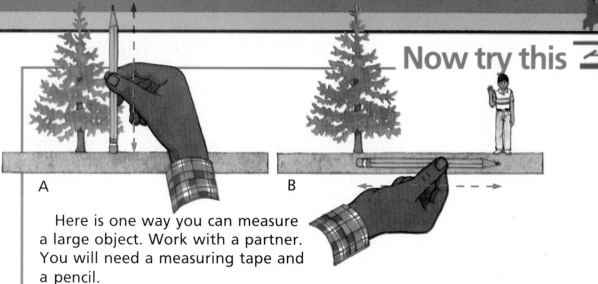

Here is one way you can measure a large object. Work with a partner. You will need a measuring tape and a pencil.

Select a tall tree whose height you wish to measure. Have your partner stand next to the tree. As you look at the tree, close one eye. Extend your arm to hold a pencil upright in front of you. Line up the pencil with the tree as shown in picture A. Move toward or away from the tree until the pencil and the tree appear to be the same size. Turn the pencil as shown in picture B. Keep the pencil in this position.

Now direct your partner to turn sideways and walk away from the tree. Tell your partner to stop walking when he or she is lined up with the end of the pencil. Use a measuring tape to measure the distance between the tree and your partner. This distance is the same as the height of the tree. How tall is the tree?

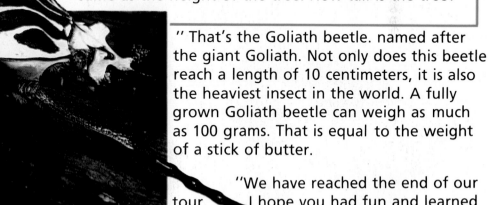

Goliath Beetle-life size.

" That's the Goliath beetle. named after the giant Goliath. Not only does this beetle reach a length of 10 centimeters, it is also the heaviest insect in the world. A fully grown Goliath beetle can weigh as much as 100 grams. That is equal to the weight of a stick of butter.

"We have reached the end of our tour. I hope you had fun and learned some measurement facts. In this chapter you will learn about more things that can be measured. You will also learn how to measure them."

93

The Properties of Matter

What is a property?

What kinds of things have you measured? You may have measured how tall you are. You may have measured the amount of milk to put in a recipe. You may have measured how much you weigh.

All these things that you can measure are matter. **Matter** is anything that has mass and takes up space. Water is matter, and air is matter. You are made of matter.

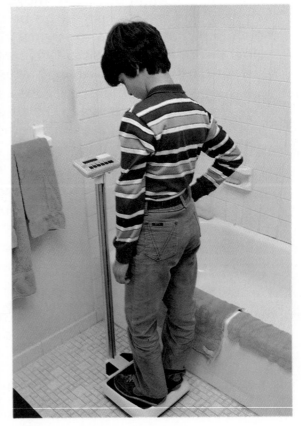

This picture shows different examples of matter. What makes these kinds of matter different? To answer this, you might make a list. Your list might say that the stone is hard. The ice is cold. The gold is yellow. The apple tastes sweet and the vinegar tastes sour. You could go on until you had a long list.

Each of the things on your list is a property (prop'ər tē) of matter. A **property** is something that describes matter. Color, hardness, size, shape, and taste are examples of properties.

Some properties can be measured, while others cannot. For example, you cannot measure taste, but you can measure size. In the rest of this chapter, you will learn about some of the properties of matter that can be measured.

For Lesson Questions, turn to page 328.

The Length of Matter

How do you measure length?

The distance around this track has been measured so that the runners can race. Length is a property of matter that can be measured. **Length** is a measured distance. A metric ruler or tape measure is a tool for measuring length.

The **centimeter** (sen′tə mē tər) is a unit used to measure length. The symbol for centimeter is *cm*. The centimeter is a small unit of measurement. A pencil is about 20 cm long. Your height is probably over 120 cm.

Suppose you wanted to measure a book. First you would place the ruler on the book. The zero point of the ruler would be even with the edge of the book, as in the picture. You would then count the number of centimeters from this point to the other end of the book. If you look closely at the picture, you will see that the book measures 25 cm.

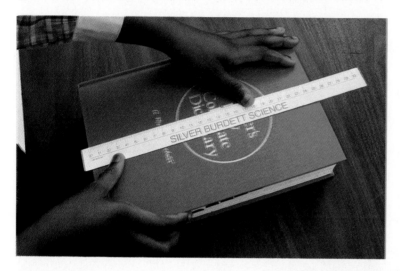

SKILL: Measuring

Finding Out

How is a ruler used to measure length?

Use a metric ruler to measure some parts of your body. Place the zero point of the ruler at the tip of your thumb. Count the number of centimeters from the tip to the base to find its length. Use a string to measure around parts such as your wrist. Then measure the string to find the length. Also measure your foot, your head, and your waist.

Large objects are usually measured in meters. A **meter** is a unit of length equal to 100 cm. The symbol for meter is *m*. Distances in sporting events are often measured in meters.

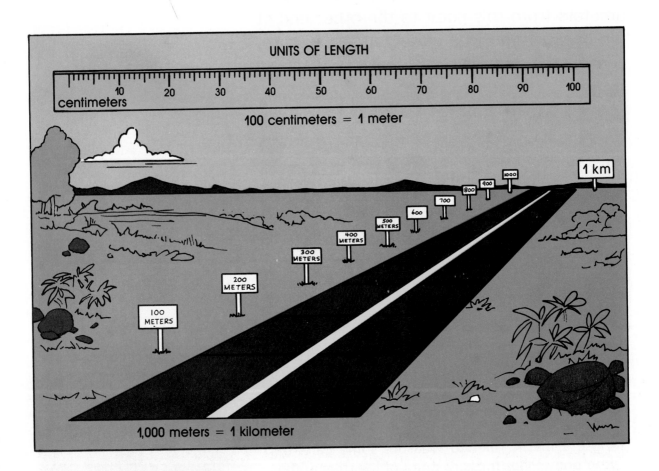

UNITS OF LENGTH

10 20 30 40 50 60 70 80 90 100
centimeters

100 centimeters = 1 meter

1 km

1000

900

800

700

600

500 METERS

400 METERS

300 METERS

200 METERS

100 METERS

1,000 meters = 1 kilometer

Very large distances are measured in kilometers (kil'ə mē tərs). A **kilometer** is a unit of length equal to 1,000 m. The symbol for kilometer is *km*. Many road signs use kilometers to give the distance between two locations. Have you ever seen a sign like this?

For Lesson Questions, turn to page 328.

Mass of Matter

How do you measure mass?

The barbells in these pictures are made of the same kind of matter. Both are made of iron. What properties do they have that are different?

One of the first things you might notice is that one barbell is larger than the other. The large barbell is also heavier than the other. The large barbell is heavier because it contains more iron. It has greater mass than the small barbell. Mass is a property of all matter. **Mass** is a measure of the amount of matter in an object. Things that contain more matter have greater mass. Things that contain less matter have lesser mass.

Empty balance

Balance with clip and masses

The pictures above show the same kind of matter—wood. Which wood object has the greatest mass? If you think the tree has the greatest mass, you are right.

Mass is a property that can be measured. A **balance,** such as the one shown in the pictures, is a tool for measuring mass. A balance has two pans. If objects having the same mass are placed in each pan, they balance each other. If objects having different masses are placed in each pan, the pan having the greater mass will be lower.

Suppose you wanted to use a balance to find the mass of a paper clip. As you can see, you would first put the paper clip on one pan. Next you would add mass to the other pan until the two pans balanced.

Each of the small pieces of metal in the pan has a mass of 1 gram. A **gram** is a unit of mass. The symbol for a gram is *g.* It took two of these 1-g masses to balance the paper clip. So the mass of the paper clip is 2 g.

A gram is too small to be a useful unit for measuring large masses. The mass of larger things is usually measured in kilograms (kil′ə-grams). A **kilogram** is a unit of mass equal to 1,000 g. The symbol for kilogram is *kg.*

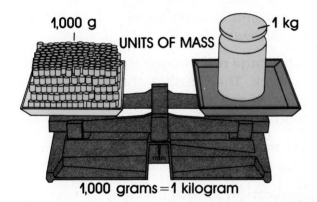

1,000 g

UNITS OF MASS

1 kg

1,000 grams = 1 kilogram

SKILL: Measuring

Finding Out

Can you use a metric balance to measure mass?

Get a balance and some metric masses. Put a pencil on one pan of the balance. Add masses to the other pan until the two pans balance. Be sure to add one mass at a time. What is the mass of your pencil? Try to find the mass of other small objects.

For Lesson Questions, turn to page 328.

Activity

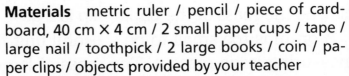

How is a balance used to measure mass?

Materials   metric ruler / pencil / piece of cardboard, 40 cm × 4 cm / 2 small paper cups / tape / large nail / toothpick / 2 large books / coin / paper clips / objects provided by your teacher

Procedure

A. Hold a metric ruler across a piece of cardboard and make a mark at 2 cm, 20 cm, and 38 cm.

B. Tape a paper cup at the 2-cm mark on the cardboard and another paper cup at the 38-cm mark, as shown.

C. Push a large nail through the cardboard at the 20-cm mark. Then push a sharp toothpick into the edge of the cardboard at the 20-cm mark. The toothpick will be the pointer of your balance.

D. Rest the nail on two large books, as shown. Make sure the toothpick stands up straight.

E. Place a coin in one of the cups.
   1. What happens to the balance?

F. Add paper clips to the other cup, one at a time, until the cups balance. You are using a paper clip as a unit of mass.
   2. How many paper clips are needed to balance the cups?
   3. What is the mass of the coin?

G. Find the masses of other objects.
   4. What do you predict the mass of each object will be?
   5. What is the mass of each object?

Conclusion

How can the balance you made measure mass?

Volume

How do you measure volume?

You have learned that mass is a property of all matter. This picture shows another property of matter. It shows that matter takes up space. These clothes are taking up more space than there is in the suitcase. The volume (vol'yəm) of the clothes is greater than the volume of the suitcase. The **volume** of an object is the amount of space it takes up.

The picture shows a cube, which we will use as a unit for measuring volume. The cube is 1 cm high, 1 cm wide, and 1 cm thick. To find the volume of something, you would find out how many cubes would fill it. For example, it takes 2,400 cubes to fill this shoebox. So the volume of the box is 2,400 cubes.

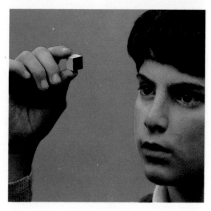

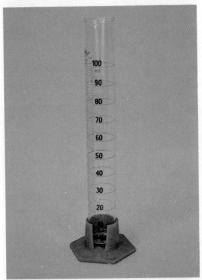

Liquids also have the property of volume. Suppose you wanted to find the volume of the water in this bottle. The bottle is not shaped like a shoebox, so you cannot measure its volume in cubes. Instead you could use a graduate (graj'ü it), like the one shown in the picture. A **graduate** is a tool used to measure the volume of liquids.

The volume of a liquid is measured in units called milliliters (mil'ə lē tərs). The symbol for milliliter is *mL.* A **milliliter** is the same amount of volume as the cube (1 cm × 1 cm × 1 cm). A tiny glass box the same size and shape as this cube would hold 1 mL of water. Liquids in small bottles are measured in milliliters.

This picture shows how to use a graduate to measure the volume of the water in the bottle. The mark on the graduate shows that the bottle holds 50 mL of water.

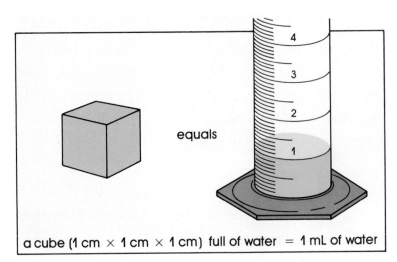

a cube (1 cm × 1 cm × 1 cm) full of water = 1 mL of water

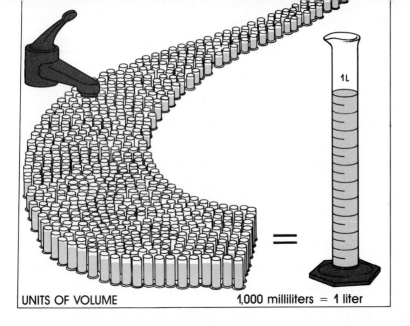

UNITS OF VOLUME   1,000 milliliters = 1 liter

Milliliters are very small units of volume. Large volumes of liquid are measured in bigger units. These units are called liters. The symbol for liter is *L*. One **liter** is equal to 1,000 mL. Juice in large jars is often measured in liters.

You can also use a graduate to measure the volume of a solid, such as a marble. Here's how. Fill a graduate with water. Drop a marble into the water. The marble takes up space that had water in it. The marble displaces (dis plās'əs), or pushes aside, the water. This is called displacement (displās'mənt). You can measure the increase of water level in the graduate to find the volume of the marble. Displacement is a good way to measure the volume of odd-shaped solids. Cubes cannot be used to measure the volume of odd-shaped solids.

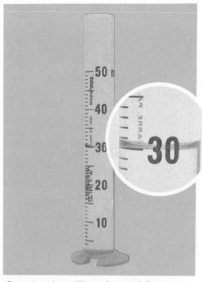

Graduate without marble

Graduate with marble

For Lesson Questions, turn to page 328.

Activity

How is a graduate used to measure the volume of an object?

Materials 50-mL graduate / water / bolt, or other small object / heavy thread

Procedure

A. Set a graduate on a table, away from the edge. Fill it with water up to the 20-mL mark.

 1. What is the volume of the water in the graduate?

B. Tie a piece of heavy thread around the bolt. Make sure the thread is long enough for you to hold onto when the bolt is lowered into the graduate.

 2. What do you think will happen to the water when you lower the bolt into the graduate?

C. Carefully lower the bolt into the water. Watch the level of the water.

 3. Describe what happens to the level of the water.

 4. What is the volume of the water in the graduate now?

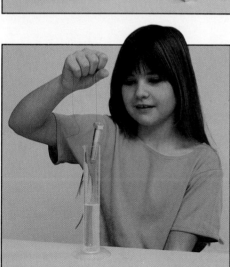

Results

1. How much did the bolt increase the volume of the water? (*Hint:* Subtract 20 mL from the new volume of water and the bolt together.)

2. What is the volume of the bolt?

Conclusion

How is a graduate used to measure the volume of an object?

Using science ideas

Use your graduate to find the volume of a crayon.

Density

How do you measure density?

Both pans of this balance hold objects with the same mass. One pan holds an iron nail. The other holds a piece of wood. You can see that the wood has a bigger volume than the nail. What do you think would happen if the piece of wood were the same size as the nail? If you think the balance would tip toward the nail, you are right.

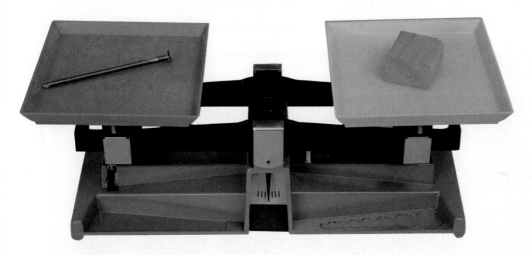

A piece of iron has more mass than a piece of wood with the same volume. Iron has a greater density (den′sə tē) than wood. Density is another property that can be measured. **Density** is the mass in a certain volume of matter. For example, the mass of one cube (1 cm × 1 cm × 1 cm) of iron is about 8 g. The mass of one cube (1 cm × 1 cm × 1 cm) of wood is less than 1 g.

You have learned that the mass of an object depends on the amount of matter it contains. Objects that have different densities have different amounts of matter in the same volume. A cube of iron contains more matter than the same sized cube of wood.

Most kinds of solid matter have greater density than most liquids. In most solids the matter is packed more tightly than in most liquids. One cube (1 cm × 1 cm × 1 cm) of iron contains more matter than one cube (1 cm × 1 cm × 1 cm) of water.

Science & TECHNOLOGY

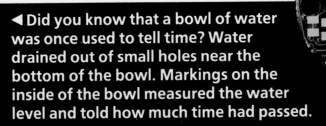

◀ Did you know that a bowl of water was once used to tell time? Water drained out of small holes near the bottom of the bowl. Markings on the inside of the bowl measured the water level and told how much time had passed.

▶ Today many people use electronic watches to tell time. Electronic watches are also called quartz watches. A vibrating quartz crystal is the time base for this watch. A microchip keeps the crystal vibrating.

▶ An atomic clock is the most accurate clock ever made. It works by counting the vibrations of certain atoms. These atoms always vibrate at the same rate. An atomic clock may gain or lose only a second in 100,000 years. Time signals from this clock are sent to the world.

You can compare the densities of different kinds of solid matter to the densities of liquids. Solid matter sinks in a liquid if the solid has a greater density than the liquid. If the solid has a lower density than the liquid, the solid floats. These two kinds of soap have different densities. Which one has more matter in one cube than water?

You can also compare the densities of different kinds of gases. Which gas has a lower density—the helium in a balloon or the air the balloon floats in?

For Lesson Questions, turn to page 328.

Ideas to Remember

▶ Matter is anything that has mass and takes up space.

▶ Length is a measured distance. Centimeters (cm), meters (m), and kilometers (km) are units of length.

▶ Mass is the measure of the amount of matter in an object. The units used to measure mass are the gram (g) and the kilogram (kg).

▶ The volume of an object is the amount of space it takes up. The volume of liquids is measured in milliliters (mL) and liters (L).

▶ Density is the mass in a certain volume of matter.

Reviewing the Chapter

SCIENCE WORDS

A. Write the letter of the term that best matches the definition. Not all the terms will be used.

1. A unit of volume
2. A measured distance
3. A unit equal to 1,000 m
4. The amount of space an object takes up
5. A tool for measuring mass
6. Anything that has mass and takes up space
7. A unit equal to 1,000 g
8. A tool used to measure the volume of liquids
9. The amount of matter in an object
10. The mass in a certain volume of matter

   a. kilometer
   b. density
   c. milliliter
   d. mass
   e. graduate
   f. length
   g. balance
   h. gram
   i. volume
   j. matter
   k. kilogram

B. Copy the sentences below. Use science terms from the chapter to complete the sentences.

1. A unit of volume equal to 1,000 mL is a ____.
2. A ____ is a small unit that can be used to measure the length of a pencil.
3. A ____ is a unit of length equal to 100 cm.
4. Something that describes matter is called a ____.
5. A good way to measure the volume of an odd-shaped solid is ____.

UNDERSTANDING IDEAS

A. Choose two tools that are used to measure matter. Explain how each tool is used. Name the unit or units of measure each tool shows.

B. Make a chart like the one shown. Fill in the empty spaces using information from the chapter.

UNITS OF MEASUREMENT		
Measurement	**Units**	**Symbol**
volume		L
	meters	m
mass	grams	
	milliliters	
		km

C. Tell which of the following sentences are true and which are false.

1. Some properties of matter can be measured.

2. All solids sink in water.
3. Air is matter.

USING IDEAS

1. Make a list of things that are longer than 1 km.
2. With help from a friend, measure the length of your shadow in centime- ters at 9:00 A.M., noon, and 2:00 P.M. on the same day.

THINKING LIKE A SCIENTIST

You may be able to answer this question just by thinking about it, or you may have to do some research.

Imagine a 1-cup container filled half way with sand. Another identical container has three fourths of a cup of sand. Both containers are then filled to the brim with water. Which cup holds the greater volume of matter? Which cup has the greater mass? Which cup has the greater density?

CHAPTER 6

Energy and Machines

Stanley Kyi raises his trophy and the crowd roars its approval. Is Stan the star of the basketball team? Is he the state chess champion? No—Stan's trophy is for something very different. He has won the contest that is the final exam for Professor Woodie Flowers's engineering course. The course is given at the Massachusetts Institute of Technology (MIT).

Dr. Flowers's course is unusual. In his course, students do not just read books and study for tests. They have to take what they have learned and do something with it. During the last 7 weeks of this course, the students use what they have learned to make a machine. This project is their final exam.

Stan, along with every other student in the course, was given a bag of objects. The objects included springs, gears, wheels, pipe cleaners, rubber bands, and motors. These objects were parts to be used to make a special kind of machine. It was to be a machine designed to win a tug-of-war contest.

All students had the same set of rules. Each student had to design a machine, build that machine, and make it work. Not only would the machine have to

work, but it would also have to be better than the other students' machines. Often a student's plan would look great on paper, but then the machine would fail. The student would have to keep changing the plan until the machine would work.

Finally the moment of truth arrived! On a Tuesday night, before a packed house, the contest began. The students had been told by Professor Flowers, "If it doesn't work, be sure and make it pretty." Indeed, all the machines looked great! And most of them worked. A machine that looked like an alligator beat another that looked like an apple. There were machines that looked like a teddy bear, a gremlin, and even Tweety bird.

Each round of the contest lasted for 30 seconds. Two machines were placed at each end

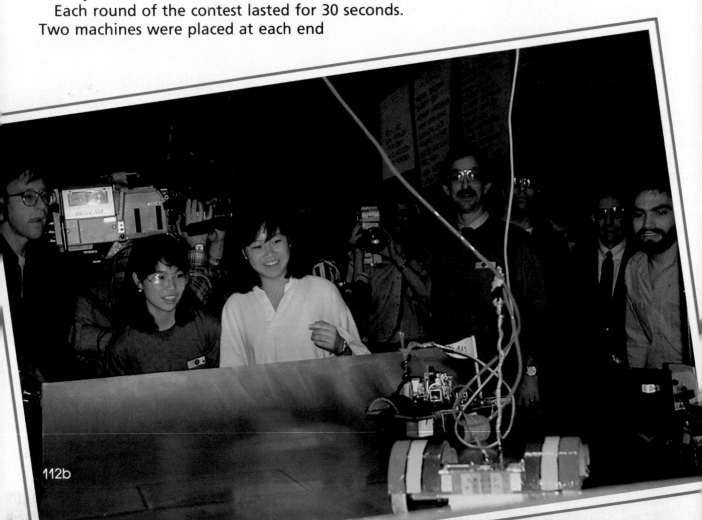

112b

of an aluminum table with a line down the center. The machines were joined by a cord that was knotted in the middle. Then the tug of war began. The first machine to pull the knot across the center won.

Some machines used barriers to block the other machines. Some machines used suction cups to firmly hold their ground. Stan Kyi's machine had a long hinged arm. This arm pulled the knot across the center line. Stan also used a device to anchor his machine. Thus his machine could not be pulled across the line. Stan's machine defeated all the others and won the contest.

112c

Now try this

Now you will have a chance to make your own machine. You will receive a bag of parts to construct a machine, just like the MIT students. Your bag of parts includes 2 large wooden spools, 2 rubber bands, 4 tacks, 4 paper clips, 4 drinking straws, 2 wooden blocks, a screw top from a jar, string, a pair of scissors, and a hammer.

What kind of machine should you build? Build one that can move from place to place. Draw a design for your machine, build it, and then test it. If it does not work, you will have to change your design and try again. Make your machine look pretty, too!

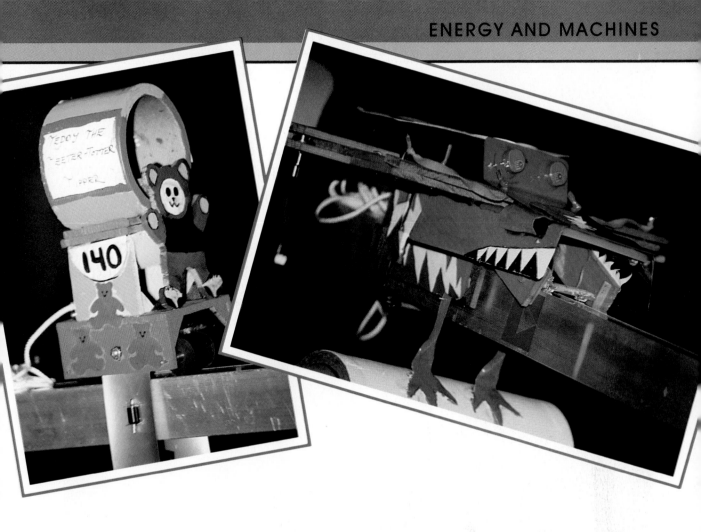

Each year Dr. Flowers thinks of a new challenge. One year it was a harvester of table tennis balls, another year it was the M.I. Teetor-Totter. What will Dr. Flowers think of next?

To build their devices, the students in Dr. Flowers's course had to know all about machines. In this chapter you will learn about different machines and how they work. You will also learn about the energy needed by these machines.

113

Forms of Energy

What are some different forms of energy?

What do the crane and the baseball player have in common? They are both doing work. You might not think of hitting a baseball as work. However, work is done whenever a force is used to move an object. The boy is moving the ball by hitting it, or by giving it a quick push. The crane is moving boxes by lifting them.

It takes energy to do work. Energy does not take up space or have mass. So energy is not matter. **Energy** is the ability to do work. Cranes get energy from gasoline. People get energy from the food they eat. Gasoline and food contain chemical (kem′ə kəl) energy. Chemical energy is just one form of energy.

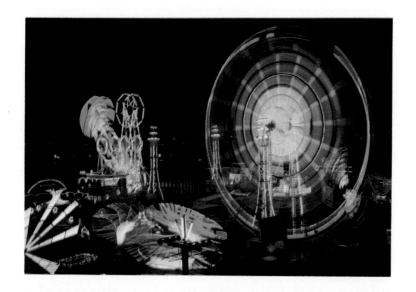

Suppose you could go to the fair shown here. What forms of energy could you find? Even before you got to the fair, you would notice two forms of energy. First you would be able to see the light bulbs on the rides. These light bulbs would be giving off light energy. As you got closer, you would hear another form of energy called sound energy.

The light bulbs at the fair would be lit by electrical (i lek′trə kəl) energy. The moving parts on the rides and games would have another form of energy. This form is called mechanical (mə kan′ə kəl) energy. Anything that moves has mechanical energy. If you got hungry at the fair, you might eat a hot dog or some popcorn. This food would have been cooked using heat energy. The light bulbs at the fair would also give off heat energy.

Did you know that energy can change from one form to another? Electrical energy can be changed to light energy and heat energy by light bulbs. Electrical energy can also be changed into sound energy by a radio.

You learned that chemical energy in gasoline can be used to make a crane move. To do this, chemical energy is burned to release heat energy. The heat energy is then changed to mechanical energy. Chemical energy stored in wood is changed to heat energy and light energy when the wood is burned. Chemical energy is also stored in fireworks. What forms of energy is the chemical energy changed into when the fireworks explode?

For Lesson Questions, turn to page 330.

Light bulbs

Fire

Fireworks

Two Kinds of Energy

What are potential and kinetic energy?

How is work being done in this picture? The wrecking ball is doing work by moving the wall of the building. The ball must have a lot of energy to do this much work. The swinging ball has a kind of energy called kinetic (ki net'ik) energy. **Kinetic energy** is the energy of motion.

What if the wall could not be moved by this ball? How could the ball be changed and still knock down the wall? Swinging the ball faster could make the wall move. Or a heavier ball could do the job. Either way, the moving ball would have more kinetic energy. The kinetic energy of an object depends on its mass and speed. If you increased the mass or the speed of the ball, you would increase its kinetic energy. Then the ball could do more work.

As you have learned, anything that moves has mechanical energy. So mechanical energy is a type of kinetic energy. Some other forms of energy are also types of kinetic energy. Light energy, heat energy, and sound energy all move from one place to another. So they are all types of kinetic energy.

Just before this picture was taken, the man was not moving. So he did not have kinetic energy. But as the man swings on the rope, he moves. He has kinetic energy.

While the man holds the rope at the top of the hill, he has potential (pə ten'shəl) energy. **Potential energy** is stored energy. As he starts to move, this stored energy will begin to change to kinetic energy. When he reaches the bottom of his swing, he will have a lot of kinetic energy. He will have little potential energy. Most of his potential energy will have changed into kinetic energy.

Some of the forms of energy you have read about are also types of potential energy. For example, a battery has chemical potential energy. The chemical energy is stored until the battery is connected in a circuit. Then it is changed to electrical energy. This electrical energy might be used to light a light bulb. A piece of wood has chemical potential energy. The chemical energy is stored until the wood is burned. What happens to it then?

For Lesson Questions, turn to page 330.

How is the height of a swinging mass related to its energy?

Materials C-clamp / 50-g mass / string / block of wood / meterstick

Procedure

A. Tie one end of a piece of string to a 50-g mass.

B. Clamp a C-clamp to the edge of a table. Tie the loose end of the string to the C-clamp.

C. Adjust the string so that the mass almost touches the floor. Place a block of wood in front of the mass. Then make a small mark on the floor in front of the block.

D. Pull back the mass until it is exactly 10 cm above the floor.
   1. Predict how far the block will move when it is struck by the mass.

E. Let the mass swing down and hit the block. Measure how far it moves from the mark on the floor.
   2. How far did the block move?
   3. How does this compare with your prediction?

F. Repeat step **E**, pulling the mass 20 cm, 30 cm, 40 cm, and 50 cm above the floor.
   4. How far did the block move each time?

Results

Make a chart like the one shown. Write the distance the block moved each time.

Conclusion

How is the height of the mass related to the amount of work done?

Height of mass from floor	Distance block was moved by mass
10 cm	
20 cm	
30 cm	
40 cm	
50 cm	

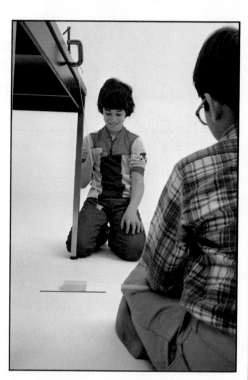

Simple Machines and Energy

How is energy used by different simple machines?

Have you ever tried to lift a car? Probably not. A car is very heavy. Lifting even one end of a car would be a lot of work. Yet this man is lifting a car. He is able to do this by using a jack. A jack consists of a simple machine called a lever. A **simple machine** is a machine made of very few parts.

A **lever** is a machine made of a bar or rod that turns on a point. The point on which a lever turns is called the fulcrum. A force, or effort, is used on one end of the lever. This force moves an object that is attached to the other end. This object is called the load. The closer the fulcrum is to the load, the easier the load is to lift.

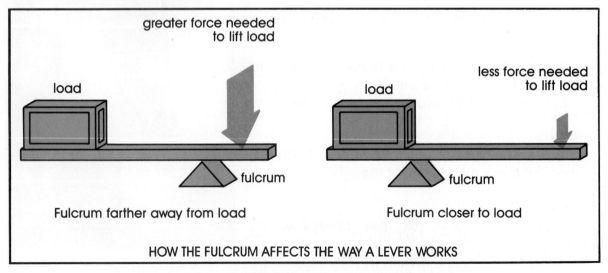

greater force needed to lift load

load

fulcrum

Fulcrum farther away from load

less force needed to lift load

load

fulcrum

Fulcrum closer to load

HOW THE FULCRUM AFFECTS THE WAY A LEVER WORKS

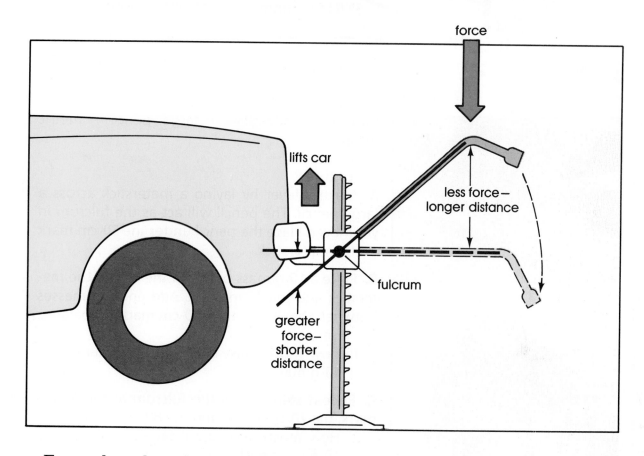

force

lifts car

less force— longer distance

fulcrum

greater force— shorter distance

Even though using a lever makes work easier, it does not save energy. Look at the drawing of the car jack. It takes less force to push down on the jack handle than it would take to lift the car by hand. But you have to push the handle a long distance to lift the car a short distance. If you move the handle 40 cm, the car may be lifted only 2 cm. So why use a car jack? The answer is to decrease the force needed to lift the heavy car. The only way you can lift the car is to decrease the force. The jack is a simple machine that decreases the force needed to lift the car. That is the advantage of a simple machine.

Activity

How does changing the fulcrum affect a lever?

Materials meterstick / large pencil / metric masses

Procedure

A. Make a lever by laying a meterstick across a large pencil. The pencil will act as the fulcrum in your lever. Place the pencil under the 50-cm mark on the meterstick.

B. Place a 10-g mass between the end of the meterstick and the 1-cm mark. Add enough masses between the 99-cm and 100-cm marks to balance the lever.

   1. How much mass did it take to balance the 10-g mass?

C. Repeat step **B** with the fulcrum at the 60-cm mark, the 70-cm mark, and the 80-cm mark.

   2. How much mass did it take to balance the 10-g mass each time?

Results

Use the information from the activity to make a chart. List the different positions of the fulcrum. Then write the amount of mass it took to balance the 10-g mass each time.

Conclusion

What happens to the amount of mass needed to balance the lever as the fulcrum is moved farther away from the 10-g mass?

Using science ideas

If you were using a lever to lift a heavy load, how would you position the fulcrum to make the job easier?

Another type of simple machine is called a wheel and axle. A **wheel and axle** consists of a wheel connected to an axle. When either the wheel or the axle moves, the other moves, too.

A doorknob is a wheel and axle. Have you ever tried to open a door by just turning the axle of a doorknob? It takes a large force to do this. By attaching a larger handle to the axle, less force is needed. But, as with levers, this force is used over a long distance. So a wheel and axle does not save energy.

axle

wheel

This ramp is a third kind of simple machine called an inclined plane. An **inclined plane** is a machine made of a slanted surface. Pushing the box up the inclined plane takes a small force. Lifting the box straight up takes a larger force. But the distance the box is pushed across the inclined plane is long. The distance the box would be lifted is shorter. The smaller force needed to push the box is used over a long distance. The larger force needed to lift the box is used over a shorter distance. Inclined planes make work easier without saving energy.

A pulley is still another type of simple machine. A **pulley** is made of a wheel that has a groove in it. A rope, chain, or belt fits into the groove. Pulleys can be used in two ways. The pulley used on a flagpole is a fixed pulley. A fixed pulley can change the direction of your force. You pull down on one end of the rope. The load is pulled up by the other end. It takes the same force to lift a load with a fixed pulley as it does without a fixed pulley.

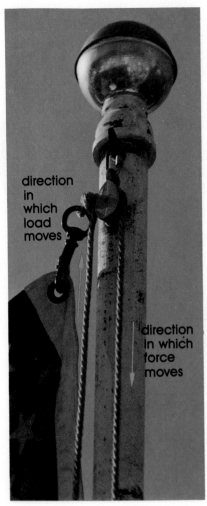

Fixed pulley

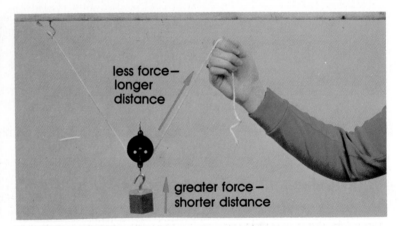

Movable pulley

The pulley shown above is a movable pulley. A movable pulley does not change the direction of your force. Like a lever, a movable pulley lets you use less force to lift a load. But you must pull the rope a longer distance than the load moves. The smaller force needed to lift a load with a movable pulley is used over a longer distance. So a movable pulley does not save energy.

Not all the energy you put into a machine is used to move a load. A small part of the energy is used to overcome a force called friction (frik'shǝn). **Friction** is a force that slows down or stops motion. There is friction when two parts of a machine rub against each other. In the inclined plane there is friction between the box and the surface of the ramp. In the pulley there is some friction between the rope and the wheel of the pulley.

One way to reduce friction is by covering surfaces that rub together with grease or oil. Another way is by using wheels. A box with wheels can be pushed up a ramp much easier than can a box without wheels.

For Lesson Questions, turn to page 330.

Science & TECHNOLOGY

▶ **Did you know that robots can be used to save lives? Robots can do jobs that are too dangerous for people to do. The robot in this picture is used by a police department. It can pick up and carry objects that may injure people.**

◀ **There are more than 20,000 robots at work in factories. Most of them help to build cars. These robots stay in one spot. Their arms move up and down and back and forth. They can hold tools and lift things. They do welding and drilling. These robots are good helpers. But they cannot build cars by themselves.**

125

Compound Machines and Energy

What is a compound machine?

How many simple machines can you name in this can opener? The two long handles are levers. The key that you turn to open a can is a wheel and axle. The cutting blade is a type of inclined plane. A can opener is made of many simple machines. Any machine that is made up of two or more simple machines is called a **compound machine.**

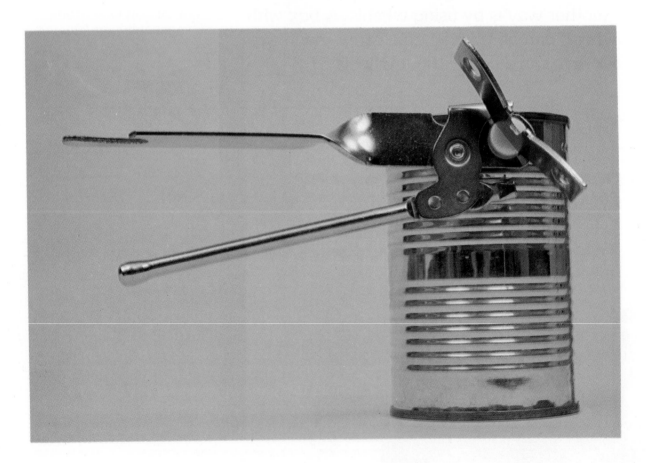

There are many different kinds of compound machines. Some, such as a wheelbarrow, are made up of only a few simple machines. Other compound machines, such as a car, are made of hundreds of wheels, levers, and pulleys. Some compound machines, such as a wheelbarrow, use mechanical energy. Others, such as a car, use chemical energy.

A bicycle is a compound machine. Study the bicycle shown here. How many simple machines can you name?

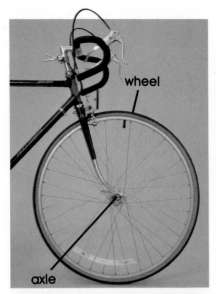

wheel

axle

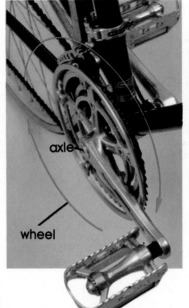

axle

wheel

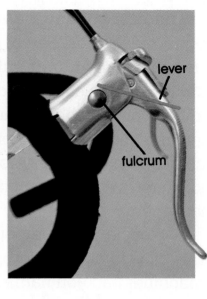

lever

fulcrum

wheel

axle

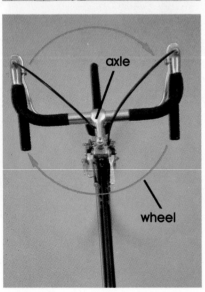

axle

wheel

A bicycle is made of many simple machines. There are several wheel-and-axle machines on this bicycle. The wheels of the bicycle are connected to axles. So they form a wheel-and-axle machine. The pedals are two other wheel-and-axle machines. First the pedals turn a gear. This gear is connected to a gear on the rear wheel of the bicycle by a chain. The gears and the chain that connects them form a third wheel-and-axle machine. The handlebars make up a fourth wheel and axle. This bicycle also has brake handles, which are levers. These levers help to make it easier to stop the bicycle. Where does the energy used by each of these simple machines come from?

For Lesson Questions, turn to page 330.

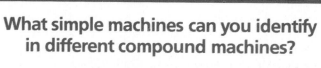

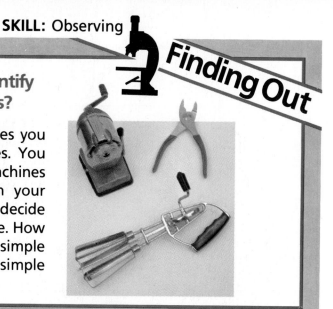

What simple machines can you identify in different compound machines?

See how many different simple machines you can find in different compound machines. You may use some of the compound machines shown here, or others that you find in your home. For each simple machine you find, decide what job it does in the compound machine. How would the compound machine work if the simple machine were removed? How does the simple machine get the energy it uses?

Ideas to Remember

▶ Energy is the ability to do work. Chemical energy, light energy, sound energy, heat energy, electrical energy, and mechanical energy are different forms of energy.

▶ The energy of motion is called kinetic energy. Stored energy is called potential energy.

▶ A simple machine is a machine made of very few parts. A lever, an inclined plane, a wheel and axle, and a pulley are simple machines.

▶ A simple machine makes it easier to do work, but it does not save energy.

▶ A compound machine is a machine made of two or more simple machines.

Reviewing the Chapter

SCIENCE WORDS

A. Use the science terms to identify the following.

compound machine   pulley   simple machine
inclined plane   lever   wheel and axle

1. I am any machine made of very few parts. What am I?
2. I am a machine made of a slanted surface. What am I?
3. I am any machine made up of two or more other machines. What am I?
4. I am a machine made of a bar or rod that turns on a point. What am I?
5. I am a machine made of a wheel connected to an axle. What am I?
6. I am a machine made of a wheel that has a groove in it. A rope, chain, or belt fits into this groove. What am I?

B. Copy the sentences below. Use science terms from the chapter to complete the sentences.

1. The energy of motion is called ＿＿.
2. Stored energy is called ＿＿.
3. A force that works to keep one object from sliding across another is called ＿＿.
4. The ability to do work is called ＿＿.
5. Light bulbs are lit by energy called ＿＿.
6. Gasoline and food contain ＿＿ energy.

UNDERSTANDING IDEAS

A. Explain the difference between kinetic energy and potential energy. Use examples in your answer.

B. Explain why a simple machine makes work easier to do but does not save energy. Use a lever in your explanation.

C. Identify at least one form of energy in each of these pictures. Explain how one of the forms of energy comes from another form of energy.

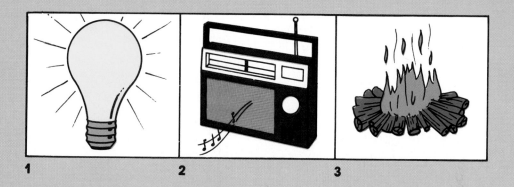

1

2

3

USING IDEAS

1. Make a list of different forms of energy in your home. Identify which forms of energy come from other forms of energy.
2. Find out how changing the angle of a ramp changes the force needed to move an object up it.
3. As you learned in this chapter, some of the energy put into a machine is used to overcome friction. Yet friction is helpful in many ways. Describe what the world would be like if there were no friction.

THINKING LIKE A SCIENTIST

You may be able to answer some of these questions just by thinking about them. To answer other questions, you may have to do some research.

1. How many different kinds of energy are used in making a loaf of wheat bread? List as many kinds of energy as you can, beginning with the seeds that produced the wheat plant.
2. How could each of these things be used to reduce friction: baby powder, a plastic bag, a pencil, marbles, and soap?

CHAPTER 7

Heat Energy

A plane flies overhead
and Chris runs outside.
He lives near an airport.
Chris often listens for the
whrrr of the small plane
motors. When Chris hears
this sound, he looks up in
the sky to see if he recognizes
any of the planes. Chris knows
many of the pilots and the planes
they fly. He enjoys spending time
at the airport talking to the pilots.

One warm, clear day something special happened. Chris was riding his bicycle
near the airport. He happened to look up and
saw a small plane with long wings. Chris was surprised because he hadn't heard the sound of an airplane
motor. How could this plane be flying? Had the motor stopped
working? Was the plane going to crash? Chris watched in
awe as the plane circled and glided smoothly to the ground.

The plane had NO motor!

Chris ran over to the plane. He had a lot of questions for the pilot. He knew he had to find out about this unusual plane. When he reached the plane, the pilot was getting out. Some people were walking toward the plane with a wheelchair. The pilot transferred himself into the chair. Now Chris was really amazed. The pilot couldn't walk, but he could fly a plane that didn't have a motor!

132a

The pilot, Ray, said that the plane was a sailplane and belonged to a club named Freedom's Wings. Freedom's Wings provides special planes and flight training for people with physical handicaps. Many of the club's members are in wheelchairs.

Ray told Chris that wings are a symbol of freedom and that people feel freed from their handicaps when they are flying. Because the plane has a hand-operated control system, people who cannot use their legs or feet can fly it.

Chris still wanted to know what kind of a plane could fly without a motor. Ray explained that the sailplane does not need a motor to fly. But a sailplane must be towed into the sky by a plane that has a motor.

After being released from the tow plane, the sun provides power for a sailplane. This type of flying is called thermal (thĕr′ məl) flying.

How does thermal flying work? The sun heats the surface of the earth. Heat from the earth's surface warms the air. Different surfaces heat up at different rates. So the air above the earth's surface is heated unevenly. The air above the warmest surfaces rises very fast. This rising air has a lot of power to lift the sailplane higher into the sky.

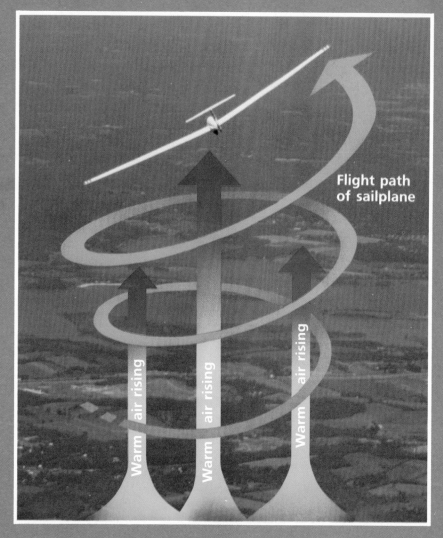

Flight path of sailplane

Warm air rising

Warm air rising

Warm air rising

Now came a great moment for Chris. Ray offered to take him for a ride. Chris ran home to get permission from his parents. They came back with Chris to the airport. After they met Ray and talked with him, Chris was allowed to go up for a ride.

As he sat behind Ray in the plane, Chris could hardly wait for takeoff. Chris watched with excitement as the sailplane was being attached to the tow plane. Ray told Chris, "We're going to climb to 915 meters. When I give you the signal, pull the yellow knob and we'll be free from the tow rope.

Now!"

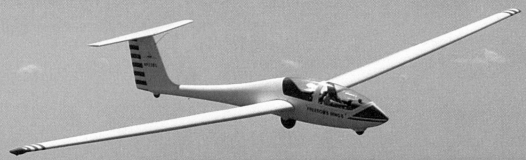

Flying in the sailplane was the closest thing to flying like a bird. Now Chris understood the meaning of freedom. It was so quiet as they soared through the sky on Freedom's Wings!

A sailplane moves higher in the sky because of heat energy. You can show how heat energy can cause an object to move. You will need a sheet of paper, a pencil, a straight pin, a pair of scissors, a 12 cm piece of thread, and a lamp.

Turn the lamp on. Then trace the spiral on a sheet of paper. Make a pinhole in the center of the spiral. Cut the paper in a spiral as shown. Put the thread through the pinhole and make a knot. Hold the thread so that the spiral is about 1-2 cm above the hot light bulb. What happens to the spiral?

The sailplane uses heat energy from the sun to move higher in the sky. The spiral moves because of heat energy, too. In this chapter you will learn more about heat energy. You will also learn how heat moves from one place to another.

Heat

What is heat?

In what ways have you experienced heat? Maybe you can remember hot summer days when you played in the shade all day. You might remember trying to cool some hot soup before you ate it. Or maybe you have felt the warmth of a campfire.

As you can see, heat can be experienced in many ways. But what is heat? **Heat** is a form of energy. As more heat energy is added to matter, it becomes hotter. For example, if you add more heat energy to a pot of soup, it will become hotter.

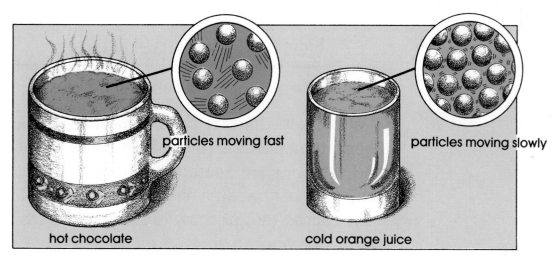

particles moving fast

particles moving slowly

hot chocolate

cold orange juice

All matter is made of tiny particles. The particles are always moving. The more heat energy the matter has, the faster the particles vibrate (vī'brāt), or move back and forth. As particles vibrate faster, they also move farther apart. For example, the particles in hot chocolate vibrate fast and are far apart. But the particles in cold orange juice vibrate more slowly and stay closer together. The hot chocolate has more heat energy than the cold orange juice.

How can you find out how much heat energy matter has? One way is to measure its temperature. Think about two cups filled with the same amount of water at 0°C. One cup is then heated to 10°C. The other cup is heated to 20°C. To which cup has more heat energy been added?

Heat energy is measured in a unit called a **calorie** (kal'ər ē). Adding calories of heat energy to matter raises its temperature.

For Lesson Questions, turn to page 332.

Heat and Temperature

How are heat and temperature different?

When you think of heat, you often think about temperature (tem'pər ə chər). Heat and temperature seem to go together. But they are not the same. As you have learned, heat causes the particles in matter to move faster. **Temperature** is a measure of how fast the particles move. The faster the particles in matter move, the higher the temperature of the matter.

Science & Technology

◄ The next time your temperature is taken, a new type of thermometer may be used. Both of the thermometers at the left are made of plastic and have liquid crystals. Liquid crystals change color at certain temperatures. The thermometer at the top is held against the forehead. The bottom one is held under the tongue.

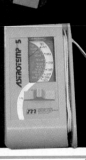

▶ Both thermometers at the right have a small probe that is held under the tongue. The probe is made of copper or platinum. Differences in temperature cause changes in the way these metals conduct electricity. When the probe is put into your mouth, your temperature causes these changes. What is a normal body temperature? When does your temperature change?

Pleasant summer day—27°C

Ice—0°C

Temperature can be measured in units called **degrees Celsius** (di grēz′ sel′sē əs). The symbol for degrees Celsius is °C. Water boils at a temperature of 100°C. Water freezes at a temperature of 0°C. On a summer day, the air temperature might be 27°C.

Boiling water—100°C

SKILL: Measuring

What is the difference in temperature of different forms of water?

Fill a bowl halfway with cold tap water. Put the bulb end of a Celsius thermometer into the water. Wait until the level of the liquid in the thermometer stops changing. Then read the thermometer. Repeat these steps with hot tap water and then with crushed ice. What is the difference in temperature between these three bowls of water?

Finding Out

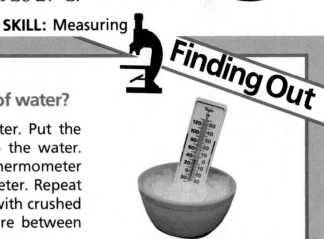

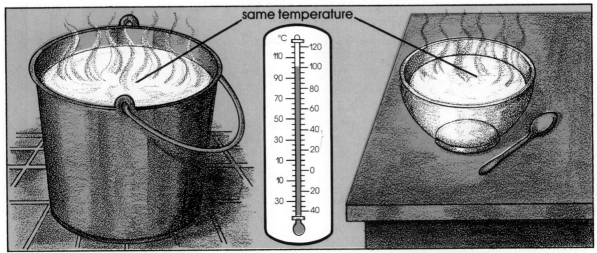

same temperature

°C
110
90
70
50
30
10
10
30

120
100
80
60
40
20
0
20
40

pail full of boiling water:
more particles — more heat

bowl full of boiling water:
fewer particles — less heat

To see how heat is different from temperature, think of this example. Suppose you have a pail and a bowl. Someone pours boiling water into each of them. The pail holds much more boiling water than does the bowl. You know that the temperature of the water in each is about the same. But does the water in the pail have the same amount of heat energy as the water in the bowl?

You have learned that heat is the vibration of the particles in matter. The pail holds more particles of water than does the bowl. So the water in the pail contains more heat energy than does the water in the bowl.

Now you can see that two different amounts of matter can have the same temperature. But the larger amount of matter will always have more heat energy.

For Lesson Questions, turn to page 332.

How Heat Moves Through Solid Matter

How does heat move through a solid?

Have you ever touched the metal handle of a pan before it was placed on the stove? If so, then you may have noticed that the handle felt cold. But what happened after the pan was put on the stove and used to cook food? If you were to touch the handle then, you might feel it getting hotter. You might have to use a pot holder to protect your hand from the heat in the handle. Why does the metal handle of a pan get so hot?

The pan is made of metal, a solid. The particles in a solid vibrate back and forth. In the drawing you can see how the particles in the cold pan move.

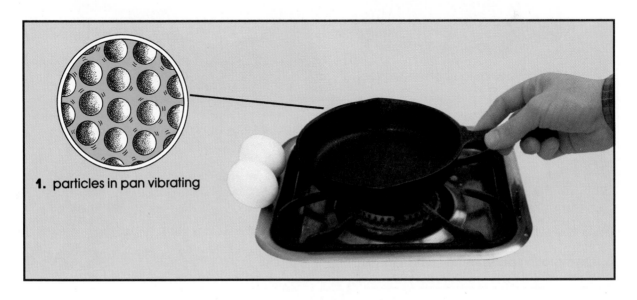

1. particles in pan vibrating

As the pan starts to get hot, the particles in the large part of the pan begin to vibrate faster. Then these particles bump into the slower-moving particles in the handle. This causes the particles in the handle to vibrate faster. This continues to happen all along the handle. Soon all the metal particles are vibrating rapidly. Now the handle feels hot. The heat energy has been passed along through the whole pan. This movement of heat through a solid is called **conduction** (kən duk'shən).

2. particles in pan vibrating faster

4. heat energy moving along handle

3. fast-vibrating particles bumping into slower-vibrating particles in handle

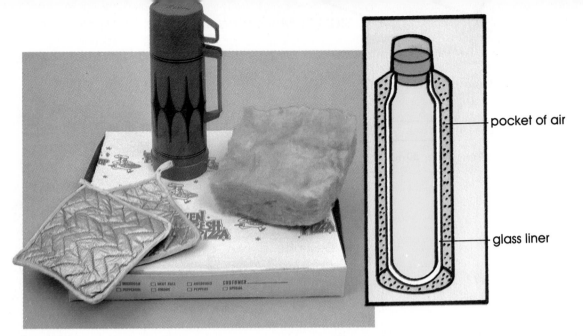

pocket of air

glass liner

Insulators

Heat energy does not move at the same speed through all kinds of matter. Heat energy does not move easily through some materials. These materials are called good **insulators** (in′sə lā tərs). The particles that make up a good insulator are spaced far apart. The pizza box, pot holders, and home insulation shown above are made of good insulating materials. So is the thermos. It uses a layer of air to keep hot liquids hot and cold liquids cold. Particles of air are spaced far apart.

Heat energy can move easily through other materials. These materials are called good **conductors** (kən duk′tərs). The particles that make up a good conductor are close together. The pans and iron shown here are made of good conducting materials.

Conductors

For Lesson Questions, turn to page 332.

141

Activity

What kinds of fabrics make good insulators?

	WATER TEMPERATURE	
	At beginning	After 30 min.
Jar wrapped with cotton cloth		
Jar wrapped with wool cloth		
Jar wrapped with polyester cloth		
Unwrapped jar		

Materials 4 identical jars with lids / hot tap water / 4 thermometers / tape / pieces of cotton, wool, and polyester cloth / hand lens

Procedure

A. Use a hand lens to look at pieces of cotton, wool, and polyester cloth.

   1. Describe how the threads in each kind of cloth are woven.

B. Make a chart like the one shown.

C. Half fill four jars with hot tap water. Place a thermometer in each jar. Screw the lids on tightly. Measure the temperature of the water in each jar. Make sure the temperatures are about the same. Write the temperatures in the chart.

D. Cover three of the jars with cloth. Wrap the piece of cotton cloth around one jar. Wrap the piece of wool cloth around the second jar and the piece of polyester cloth around the third jar. Fasten each piece of cloth with tape.

   2. How do you think the temperature in each jar will change?

E. Unwrap the jars after 30 minutes. Write the temperatures in the chart.

Results

1. The cloth covering the jar whose water temperature fell the least was the best insulator. Which cloth was the best insulator?

2. The cloth covering the jar whose water temperature fell the most was the poorest insulator. Which cloth was the poorest insulator?

Conclusion

What kinds of fabrics make good insulators?

How Heat Moves Through Liquids and Gases

What is convection?

Heat energy can easily move through conductors. But most liquids and gases are not good conductors. So how does heat move through liquids and gases?

The way heat energy moves through liquids and gases is called **convection** (kən-vek'shən). Like conduction, convection is caused by the movement of particles in matter. But unlike conduction, in convection the particles move from one place to another.

To help you understand convection, think of a room in a house. The room contains a radiator. How is a whole room heated by one radiator?

Look at the picture below. At first, only the air near the radiator is heated. As this air becomes warmer, the particles that make up the air begin to move faster. The particles also move farther apart. So the warm air takes up more space. This air is now less dense than it was before it was heated.

The particles in cool air move more slowly and are closer together than those in warm air. So cool air is more dense than warm air. The cool air pushes the warm air up toward the ceiling. The warm air cools as it rises. It becomes more dense, and then it sinks. The cool air is heated by the radiator. This happens over and over. In this way the air in the room is heated by convection.

cooler air moving down

warm air beginning to rise

air becoming warm

cool air pushes warm air up

144

For Lesson Questions, turn to page 332.

Heat from Sunlight

How does the sun warm matter on earth?

Have you ever been warmed by the sun on a cold day? As long as you stayed in the sunlight, you were warm. If the sun went behind a cloud, you were chilly. Why did this happen?

As you can see in the drawing, the sun gives off other forms of energy besides light. These forms of energy cannot be seen. But like light, the other forms of energy travel in waves. One of the other forms of energy changes to heat when it strikes matter. The movement of heat energy in waves is called **radiation** (rā dē ā'shən).

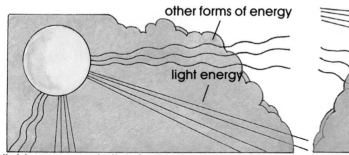
other forms of energy

light energy

light energy and other forms of energy leaving sun

waves of energy striking matter changing to heat

Your body is made of matter. When you stand in sunlight, waves of energy from the sun strike you. Some of the energy changes to heat. You are warmed by the heat. This is why you can be warmed by the sun on a cold day.

Activity

How can heat from the sun be trapped?

Materials   2 thermometers / glass jar with lid

Procedure

A. Make a chart like the one shown.

B. Place a thermometer in a glass jar. Screw the lid on tightly.

C. Place the jar in direct sunlight on a table or windowsill. Place a second thermometer next to the jar. Read both thermometers. Write the temperatures under the heading *0 minutes.*

   1. How do you think each thermometer will change after 20 minutes?

D. Read the thermometers every 5 minutes for 20 minutes. Write the temperatures in the chart.

Results

1. What happened to the temperature inside the glass jar during the 20-minute period?

2. What happened to the temperature outside the jar during the same time?

3. Which temperature was higher after 20 minutes?

Conclusion

How were you able to trap heat from the sun?

Using science ideas

Some people are beginning to use heat from the sun to heat their homes. Find out about solar collectors. How are they like the jar you used in this activity? How are they different?

Time	Temperature inside jar	Temperature outside jar
0 min.		
5 min.		
10 min.		
15 min.		
20 min.		

Have you ever seen a greenhouse? Much of the heat in a greenhouse comes from the sun. Waves of energy from the sun travel through the glass roof of the greenhouse. When the waves strike matter inside the greenhouse, they change to heat. Heat cannot escape through the glass, so the heat gets trapped inside. This warms the greenhouse. A greenhouse can be warmed even on the coldest day of winter. Have you ever entered a closed-up car that was sitting in the sun? Why was the inside of the car very hot?

Greenhouse

For Lesson Questions, turn to page 332.

Ideas to Remember

▶ Heat is a form of energy measured in calories.
▶ Temperature is a measure of how fast the particles in matter move.
▶ The way heat energy moves through a solid is called conduction.
▶ The way heat energy moves through a liquid or gas is called convection.
▶ The movement of heat energy in waves is called radiation.

Reviewing the Chapter

A. Use all the terms below to complete the sentences.

convection   conduction   insulator
conductor   radiation

Heat energy moves in different ways through different kinds of matter. The way heat energy moves through a solid is called __1__. Heat energy does not move at the same speed through all kinds of solids. Heat energy can easily move through a type of solid called a/an __2__. Heat energy cannot easily move through another type of solid called a/an __3__. The way heat energy moves through liquids and gases is called __4__. Heat energy also comes from waves of energy from the sun. This movement of heat energy in waves is called __5__.

B. Write the letter of the term that best matches the definition. Not all the terms will be used.

1. A unit of heat energy
2. A measure of how fast the particles in matter move
3. A form of energy
4. A unit used to measure temperature

a. heat
b. conductor
c. calorie
d. degree Celsius
e. temperature

A. Cross out the term that does not belong in each group below. Then describe what the remaining terms have in common.

1. thermometer, degrees Celsius, heat, temperature
2. convection, liquid, insulator, gas
3. solid, insulator, conduction, convection
4. conductor, radiation, waves, sun

B. Look at the drawing. Draw what the particles that make up liquid A and liquid B would look like.

A

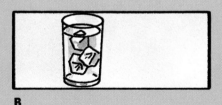

B

C. Which cup of soup needed more calories to get hot? Explain your answer.

A

B

D. Explain the difference between an insulator and a conductor. Use examples of each in your explanation.

USING IDEAS

Make a list of the different insulators and conductors found in your home.

THINKING LIKE A SCIENTIST

You may be able to answer some of these questions just by thinking about them. To answer other questions, you may have to do some research.

1. Some people make cooking pans for a living. What should these people know about the movement of heat?

2. Some people use ceiling fans in winter to keep their heated houses warmer. How do you suppose the fans help to do this?

CHAPTER 8
Electricity and Magnetism

BONG!   BONG!   BONG!

This was a sound heard when there was lightning in the sky in the 1700s. People believed that if they rang church bells, the lightning would be kept away. However, the people who rang the bells were often struck by lightning and killed.

After a while, people realized that bell ringing did not keep lightning away. They learned that lightning would strike high church spires. It would travel down the wet rope used to ring the bell and would strike the bell ringer. So laws were passed to stop bell ringing when lightning occurred.

In 1752, Benjamin Franklin showed that lightning is electricity. Perhaps you have seen pictures of Franklin standing in a rainstorm with his kite. Franklin attached a stiff wire to the top of his kite. Then he tied a piece of silk thread near the free end of the kite string. He tied a metal key to the thread. Lightning struck the wire, and electricity traveled down the wet string, through the thread, and to the key. The electricity caused a spark to jump from the key to Franklin's hand, which was near the key. Franklin could have been killed.

Today, scientists are still studying lightning. They know lightning occurs when energy builds up and then releases suddenly. This build-up of energy takes place in clouds. What scientists are not sure of is just how this happens. Some say rain causes charges to build up. Others say it is the wind.

150a

Now try this

You can see lightning in the sky during a thunderstorm. In a darkened room you can make you own "lightning" on a very small scale. You will need a roll of black bicycle tape and a comb.

Pick a dry, cool day. In a darkened room, pull a length of tape away from the roll of bicycle tape. What can you see?

Long hair can be combed to produce sparks you can see. Continue combing the hair until you hear a crackling sound. How are the sparks similar to lightning?

No matter what causes lightning, it continues to be a threat. It injures and kills people. It causes fires that burn homes and destroy trees. Scientists hope that by learning more about lightning, they can predict where it will strike next. This would prevent people from being hurt, and damage from being done.

Since lightning is such a threat, you should remember these safety rules when you see lightning. Electricity travels through water, so stay away from water. Metal may attract lightning, so do not ride a bike. Since lightning often hits something tall, do not take shelter under a tree. When outdoors, go indoors or sit in a car. If you are not able to do either, drop to the ground. When inside a building, stay away from open doors and windows. Do not touch any electric appliances.

Lightning is a type of electricity. In this chapter you will learn about different types of electricity. You will also learn how electricity is related to magnetism.

Static Electricity

There are two types of electricity. One type is called current electricity. You use this type of electricity to light your home and classroom. The second type is called static electricity. **Static electricity** is made by friction, or rubbing. Static electricity makes your hair rise when you pull a sweater over your head. It also causes lightning. But what causes static electricity?

All matter is made up of tiny particles that have electric charges. Some of these particles have a positive charge. Other particles have a negative charge. Rubbing two objects together may cause some of the negative charges to rub off one object. The charges move to the second object. This gives the second object a greater negative charge than the first object.

1 negative and positive charges on both sweater and hair

2 negative charges from sweater moving to hair

What happens when you pull off a sweater over your head? Look at the drawings. As you take off the sweater, you rub off some of the negative charges from the sweater. These negative charges move to your hair. Now your hair has more negative charges than your sweater does. Your sweater has more positive charges than negative charges. Negative and positive charges attract each other, or are drawn together. So the positive charges from the sweater attract the negative charges on your hair. This makes your hair rise.

Can you name other ways you have experienced static electricity? Static electricity causes clothes to stick to each other in a clothes dryer. You can also experience static electricity while you comb your hair. Try combing your hair, and then hold the comb close to your hair. What happens? Why does this happen?

3 positive charges on sweater attracting negative charges on hair

For Lesson Questions, turn to page 334.

Activity

How do charged objects affect each other?

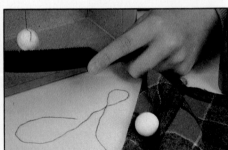

Materials   2 plastic-foam balls / tape / thread / shoebox / comb / wool cloth

Procedure

A. Tape a plastic-foam ball to one end of a piece of thread. Tape the other end of the thread to a shoebox as shown.

B. Rub a comb with a wool cloth. This gives the comb a negative charge.

   1. Predict what will happen if you bring the comb near the ball.

C. Bring the comb near the ball.

   2. What happens?

   3. Is the charge on the ball the same as the charge on the comb? How do you know?

D. Tape another ball to a second piece of thread. Hang this ball next to the first ball. Make sure the balls are touching.

E. Rub the comb with the cloth again. Bring the comb near one of the balls.

   4. What happens?

   5. What kind of charge must each of the balls have for this to happen? How do you know?

Results

1. What happens when an object that has one type of charge is brought near an object that has the opposite charge?

2. What happens when an object that has one type of charge is brought near an object that has the same type of charge?

Conclusion

How do charged objects affect each other?

Current Electricity

How is current electricity produced?

Whenever you turn on a television, a radio, or a lamp, you are using current electricity. **Current electricity** is produced when negative charges move along a path. How is this different from static electricity?

The path along which negative charges move is called a **circuit** (sêr′kit). The picture shows four parts of an electric circuit. (1) There is a source of electricity. In this circuit the source of electricity is a battery. (2) There is a path along which charges can move. In this circuit a wire forms the path. (3) There is a switch that opens and closes the circuit. (4) There is some object that uses the electricity. In this circuit the object is a light bulb.

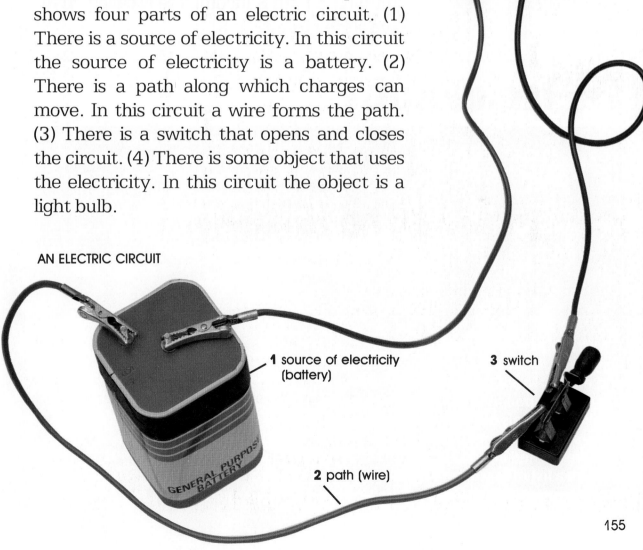

AN ELECTRIC CIRCUIT

4 user of electricity (light bulb)

1 source of electricity (battery)

3 switch

2 path (wire)

In this electric circuit the charges move from the battery, through the wire, to the switch. Then they move through the light bulb and back to the battery. When the switch is closed, or turned on, the path is complete. The charges can move. A circuit whose path is complete is called a **complete circuit.** When the switch is open, or turned off, the path is broken. The movement of charges stops. The path is incomplete. A circuit whose path is incomplete is called an **incomplete circuit.**

Science & Technology

◄ Microchips are important parts of computers and other machines. They store information in computers. They control machines like calculators and VCR's. Each microchip contains thousands of circuits. They must all fit on a tiny square that is smaller than a fingernail.

► Microchips must be made in rooms that are very clean. Workers must wear white gowns and masks. This is because the smallest bit of dust can spoil the chips. Chips are made of silicon crystals that are sliced into wafers. Then the circuit patterns for each chip are burned into the wafer.

Make a list of machines that use microchips.

Overloaded outlet

Electricity is useful, but it can also be dangerous. Electric wires should be handled carefully. If the outer covering of an electric wire is cracked or peeled, you can get a shock. Because of this, electric wires should never be pulled, stretched, or moved more than necessary.

Heat is produced as electricity moves through wires. If too many wires are plugged into one outlet, too much heat is produced. This can cause a fire.

Fires can also be caused by a short circuit. A short circuit can happen when the outer covering of the wires is worn and the wires touch each other. You can prevent short circuits by not using old or worn electric wires. Short circuits can also be prevented by handling all electric wires carefully.

For Lesson Questions, turn to page 334.

Making Electricity

What are some ways electricity can be made?

This flashlight needs electricity to work. The electricity used by a flashlight comes from a battery. A **battery** is an object that changes chemical energy into electricity.

There are two types of batteries. A dry cell battery is the type of battery used in a flashlight. A **dry cell battery** is a battery that is made up of a zinc case with a carbon rod in the center. The space in between is filled with a chemical paste. A chemical reaction takes place inside the battery. The reaction produces electric charges. Turning on a switch connects the zinc and the carbon. They form a circuit through which charges can move. The moving charges light the bulb.

light bulb

carbon rod

zinc case

paste

dry cell battery

wire

PARTS OF A FLASHLIGHT

The electricity from a car battery also comes from chemical action. A car battery is a wet cell battery. A **wet cell battery** is a battery that is made of layers of lead instead of zinc and carbon. The case has water and acid in it instead of paste. The lead and acid cause a chemical action that produces electricity.

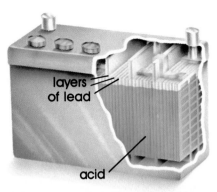
layers of lead
acid

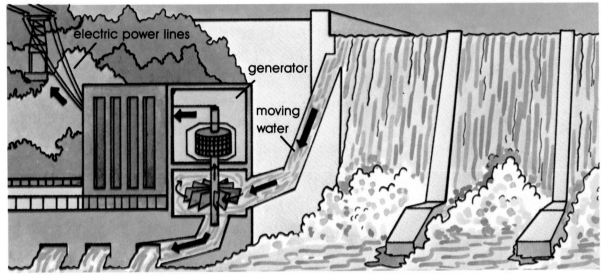
electric power lines
generator
moving water

Hydroelectric power plant

Electricity can also be produced by a generator (jen'ə rā tər). A **generator** is a machine that uses a magnet to produce electricity. Power plants use large generators to make electricity for whole towns. Generators have moving parts. They need a source of energy to move the parts. The generator in the power plant shown above uses moving water. This kind of power plant is called a hydroelectric (hī drō i lek'trik) power plant.

For Lesson Questions, turn to page 334.

Magnetism

What is a magnet?

Have you ever used a magnet? If you have, you know that a **magnet** is an object that attracts metals, such as iron and steel. You may also know that a magnetic force can be found in the space around a magnet. This space is called the **magnetic field.** A magnetic field can be seen when iron filings are sprinkled near a magnet. The iron filings form a pattern of lines. These lines are called lines of force. Lines of force show where the magnetic field is and what it looks like.

Magnetic field of one magnet

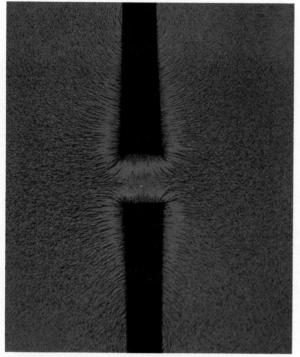 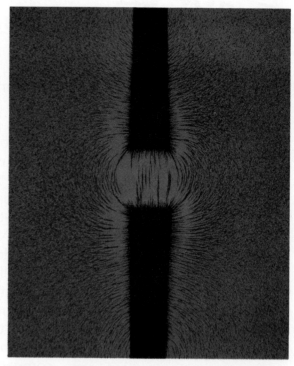

Magnetic field of two poles that are alike
Magnetic field of two poles that are not alike

The ends of a magnet are called the **poles.** A magnetic field is strongest at the poles. A magnet has two poles—a north pole and a south pole. The poles are equal in strength. Do you know how the poles are different from each other?

The north pole of one magnet attracts the south pole of another magnet. The south pole of one magnet attracts the north pole of another magnet. But the north pole of one magnet repels, or pushes away, the north pole of another magnet. In the same way, the south pole of one magnet repels the south pole of a second magnet.

Finding Out

How can you make a compass?

A compass is used to show direction. It has a needle that is a magnet. One end of the needle always points to the north. By looking at a compass, you can tell which direction is north.

You can make a compass by using a small bar magnet. Identify the north pole of the magnet. Use a piece of tape to mark the north pole on the magnet. Center the magnet on a piece of plastic foam. Next fill a shallow aluminum tray with water. Add 20 drops of liquid soap to the water. Carefully place the magnet and plastic foam on the water. In which direction does the north pole of the magnet point? Slowly turn the tray of water so that it points in another direction. What happens to the magnet? How could you use your compass to find which direction is south?

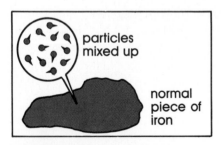
particles mixed up

normal piece of iron

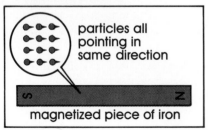
particles all pointing in same direction

magnetized piece of iron

What makes a magnet magnetic? Most magnets are made of iron. The particles that make up iron are like tiny magnets. Look at the first drawing. It is a normal piece of iron. As you can see, the particles are all mixed up. They point in different directions. Now look at the second picture. It is a magnetized piece of iron. All the particles point in the same direction. Can you think of any way you could make a magnet out of a piece of iron?

162

For Lesson Questions, turn to page 334.

What does a magnetic field look like?

Materials 2 bar magnets / piece of thin cardboard / iron filings

Procedure

A. Place a bar magnet on a table. Cover the magnet with a piece of thin cardboard.

B. Sprinkle iron filings on the cardboard. Tap the side of the cardboard gently.

  1. Make a drawing of the pattern formed by the iron filings.

C. Carefully slide another magnet under the cardboard. The north poles of the two magnets should be end to end, but not touching. Tap the side of the cardboard gently.

  2. Make a drawing of the new pattern.

D. Now arrange the two magnets so that the north pole of one magnet is next to the south pole of the other magnet. Place the magnets end to end, but not touching. Tap the cardboard again.

  3. Make a drawing of the new pattern.

Conclusion

1. Iron filings line up along the magnetic field of a magnet. Describe the magnetic field of a magnet.

2. Describe the magnetic field of two magnets whose same poles are next to each other.

3. Describe the magnetic field of two magnets whose opposite poles are next to each other.

Using science ideas

Repeat steps **A** and **B** using different-shaped magnets.

Electricity and Magnetism

What is an electromagnet?

Did you know that electricity and magnetism are related? First of all, magnetism can be used to produce electricity. This can be done by moving a magnet through a coil of wire. Electricity is produced as long as the magnet moves through the coil. A generator produces electricity in this way.

Electric current can be used to make a magnet. This can be done by wrapping wire around an iron nail. When electricity moves through the wire, a magnetic field is formed around the nail. The nail becomes a magnet. This type of magnet is called an electromagnet (i lek trō mag'nit). Electromagnets are often used in scrapyards to lift metal and move it. Many electromagnets are strong enough to lift heavy objects, such as cars. Electromagnets are also used in telephones.

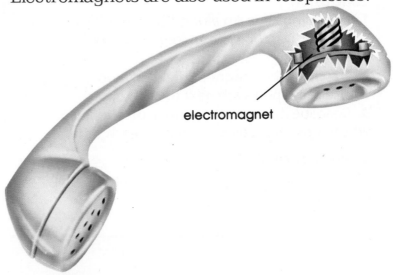

electromagnet

Electromagnet in scrapyard

For Lesson Questions, turn to page 334.

Finding Out

How can you make an electromagnet?

You can make an electromagnet by wrapping 90 cm of wire around a large nail. Be sure to make at least 20 turns around the nail. Then attach the free ends of the wire to the posts of a dry cell. Use your electromagnet to pick up paper clips. How many paper clips can you pick up? How could you make your electromagnet stronger without using a different source of electricity?

Ideas to Remember

▶ Static electricity is electricity made by friction, or rubbing.

▶ Current electricity is produced when negative charges move along a path called a circuit.

▶ Electricity can be produced using a battery or a generator.

▶ A magnet is an object that attracts certain metals, such as iron and steel.

▶ Magnetic poles that are alike repel, while magnetic poles that are not alike attract.

▶ Magnetism can be used to produce electricity. Electricity can be used to produce a magnet.

Reviewing the Chapter

SCIENCE WORDS

A. Write the letter of the term that best matches the definition. Not all the terms will be used.

1. The ends of a magnet
2. Something produced when negative charges move along a path
3. A battery made of lead, water, and acid
4. The space around a magnet in which a magnetic force can be found
5. An unbroken electrical path
6. Any object that changes chemical energy into electricity
7. A broken electrical path
8. A path along which negative charges move

    a. dry cell battery
    b. magnetic field
    c. incomplete circuit
    d. poles
    e. circuit
    f. complete circuit
    g. battery
    h. current electricity
    i. wet cell battery

B. Copy the sentences below. Use science terms from the chapter to complete each sentence.

1. A battery made of a zinc case with a carbon rod in the center is called a/an ＿＿.
2. A/An ＿＿ is a machine that uses a magnet to produce electricity.
3. Electricity produced by friction is called ＿＿.
4. A/An ＿＿ is an object that attracts steel.

UNDERSTANDING IDEAS

A. A girl rubbed a balloon with a piece of wool cloth. Then she held the balloon near her hair. She noticed that her hair was attracted to the balloon. Explain what happened.

B. Match each numbered item with its source of electricity.

1. car
2. flashlight
3. town

a. power plant
b. dry cell battery
c. wet cell battery

C. These two magnets are attracting each other. Identify poles 1, 2, and 3.

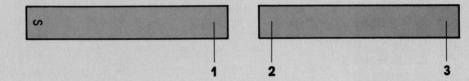

USING IDEAS

1. Make a list of the different rooms in your home. Look for electrical outlets in each room. Write down what things are plugged into each outlet in each room.
2. Find out what objects around your home and school are attracted to a magnet. You can do this by touching different objects with a magnet. You might want to test a copper penny, a sheet of aluminum foil, and an iron nail. Make lists of which objects were attracted to the magnet and which were not.

THINKING LIKE A SCIENTIST

You may be able to answer this question just by thinking about it, or you may have to do some research.

Large generators have a special part called a turbine. A turbine must move or spin before a generator can make electricity. The turbine in the drawing on page 159 is turned by moving water. Name two other sources of power that could be used to turn the turbine and produce electricity.

Science in Careers

Many people must do their jobs correctly before you can receive electricity in your home. Electricity is often used to supply heat and light and to run many machines found in your home.

Electricity is usually produced at some type of power plant. The machines that produce electricity have been developed with the help of **engineers.** Engineers are also in charge of the power plant. **Operators** run the generators. **Mechanics** make the generators run smoothly.

After leaving the power plant, electricity travels along wires and enters your home. The electrical wires in your home were put in by **electricians.** Electricians must also make sure the wires are safe to use.

Electrician

Some of the electricity in your home is used for lighting. Some of it may be used to provide heat. Heating equipment must be put in by **heating mechanics.** It must also be repaired by these mechanics.

Mechanic at an energy plant

People in Science

LEWIS LATIMER
(1848–1928)

Lewis Latimer was born in Chelsea, Massachusetts. He was an engineer. His work with carbon led Thomas Edison to use the material in the first light bulb. Later, Latimer invented an easy way to attach the carbon to electric wires in the bulb. He also found a cheap method for making large numbers of these pieces of carbon. This lowered the cost of light bulbs.

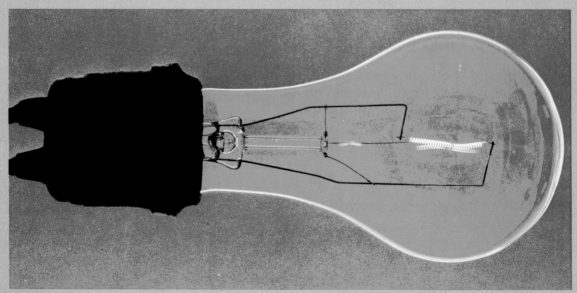

Light bulb

Developing Skills

WORD SKILLS

A prefix is one or more letters added to the beginning of a base word. A suffix is one or more letters added to the end of a base word. Prefixes and suffixes change the meanings of base words.

Use the tables to help you determine the meaning of each of the words listed.

If you do not know the meaning of a base word, look it up in a dictionary.

1. bipolar

2. discharge

3. frictional

4. magnetize

5. preheat

6. unlighted

Prefix	Meaning	Example
bi-	two	bicycle
dis-	not	dislike
pre-	before	preview
un-	not	unnecessary

Suffix	Meaning	Example
-al	of, like	natural
-ize	cause to become	magnetize

READING A CIRCLE GRAPH

A circle graph shows how something is divided. The circle graph on the next page shows different ways all the electricity used in the United States is produced. Use the circle graph to answer the following questions.

1. Which of the sources shown is the most common way to produce electricity?

2. Which is the more common way to produce electricity–petroleum or hydroelectric power?

3. Which is the least common way to produce electricity?

4. How much of the electricity used in the United States is produced by nuclear fuel?

5. How much of the electricity used in the United States is produced by hydroelectric power?

6. How much more electricity is produced with coal than with natural gas?

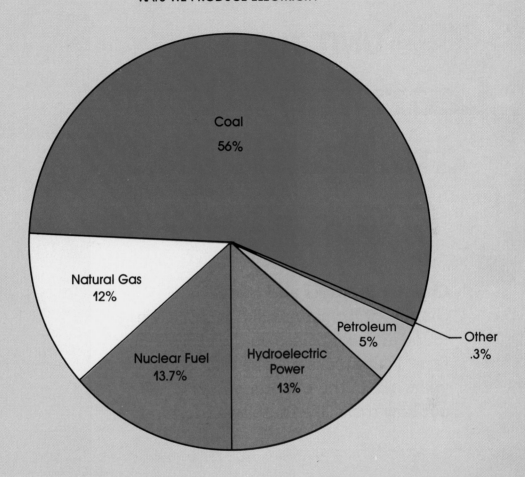

WAYS WE PRODUCE ELECTRICITY

Coal
56%

Natural Gas
12%

Nuclear Fuel
13.7%

Hydroelectric
Power
13%

Petroleum
5%

Other
.3%

USING THINKING SKILLS

There are many problems with producing electricity. Some people think that using nuclear power to produce electricity is unsafe. Using coal often causes pollution. Using petroleum to produce electricity can be costly. Keep these ideas in mind as you answer these questions.

1. Use reference books to find out about each of the sources of electricity.

2. Which source of electricity do you think is the best one to use? Explain your answer.

UNIT THREE

Learning About the Earth and the Planets

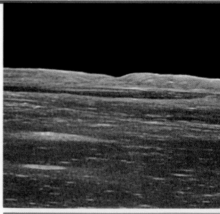

Chapter 9—Rocks and Minerals

Giant rock formations like this one are found in many places on the earth's surface. These rocks may be millions of years old. In this chapter you will find out how rocks like these were formed.

Chapter 10—The Earth's Oceans

If you were to visit this beach several times during the same day, you would find that it looked different each time. In this chapter you will learn how changes in the ocean can affect the way a beach looks.

Chapter 12–The Solar System This picture was taken from the surface of the moon. The body out in space is the earth. It is daytime on the part of the earth you can see.

Chapter 11–Measuring Weather
Clouds are formed from water that is in the air. In this chapter you will learn what happens when the air inside a cloud cools.

CHAPTER 9
Rocks and Minerals

HOT SPRINGS, SOUTH DAKOTA, 1974—George Hanson put his bulldozer in gear and began clearing a site to build some houses. Suddenly, he saw something white in the soil. George shut off the bulldozer and jumped down to take a closer look. Little did he realize what he had uncovered.

What George Hanson found was a tusk from a mammoth. As a result, he never finished clearing the site. And not one house was ever built there. Instead, the area is being used to find out about plants and animals that lived long ago.

The tusk found in Hot Springs came from a Columbian mammoth. The Columbian mammoth lived in a warm climate about 26,000 years ago. Unlike the wooly mammoth, it did not need a thick fur. It stood about 4 meters tall and weighed about 7 metric tons. This mammoth ate mainly grass and herbs.

Excited about finding the one mammoth tusk, scientists soon realized that there were more bones to be found there. In fact, the remains of about 39 mammoths have been found since 1974. Scientists have also uncovered the remains of other animals that lived long ago.

174a

Now try this

From clues on bones, scientists are able to piece facts together about animals that lived long ago. Pretend that you are a scientist in the year 3000. You are at a site where the following objects have been found. Your job is to identify each object.

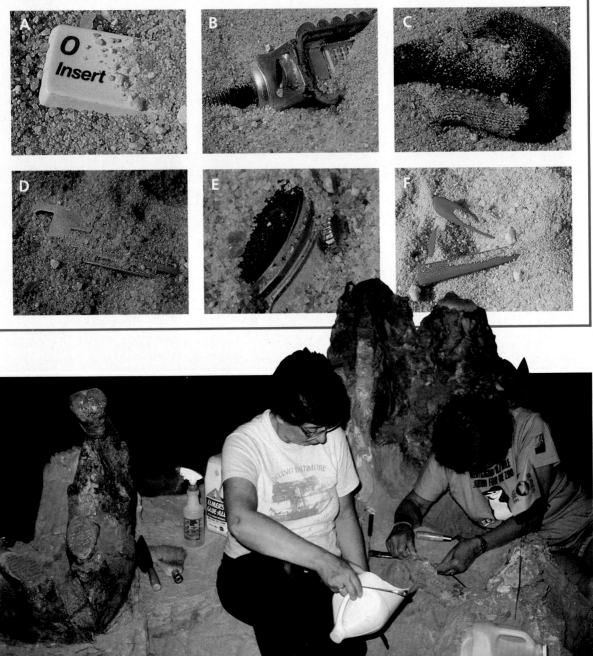

This area is now called the Mammoth Site. A building was constructed around the very place where the bones were found. There visitors can watch the careful digging being done to uncover these bones. The bones are left as they are found so that people may view them.

Why are the remains of so many mammoths buried at this site? Scientists think the site might have been a watering hole. When mammoths fed or drank at the watering hole, some may have fallen in. Unable to get out because of the steep, slippery banks, the mammoths either drowned or starved to death. Over a period of time, sand and dirt filled the hole and covered the mammoths. The mammoths remained buried until Hanson started to clear the land.

At the Mammoth Site, scientists are learning about the past by studying remains found in the earth. In much the same way, you were able to learn about an object from just one clue. In this chapter you will take a close look at rocks. You will learn how rocks help us learn about the past and why rocks are important to us today.

Inside the Earth

What are the three layers of the earth?

The parts of a fresh peach are like the three layers of the earth. A peach is covered by a thin outer skin. Under the skin there is a thick, fleshy layer. At the center of the peach, there is a pit. If you break open the pit, you will find a seed inside.

The crust of the earth can be compared with the skin of a peach. The **crust** is a thin layer of rock that covers the earth. The crust is about 4 to 7 km thick under the oceans. On land, the crust is about 35 km thick.

The **mantle** (man'təl) makes up most of the earth. The mantle is like the fleshy part of a peach. Scientists believe that the earth's mantle is made of very hot rocks.

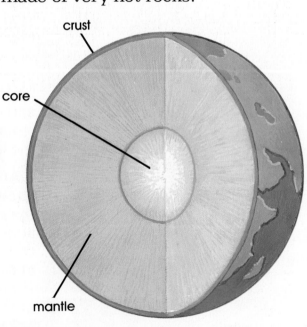

crust

core

mantle

The **core** is the inner layer of the earth. It lies below the mantle. Like a peach's pit, the earth's core has two parts—an outer part and an inner part. Many scientists think the core is made mostly of iron. Compare the crust, mantle, and core in the drawing on page 176. How are they different?

Mountains

Fuel

Food

Water

How is the earth important to us? The earth is important to us in many ways. We grow food in its soil. We drink the water it contains. It holds coal, oil, and gas, which we use as fuel. It also provides us with materials for making things.

For Lesson Questions, turn to page 336.

Minerals

What properties can be used to identify minerals?

Quartz crystals

Rocks are made up of one or more minerals (min′ər əlz). **Minerals** are pure solid materials found in the earth's crust. The particles that make up minerals join to form different-shaped crystals (kris′təlz). Different minerals can be identified by the shape of their crystals. A grain of salt is a crystal. If you look closely at salt, you will see little square blocks like those in the picture. These blocks are salt crystals.

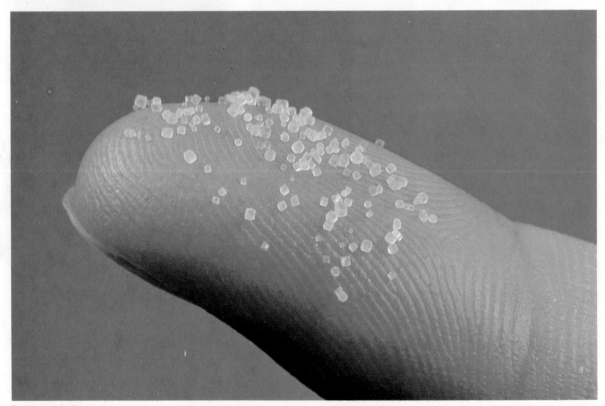

Salt crystals

There are hundreds of different minerals in the earth's crust. Each mineral has its own special properties. Scientists name, or identify, minerals by testing their properties. One property is magnetism. Magnetite (mag′nə tīt) is a magnetic mineral. Another property of a mineral is the shape of the crystals. You have already seen quartz and salt crystals. The color and the shine of the mineral are two other properties. Graphite (graf′īt) is black. Galena (gə lē′nə) is very shiny. Scientists often test for several properties before they are able to identify a mineral.

Graphite

Galena

The hardness of the mineral is another property used to identify it. Scientists test hardness by trying to scratch the mineral. Hardness is measured on a scale of 1 to 10.

The following table shows the hardness of some minerals. Which of these minerals have you seen?

MINERAL HARDNESS

Hardness	Mineral	
1 (Can be scratched with a fingernail)	TALC Talc is the softest mineral. It is used to make talcum powder.	
3 (Can be scratched with a copper penny)	CALCITE Calcite is used to make cement and fertilizer.	
7 (Can be scratched with a steel file)	QUARTZ Quartz is the most common mineral. It is used to make glass.	
10 (Can scratch glass)	DIAMOND A diamond is the hardest mineral. It cannot be scratched by any other mineral.	

For Lesson Questions, turn to page 336.

Melted Rock

What are three ways rocks can form from melted rock?

It is very hot deep within the earth. It is so hot that the rock there is melted. Melted rock within the earth is called magma (mag′mə). Magma is found in the mantle of the earth. Sometimes it moves toward the surface through cracks in the crust.

Have you ever cooled a cup of hot water? If you cool water enough, it changes to solid ice. In a similar way, if magma cools enough, it changes to solid rock. Rocks formed from magma are called **igneous** (ig′nē əs) **rocks.**

When magma gets trapped in cracks below the earth's surface, it cools slowly. Rocks formed when magma cools slowly contain large crystals. Large crystals that make up a piece of granite (gran′it) are shown here.

Granite

Obsidian

Sometimes magma reaches the surface through a crack or opening in the earth. The magma that reaches the surface is called lava (lä′və). At the surface, lava cools and hardens quickly to form small crystals.

Some of the rocks formed by lava contain such tiny crystals that they look like glass. Obsidian (ob sid′ē ən) is a rock that looks like glass. Compare obsidian with the granite on page 181. How are they different?

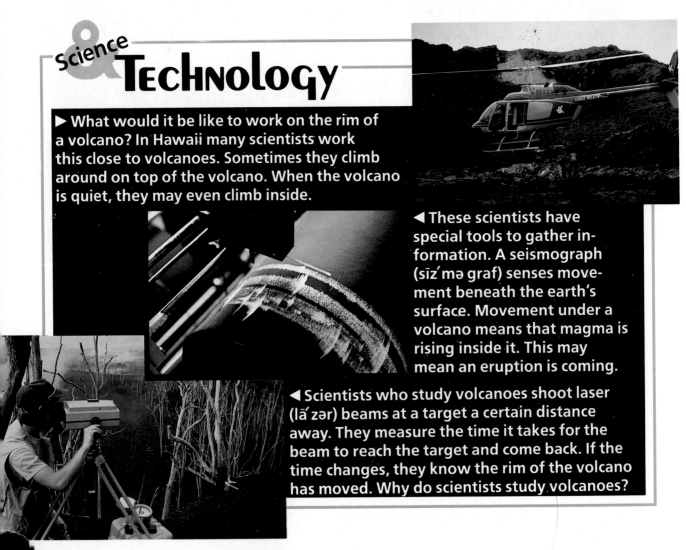

Science & TECHNOLOGY

▶ What would it be like to work on the rim of a volcano? In Hawaii many scientists work this close to volcanoes. Sometimes they climb around on top of the volcano. When the volcano is quiet, they may even climb inside.

◀ These scientists have special tools to gather information. A seismograph (sīz′mə graf) senses movement beneath the earth's surface. Movement under a volcano means that magma is rising inside it. This may mean an eruption is coming.

◀ Scientists who study volcanoes shoot laser (lā′zər) beams at a target a certain distance away. They measure the time it takes for the beam to reach the target and come back. If the time changes, they know the rim of the volcano has moved. Why do scientists study volcanoes?

Volcano and a piece of pumice

Lava that shoots out of a volcano may have steam and gases in it. This lava can also cool very quickly. It can cool so quickly that the gases do not have time to escape. Pumice (pum'is) forms from this type of lava. The trapped gases leave the holes you can see in a piece of pumice. The holes make pumice a very light igneous rock. Pumice is so light that it floats in water.

For Lesson Questions, turn to page 336.

Activity

How are crystals formed?

Materials 2 paper cups / hot sugar water / string / 2 pencils / 2 pieces of paper, 3 cm × 6 cm / tape / ruler / hand lens

Procedure

A. Write your name on two pieces of paper. Write *Cooled slowly* on one. Write *Cooled quickly* on the other. Tape each paper label to a different paper cup.

B. Use a ruler to measure the height of the paper cups. Tie a piece of string to each pencil. Cut the string 1 cm shorter than the height of the cups.

C. Rest the pencils on the cups as shown.

D. Ask your teacher to pour some hot sugar water into the cups.

E. Place the cup labeled *Cooled quickly* in a cold place. Place the cup labeled *Cooled slowly* in a warm place.

F. After several days, remove the strings. Examine them with a hand lens. Compare the crystals on the two strings.

Results

Describe the size of the crystals that formed in each cup.

Conclusion

1. What made the crystals form?
2. Why did one cup have larger crystals?

Using science ideas

On the earth, where would melted rock cool slowly? Where would melted rock cool quickly?

Rocks from Sediment

How are sedimentary rocks formed?

A second type of rock is formed from sediment (sed'ə mənt). Sediment is material such as mud, sand, or gravel. Sediment is often carried by wind and water moving across land. Water from heavy rains or melting snows often carries sediment into rivers and streams. Rivers and streams carry the loose sediment to lakes and oceans, where it settles to the bottom. There the sediment builds up in layers. The heavy top layers press down on the bottom layers.

River depositing sediment

After many years the sediment slowly hardens into a type of rock called sedimentary (sed ə men'tər ē) rock. A **sedimentary rock** is a rock formed from sediment. When you examine sedimentary rocks, you can often see the layers of sediment. Look at the layers in these sedimentary rocks.

Sedimentary rock layers

SKILLS: Observing, Interpreting data

Finding Out

How are rocks formed from layers of sediment?

Fill a clear plastic jar halfway with water. Add a mixture of sand and cement to form a layer about 2 cm deep. Wait for the mixture to settle. Add some plaster of paris to form another layer. Add other different layers. Wait a few days for the layers to harden. How are the layers in the jar like sedimentary rock?

Different sediments form different sedimentary rocks. Look at the picture of sandstone. Sandstone is formed from sediments of sand. Different materials cement the sand together. The material that cements the sand gives sandstone its color. Sandstone may be red, brown, yellow, or white.

Limestone is a sedimentary rock formed from many materials in water. Some limestone is very fine. It contains the remains of very tiny plants and animals. Other limestone is rough and contains large pieces of shells. Chalk is a type of limestone. When you write with chalk, you might be using a rock made from the shells of animals that lived long ago.

Sandstone

Fine limestone

For Lesson Questions, turn to page 336.

Limestone containing shells

Plants and Animals from Long Ago

Sometimes scientists find traces of plants and animals in sedimentary rocks. These traces are called **fossils** (fos′əlz). Some fossils are bones, footprints, or the bodies of animals from long ago.

Another type of fossil is formed when a plant or animal dies and is covered with sediment. As the sediment hardens, the body of the plant or animal decays. This leaves an empty space in the sediment where the plant or animal used to be. This empty space is a **mold fossil.**

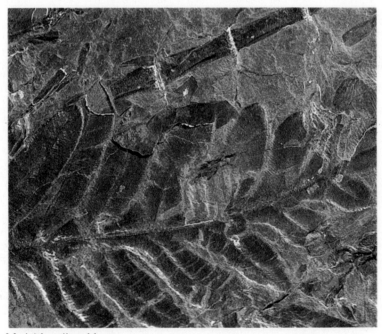

Mold fossils of ferns

Cast fossils of shells

Sometimes sediments or minerals may fill the mold. These materials may harden to form a cast fossil. The **cast fossil** is a rock with the exact shape of the original plant or animal. A cast fossil is like a gelatin mold. Gelatin hardens into the shape of the mold.

The tree trunks in the picture are cast fossils. The trees are petrified (pet′rə fīd), or changed to rock. They formed when the buried trees began to rot. Minerals slowly took the place of the material in the trees. This formed the exact copy you see.

Petrified wood

Some plants that were buried long ago changed into coal. Coal is called a fossil fuel. Today we use this fuel for energy. The drawings show how coal forms. Gas and oil are other fossil fuels. They formed from layers of tiny dead animal matter. The animals lived in the sea long ago.

For Lesson Questions, turn to page 336.

Plants and animals lived and died in large swamps.

Layers of dead plant matter built up over many years.

The swampy land sank and was covered with water and many layers of sediment.

The heat and pressure of the sediments pressed down. After many years, coal was formed.

Activity

How are mold fossils and cast fossils different?

Materials 2 milk cartons / plaster of paris / plastic spoon / water / shells / petroleum jelly / scissors / hammer / hand lens

Procedure

A. Use scissors to cut off one side of a milk carton. Cut off the top of a second milk carton. Fill the second milk carton halfway with water. Slowly stir in plaster of paris until it is as thick as soft ice cream. Pour the plaster into the first carton.

B. Cover some shells with petroleum jelly. Press them halfway into the plaster. Let the plaster harden.

C. Remove the shells to see the imprints they made.
   1. What kind of fossil does this show?

D. Lightly cover the plaster and imprints with more petroleum jelly.

E. Mix more plaster to cover the imprints. Let the plaster harden.

F. Remove the milk carton. Use a hammer to break apart the two layers of plaster. Use the hand lens to compare the two fossils.
   2. What kind of fossil does this show?

Conclusion

1. How are mold fossils and cast fossils different?
2. Explain how each of these fossils form.

Shale changes to slate

Rocks That Change into Other Rocks

How are metamorphic rocks formed?

Sometimes igneous and sedimentary rocks are buried deep in the earth. Great heat and pressure within the earth change the igneous and sedimentary rocks into a new kind of rock. This new kind of rock is called **metamorphic** (met ə môr'fik) **rock.**

Coal is one type of sedimentary rock that can be changed. Soft coal is a sedimentary rock. If soft coal is buried deep in the earth, heat and pressure may change it into hard coal. This metamorphic rock is much harder and is a better fuel than soft coal. More heat and pressure can cause the hard coal to form the mineral graphite. Graphite is not useful as a fuel. We use this mineral in making pencils. These pictures show examples of other metamorphic rocks.

Limestone changes to marble

Sandstone changes to quartzite

Granite changes to gneiss

Sandstone is a sedimentary rock that is easily scratched and broken. You can crush sandstone with a hammer. Heat and pressure change sandstone into quartzite (kwôrt′sīt). Quartzite is a metamorphic rock. Unlike sandstone, quartzite is very hard.

Limestone is a sedimentary rock that can change into marble. Marble is a very hard metamorphic rock used in buildings. Have you ever seen a marble building? Many of the buildings and other structures in Washington, D.C., are made of marble.

For Lesson Questions, turn to page 336.

Ideas to Remember

- ▶ The earth has a crust, a mantle, and a core.
- ▶ Minerals can be identified by testing their properties.
- ▶ Igneous rocks are formed from melted rock.
- ▶ Sedimentary rocks are formed from layers of sediment.
- ▶ Fossils show us what plants and animals from long ago looked like.
- ▶ Metamorphic rocks are formed from igneous and sedimentary rocks.

Reviewing the Chapter

SCIENCE WORDS

A. Write the letter of the term that best matches the definition. Not all the terms will be used.

1. A trace of a plant or animal that lived long ago
2. The layer of the earth we live on
3. A pure solid material found in the ground
4. The middle layer of the earth
5. A rock formed from melted rock
6. The inner layer of the earth
7. A rock formed from sediment
8. A rock formed from other rocks that have been changed

   a. crust
   b. magma
   c. core
   d. metamorphic rock
   e. mineral
   f. fossil
   g. igneous rock
   h. mantle
   i. sedimentary rock
   j. sediment

B. Use science terms from the chapter to answer the questions.

1. I am the empty space in a sedimentary rock where a plant or animal once was. What am I?
2. I am the trace of an animal that lived long ago. Sediments and minerals filled the empty space where the animal once was. What am I?
3. I am melted rock within the earth. What am I?

UNDERSTANDING IDEAS

A. Describe three properties that can be used to identify a mineral. Give an example of a mineral for each property.

B. Metamorphic rocks are sometimes called "changed rocks." In complete sentences, tell why this term can be used to describe metamorphic rocks.

C. Match the description of the rock with its picture. Then tell whether the rock is an igneous rock, a sedimentary rock, or a metamorphic rock.

1. A glassy rock formed when lava cools

2. A rough rock formed when large pieces of shells are pressed together

3. A light rock formed from lava that contained steam and gases

USING IDEAS

1. Collect rocks in your neighborhood. Use reference books to identify them. Label the rocks. You can display your rock collection in a shoe box or an egg carton.

2. In your mind, make up an animal that might have lived long ago. Make a drawing of a fossil from your animal.

THINKING LIKE A SCIENTIST

You may be able to answer some of these questions just by thinking about them. To answer other questions, you may have to do some research.

1. Is a wooden fence standing in a deserted field likely to become petrified after many years? Why doesn't all wood petrify eventually? Explain your reasoning.

2. Why are ancient Greek and Roman buildings that are still standing today made of marble? Didn't the Greeks and Romans construct any buildings with wood?

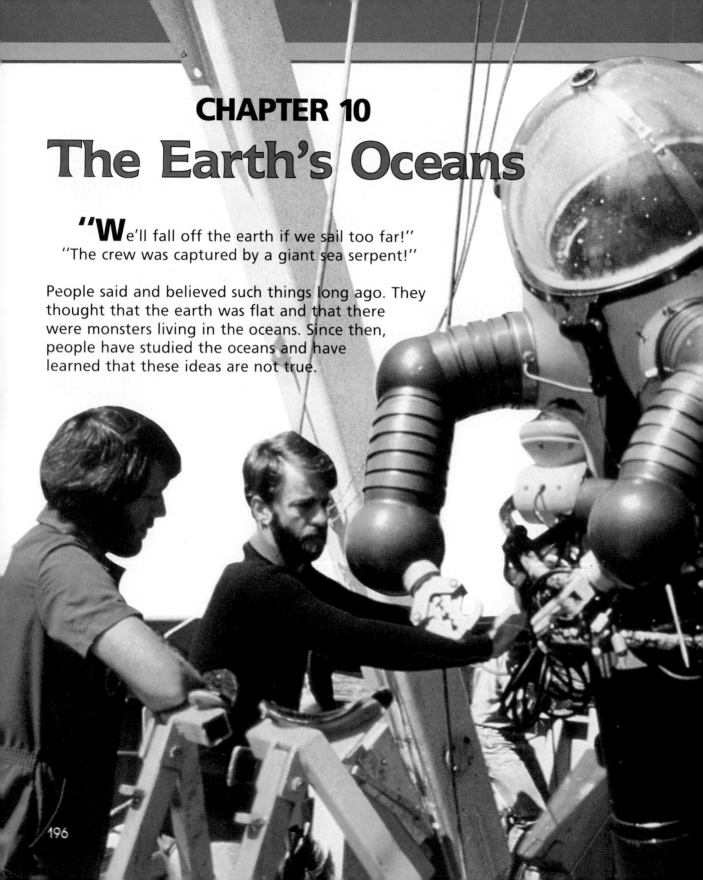

CHAPTER 10
The Earth's Oceans

"**W**e'll fall off the earth if we sail too far!"
"The crew was captured by a giant sea serpent!"

People said and believed such things long ago. They thought that the earth was flat and that there were monsters living in the oceans. Since then, people have studied the oceans and have learned that these ideas are not true.

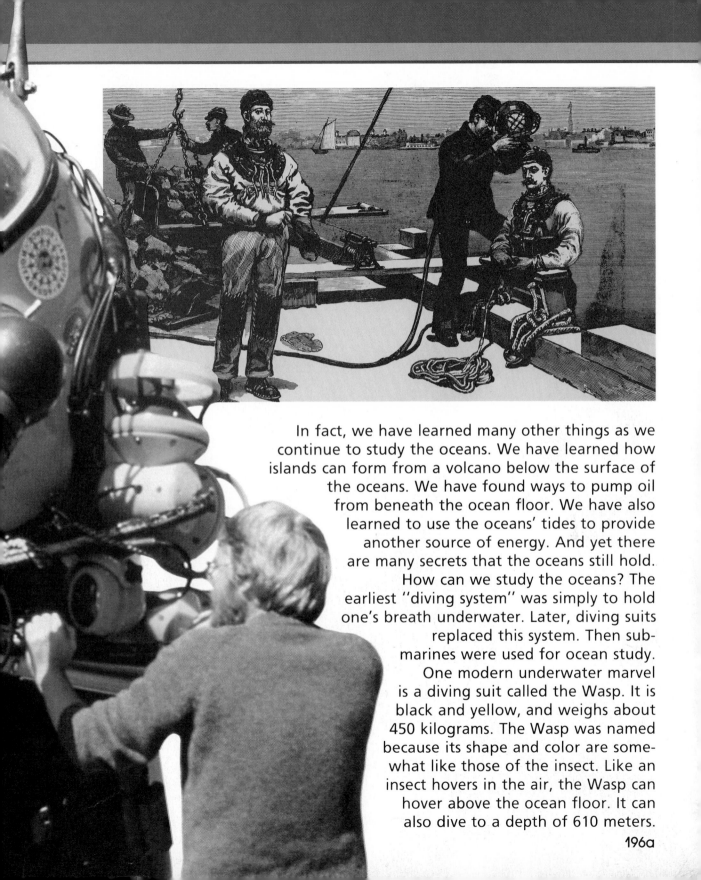

In fact, we have learned many other things as we continue to study the oceans. We have learned how islands can form from a volcano below the surface of the oceans. We have found ways to pump oil from beneath the ocean floor. We have also learned to use the oceans' tides to provide another source of energy. And yet there are many secrets that the oceans still hold.

How can we study the oceans? The earliest "diving system" was simply to hold one's breath underwater. Later, diving suits replaced this system. Then submarines were used for ocean study.

One modern underwater marvel is a diving suit called the Wasp. It is black and yellow, and weighs about 450 kilograms. The Wasp was named because its shape and color are somewhat like those of the insect. Like an insect hovers in the air, the Wasp can hover above the ocean floor. It can also dive to a depth of 610 meters.

196a

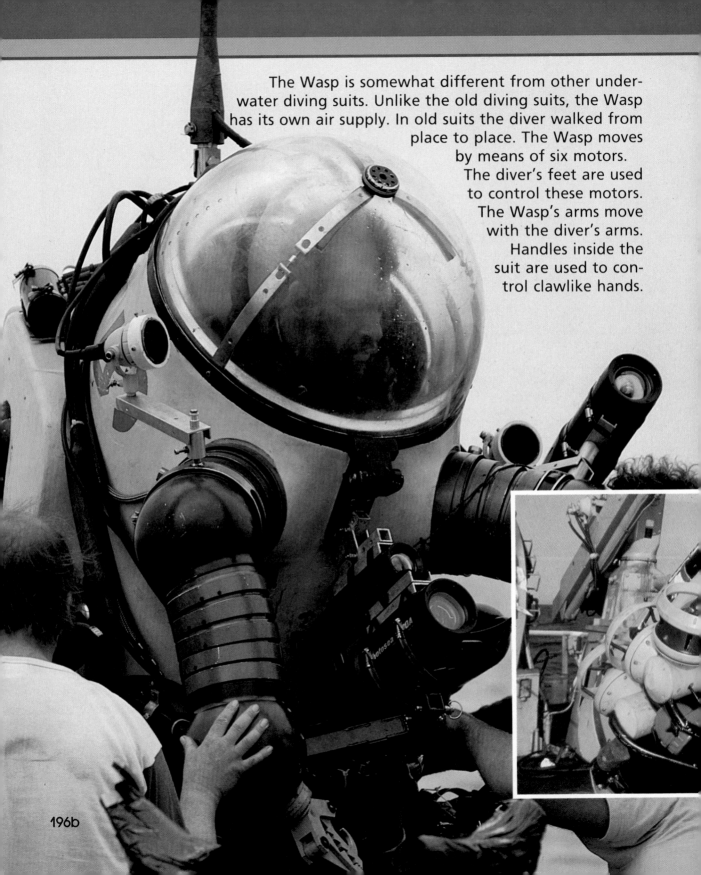

The Wasp is somewhat different from other underwater diving suits. Unlike the old diving suits, the Wasp has its own air supply. In old suits the diver walked from place to place. The Wasp moves by means of six motors. The diver's feet are used to control these motors. The Wasp's arms move with the diver's arms. Handles inside the suit are used to control clawlike hands.

196b

How can you construct a submarine? You will need a tall glass jar with a wide mouth, a glass eye dropper, a large rubber balloon, a rubber band, scissors, water, and paper towels.

Fill the jar to the rim with water. Put some water in the eye dropper and float it in the jar. The top of the dropper should be at the surface of the water. If the dropper floats too high in the water, pinch the bulb. This will remove air from the bulb. The eye dropper must float just at the surface of the water for the submarine to work.

Cut the balloon and stretch it over the mouth of the jar. Wrap the rubber band around the edge of the balloon to keep it in place. There is now a small pocket of air between the balloon and the water level inside the jar.

Lightly press the palm of your hand on the balloon. Observe what happens to the eye dropper. Now take your hand off the balloon. Again note what happens to the dropper. What caused the eye dropper to move each time? (*Hint:* Look carefully at the water level inside the eye dropper.)

These claws can collect living things from the oceans. The top of the Wasp is a clear dome. This dome allows the diver to see all around the Wasp.

The Wasp is one device that helps us learn about the oceans. Exciting things are being found in the oceans all the time. Waves and tides and how we use the oceans are some of the things you will learn about in this chapter.

A Look at the Oceans

What are the oceans like?

The oceans cover about three fourths of the earth. If you look at the map, you can see just how large the oceans are. Can you move your finger around the world, traveling only on the oceans? If you did, you showed that all the oceans are connected.

Have you ever tasted ocean water? If you have, you know it tastes salty. Has the ocean water always been salty? If not, where did the salt come from?

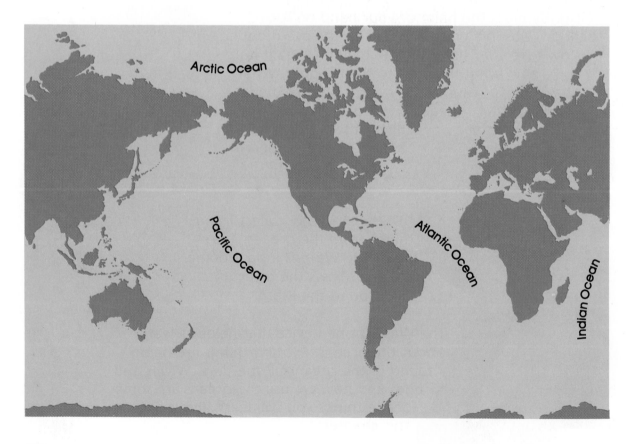

These drawings will help to show how the oceans became salty. Salt is one of many minerals found in the earth's crust. Rains washed salt from rocks and soil into streams and rivers. The streams and rivers then carried the salt to the ocean. In the ocean the salt was mixed with water. After many years the oceans became salty.

rain falling and soaking through soil

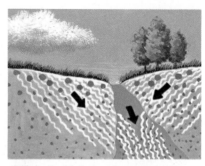

water dissolving minerals in the ground as it flows to rivers

The special submarine *Alvin*

rivers carrying minerals to the oceans

Scientists called oceanographers (ō shə-nog'rə fərs) have learned many things about the ocean. It is difficult to study the oceans because they are so large and deep. There is great pressure deep in the ocean. Oceanographers use special submarines to help them study the oceans. The special submarine shown above is named *Alvin. Alvin* has special cameras that scan the ocean floor and claws that it can use to collect samples.

For Lesson Questions, turn to page 338.

The Ocean Floor

What is it like on the ocean floor?

Imagine taking a trip in *Alvin* along the ocean floor. As you begin your trip, you notice that the floor gently slopes down. It continues to slope for many kilometers. This area is called the **continental** (kon tə-nen'təl) **shelf.** The continental shelf is really the edge of the continent that is underwater. In some places the continental shelf is only about 1 km wide. In other places it is as much as 800 km wide.

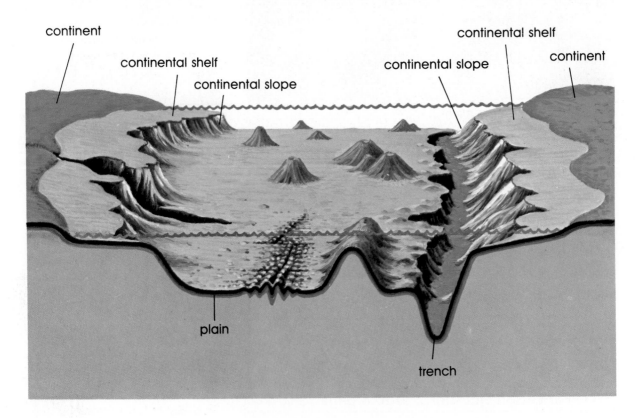

continent

continental shelf

continental slope

continental shelf

continental slope

continent

plain

trench

Hermit crab

The water on the continental shelf is shallow. Sunlight can reach the floor in many places. Many plants grow here. The plants are eaten by different types of fish. For this reason there is a great deal of fishing around the continental shelf. In these pictures you can see some of the types of living things found here.

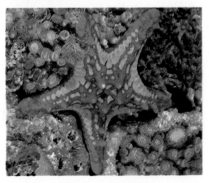
Blue angelfish

As you continue your trip, you see that the ocean floor slopes more steeply. This steep drop is called the **continental slope.** There are deep canyons in the continental slope. Some of the canyons under the oceans are even larger than the Grand Canyon in Arizona.

Red East African starfish

When you reach the bottom of the continental slope, you are on the ocean floor **plain.** Here you can see hills, mountains, and valleys. Great mountain ranges rise from the ocean floor. Find the Mid-Atlantic Ridge on the map. The Mid-Atlantic Ridge is a very large chain of mountains on the bottom of the Atlantic Ocean. This chain of mountains is 16,000 km long. Some of the mountains are bigger than any mountains found on land. The tops of some of the mountains rise above the surface to form islands.

Mid-Atlantic Ridge

Some of the mountains are volcanoes. Lava builds up to make the volcanoes bigger after each eruption. Finally the tops of the volcanoes rise above the surface of the water to form islands. The Hawaiian Islands were formed in this way.

▶ You have probably heard how robots are used in factories. But did you know that there are hundreds of robots working in the ocean?

This kind of robot is pulled through the ocean by a ship. Cameras on the robot are used by people on the ship to study the ocean floor.

◀ Robots like these can be sent deeper than people can safely and easily go. They can be used to explore under thick ice. They can collect soil. They have been used to inspect undersea pipes and cables. They can even look for sunken treasure, as they did when they searched for and explored the Titanic. What other useful things do you think undersea robots can do?

In some places you can see deep, narrow slits in the ocean floor. These slits are called **trenches**. The deepest trench in the world is the Mariana Trench in the Pacific Ocean. This trench is over 11 km deep.

As you continue your trip across the ocean floor, you reach another continental slope. This is an upward slope. Beyond it is another continental shelf. Finally you reach another continent to end your journey.

For Lesson Questions, turn to page 338.

The Moving Ocean

**What are two ways we can see
ocean water move?**

Ocean water is always moving. Waves in
the ocean show one kind of movement. Perhaps you have seen a surfer riding a large
wave like the one in the picture. How did
this wave form?

Most waves form far from the shore.
These waves are formed by wind that blows
across the surface of the ocean. Strong
winds cause large waves to form. Some
waves, formed by winds during storms, may
be as high as a house.

Not all waves are formed by the wind. Some waves are caused by earthquakes in the bottom of the ocean. These earthquakes cause a giant wave to form. A giant wave formed by an earthquake is called a tsunami (tsü nä′mē). A tsunami can destroy whole towns as it crashes onto the shore.

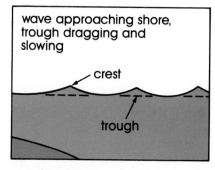

wave approaching shore, trough dragging and slowing

crest

trough

Waves crash, or break, when they come close to shore. As you can see in the drawing, the top part of a wave is called the **crest.** The bottom part of a wave is called the **trough** (trôf). As a wave approaches shore, its trough drags on the ocean floor. This slows down the trough. At the same time, the crest keeps moving forward without slowing down. Soon the crest is in front of the trough. This makes the crest fall forward. The falling wave is called a **breaker.** The surfer on page 204 is riding on a breaker.

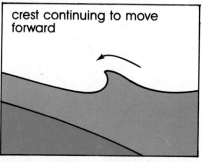

crest continuing to move forward

crest falling forward, wave breaking

SKILLS: Making a model, Observing

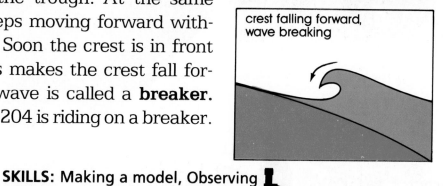

Finding Out

How can an earthquake in the ocean cause a tsunami?

Place two pieces of brick in an aquarium so that the end of one piece is resting on the end of the other. Pour enough water into the aquarium to cover the pieces of brick. Use a stick to push the higher piece off the other piece. Watch the surface of the water.

Another way ocean water moves is by rising and falling. We can see the level of the ocean rise and fall along the shore. The level changes four times during a day. This change in the level of ocean water is called a **tide.**

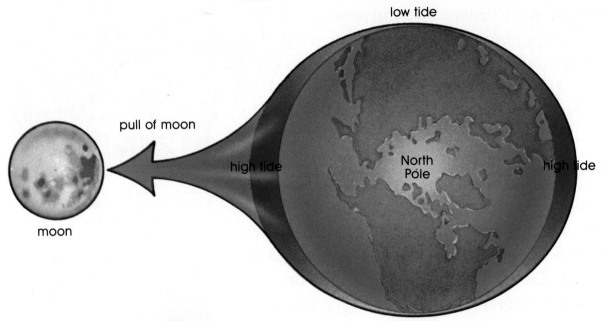

low tide

pull of moon

high tide

North Pole

high tide

moon

low tide

SKILL: Interpreting data

Finding Out

TIDE TABLE

	Tuesday	Wednesday	Thursday
Low Tide	1:49 A.M.	2:27 A.M.	3:03 A.M.
High Tide	7:55 A.M.	8:33 A.M.	9:10 A.M.
Low Tide	2:22 P.M.	3:02 P.M.	3:40 P.M.
High Tide	8:12 P.M.	8:50 P.M.	9:31 P.M.

What times are high tides and low tides?

Newspapers often print a tide chart like the one shown. Notice that the chart shows two high tides and two low tides for each day. If you were going fishing in the ocean, you would need to know the times of the tides. What time is the water deepest each day? If you were going to dig for clams, you would wait for low tide. What time is low tide each day?

High tide

Low tide

Tides are caused mainly by the gravitational pull between the moon and the earth. The moon has a strong pull on the side of the earth it is facing. The arrow in the drawing on page 206 shows this. The gravity of the moon pulls water to this side. The pull causes the water level on this side to rise. The rise in water level is called **high tide.** In other places, the water level drops. This drop in water level is called **low tide.**

Water on the side of the earth that faces away from the moon is not pulled. Only the earth is pulled, because it is denser than water. The earth is pulled away from the water. This causes a high tide here also. As the earth rotates, the tides change. Every 24 hours there are two high tides and two low tides.

For Lesson Questions, turn to page 338.

On rocky shorelines the high tide leaves behind pools of water. These tide pools are homes for many kinds of plants and animals. Crabs, starfish, and algae can be found in tide pools.

Tide pools

Living things in a tide pool

The Ocean's Rivers

What is a third way ocean water moves?

There are large moving rivers of water in the ocean called **currents** (ker′ənts). Some currents are warm and other currents are cold. At the equator the sun warms ocean water. The warm water then flows away from the equator and toward the poles. Cold water from the North Pole and the South Pole flows back to the equator. In the drawing, warm-water currents are red. Cold-water currents are blue. What types of currents affect the coastlines of North America?

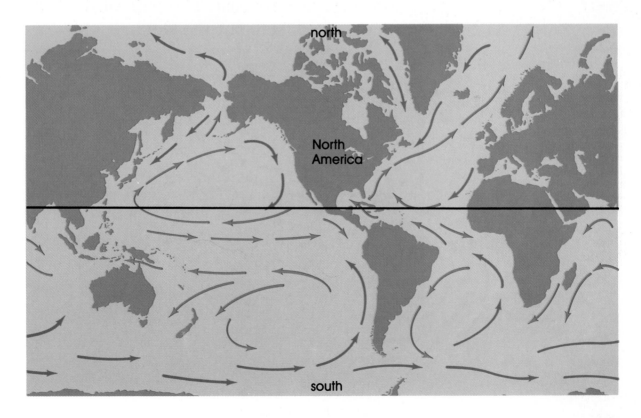

Look at the map that shows the path of the Gulf Stream. The Gulf Stream is one of the strongest ocean currents on earth. It is about 160 km wide and it travels about 5 km per hour (km/h). The Gulf Stream carries warm water north from the equator. Many fish live in this warm water. A great number of people depend on these fish for food.

Notice how the Gulf Stream moves along the east coast of North America. The land blocks and changes the path of the current. This causes the Gulf Stream to travel along the edge of North America. The spinning of the earth then causes the Gulf Stream to move toward the east. The path of the current is also affected by the wind.

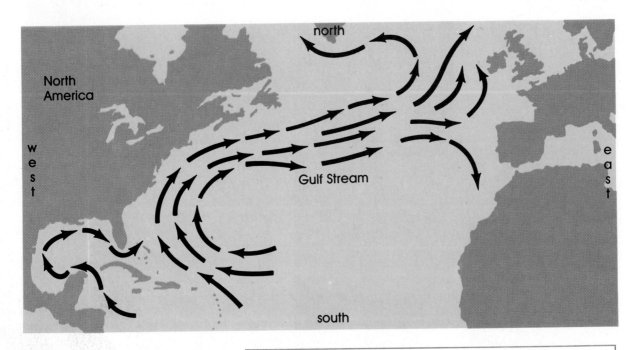

210

For Lesson Questions, turn to page 338.

What happens when hot water meets cold water?

Activity

Materials   aquarium / blue food coloring / small bottle with lid / hot water / cold water

Procedure

A. Fill an aquarium with cold water.

B. Fill a small bottle with hot water. Then add several drops of blue food coloring to the water. Place a lid on the bottle but do not tighten it.

1. Predict what will happen when the bottle is placed in the cold water and the lid is removed.

C. Hold your thumb on the lid to keep it in place. Then put the bottle into the aquarium. Set it on the bottom. Slowly lift the lid off the bottle and take your hand out of the water.

2. Does a current form?

Results

Make a drawing to show what happens when hot water meets cold water.

Conclusion

What happens when hot water meets cold water?

Using science ideas

The Gulf Stream is a warm-water current. Do you think it flows near the surface or near the bottom of the ocean? Explain your answer.

Ocean Resources

People have sailed on the oceans for hundreds of years. Transportation is still one important way people use the oceans. Can you name some other ways people use them?

One way we use the oceans is for their resources (ri sôr'siz). A **resource** is a useful material taken from the earth. Minerals are resources found in the oceans. Some minerals are found in small black rocks on the ocean floor. These rocks are called **nodules** (noj'ülz). Nodules contain minerals such as copper and nickel.

Harbor

Fishing boat

Food from the ocean is also an important resource. People eat fish and also feed fish to livestock. Seaweed has many uses. Did you know that seaweed is used to make some types of ice cream, candy, and medicines?

Natural gas and oil are resources that can be found beneath the ocean floor. As our oil and natural gas supplies on land are used up, we will need the oil and gas under the oceans.

The tides can be used to produce energy. This is called tidal power. The rise and fall of the water supplies the energy to make electricity. There is a tidal power plant in Seattle, Washington, that produces electricity. Someday tidal power may be a common energy source along the shores.

Offshore oil well

For Lesson Questions, turn to page 338.

213

Activity

How can salt be removed from salt water?

Materials   warm water / salt / paper cup / plastic spoon / shallow dish

Procedure
A. Pour some warm water into a paper cup. Slowly stir in a spoonful of salt. Keep stirring to dissolve the salt.

B. Pour the salt water into a shallow dish. Place the dish in a warm place, like near a sunny window or on a radiator.
  1. What do you think will happen? Why?

C. Make a chart like the one shown.

D. Observe the dish each day until all the water has dried up. Write down the date and your observations on the chart.

Results
1. What was left in the dish after the water dried up?
2. How long did it take for the water to dry up?

Conclusion
1. Use the chart to explain what happened to the water in the dish every day.
2. Explain how you removed the salt from the salt water.

Using science ideas
Put some salt water in a shallow dish. Think of a way to collect fresh water from the salt water. How could this be a useful thing to do?

Day	Description of salt water in dish

Ideas to Remember

▶ About three fourths of the earth is covered by water.

▶ Ocean water contains dissolved salt and other minerals.

▶ Ocean water is always moving in waves, currents, or tides.

▶ The bottom of the ocean is covered by hills, valleys, mountains, and canyons.

▶ The oceans contain valuable resources, such as oil, natural gas, and minerals.

Reviewing the Chapter

SCIENCE WORDS

A. Copy the sentences below. Use science terms from the chapter to complete the sentences.

1. The steep drop in the ocean floor after the continental shelf is called the _____.
2. The top part of a wave is called the _____.
3. The bottom part of a wave is called the _____.
4. Black rocks on the ocean floor, called _____, contain many minerals.

B. Write the letter of the term that best matches the definition. Not all the terms will be used.

1. A rise in the level of ocean water
2. A river of water in the ocean
3. A useful material taken from the earth
4. The bottom of the ocean floor
5. The edge of a continent that is underwater
6. A drop in the level of ocean water
7. A deep, narrow slit in the ocean floor
8. A falling wave
9. A change in the level of ocean water

a. tide
b. low tide
c. breaker
d. *Alvin*
e. oceanographer
f. continental shelf
g. trench
h. high tide
i. plain
j. current
k. resource

UNDERSTANDING IDEAS

A. Cross out the term that does not belong in each group below. Then describe what the remaining terms have in common.

1. plain, high tide, continental slope, trench
2. nodules, tide, current, wave
3. breaker, trough, resource, crest
4. fish, minerals, natural gas, plain

B. Make a chart with headings like the one below. Using information from the chapter, list the ocean's resources in the first column. In the second column, tell how each resource is important. Then, in complete sentences, tell what would happen if every ocean resource was suddenly used up.

Resource	How resource is important

USING IDEAS

Find a map of the world in a reference book. Trace the map. Draw the ocean currents on your map. Show how two of the currents affect the lands they touch.

THINKING LIKE A SCIENTIST

You may be able to answer some of these questions just by thinking about them. To answer other questions, you may have to do some research.

1. Imagine that you are on a ship in the middle of the ocean. The captain receives word that an underwater earthquake has occurred. Should you worry about being hit by a tsunami? Use your knowledge of waves and how they form to answer this question.

2. During the early days of exploring the world, knowledge of ocean currents was important. Explain why this was true.

CHAPTER 11

Measuring Weather

Did you know that on February 2 some people watch groundhogs to find out how long winter will last? This way of forecasting weather may seem silly to you. But Groundhog Day is a part of weather folklore. In fact, people have used weather folklore for hundreds of years to predict or explain the weather. Here is some weather folklore that has been used in the past. Which sayings or stories have you heard? Why might some of these have helped people predict weather?

A cow's tail to the west
Is weather coming at its best.
A cow's tail to the east
Is weather coming at its least.

Near the surface, quick to bite,
Catch your fish when rain's in sight.

The higher the hornets build their nests,
The harder winter will be.

Sea gull, sea gull, sit on the sand,
It's a sign of rain when you are at hand.

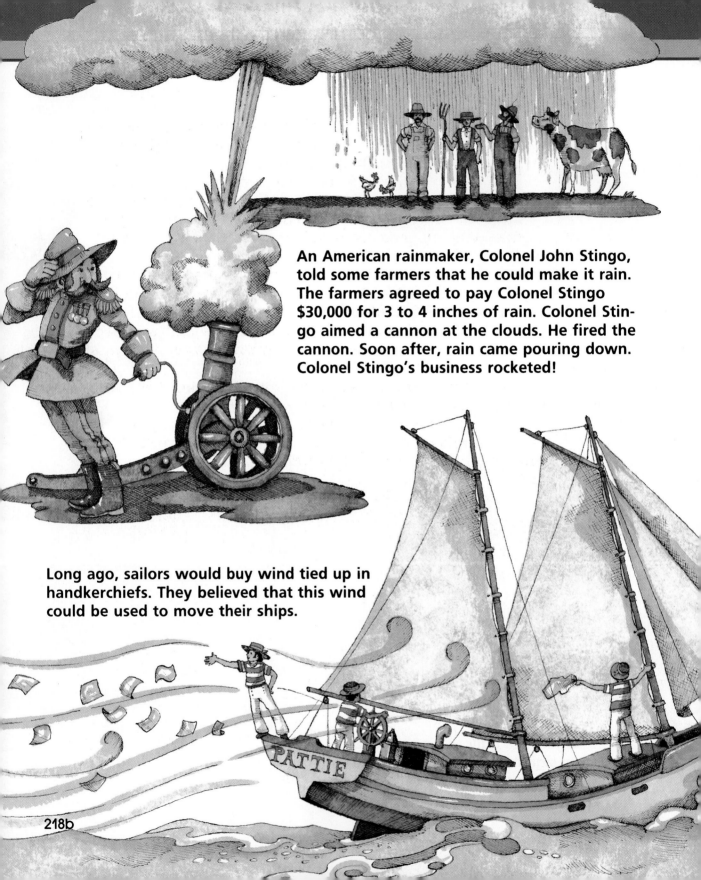

An American rainmaker, Colonel John Stingo, told some farmers that he could make it rain. The farmers agreed to pay Colonel Stingo $30,000 for 3 to 4 inches of rain. Colonel Stingo aimed a cannon at the clouds. He fired the cannon. Soon after, rain came pouring down. Colonel Stingo's business rocketed!

Long ago, sailors would buy wind tied up in handkerchiefs. They believed that this wind could be used to move their ships.

PATTIE

Weather changes every day. You can make your own instruments to measure some weather changes. Moisture in the air can be measured by using a hygrometer (hī grom' ə tər).

To make a hygrometer, you will need a toothpick, glue, a pipe cleaner, a wide-mouth jar, and a glass-marking pencil. You will also need a strand of human hair. It should be longer than the height of the glass. Wrap one end of the hair around the middle of the toothpick. Secure the hair with a drop of glue.

Bend the pipe cleaner to fit over the mouth of the jar, as shown. Holding the free end of the strand of hair, hang the toothpick inside the jar. Be sure the toothpick is just above the bottom of the jar. The toothpick should not touch the sides of the jar. Now wrap the free end of the hair around the pipe cleaner and secure it with a drop of glue.

Place the jar on a table and don't move it. As the weather changes from sunny to rainy, notice which way the toothpick points. Using the marking pencil, label the sunny and rainy positions on the jar. Keep track of the weather for several weeks. Predict how the toothpick will move each time the weather changes. How often were you correct?

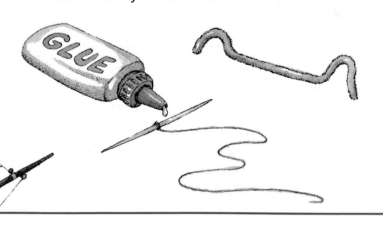

You have now made one weather instrument. In this chapter you will learn about other ways to measure weather.

Weather Around Us

What is weather?

How often have you talked about the weather with someone you just met? Weather is something we all have in common. We spend a lot of time talking about weather, but how much do we really know about it?

Weather is the condition of the air around us. Changes in the condition of the air give us many types of weather. How many different types of weather can you name? You might remember a foggy night, a cold morning, or a windy day. The words *foggy, cold,* and *windy* describe the condition of the air.

Foggy weather

Rainy weather

Snowy weather

Sunny weather

People say, "Don't count on the weather." But one thing about the weather we can count on is that it always changes. The weather may change from day to day and even from hour to hour. It may rain on one side of a city but not on the other side. When we talk about weather, we are talking about what is happening in the air in one place at one time.

Windy weather

221

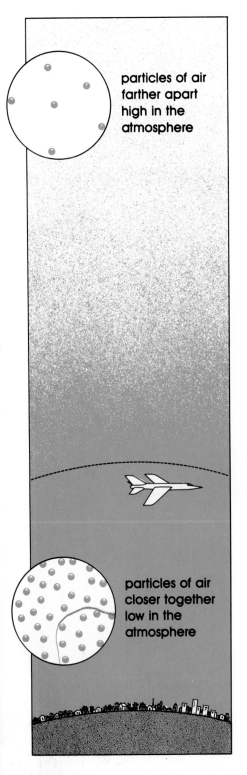

particles of air farther apart high in the atmosphere

particles of air closer together low in the atmosphere

The air that surrounds the earth is called the **atmosphere** (at′mə sfir). The atmosphere is about 2,500 km thick. There are four layers in the atmosphere.

The layer closest to the earth is the troposphere (trō′pə sfir). The troposphere is between 6 km and 16 km thick. Most of the air in the atmosphere is found here. The particles of air are packed close together in the troposphere. The air particles move farther apart as you go higher in the troposphere. The air is so thin in the upper layers of the troposphere that you would have trouble breathing. Often people who climb high mountains take a supply of oxygen with them.

The air also becomes colder as you go up in the troposphere. This is why many mountaintops are snow-covered even in the summer. The air outside a high-flying jet is about −40°C.

The troposphere is important because we breathe its air. All living things depend on water vapor in the troposphere. This is also where clouds, storms, and winds form.

You know that the weather changes from place to place and from day to day. By observing temperature, wind speed and direction, air pressure, and moisture, you can predict changes in the weather.

For Lesson Questions, turn to page 340.

Changes in Air Temperature

How does air temperature change?

It takes a lot of energy to heat the air in the troposphere. Where do you think this energy comes from? Look at the drawing. Energy from the sun warms the surface of the earth. Heat from the surface of the earth then warms the air above. How does this help explain colder temperatures in the upper troposphere?

The surface of the earth does not heat evenly. During the day, air warms more quickly over land. At the same time, air warms more slowly over water. These differences in heating the earth's surface cause changes in air temperature. The changes in temperature cause weather changes.

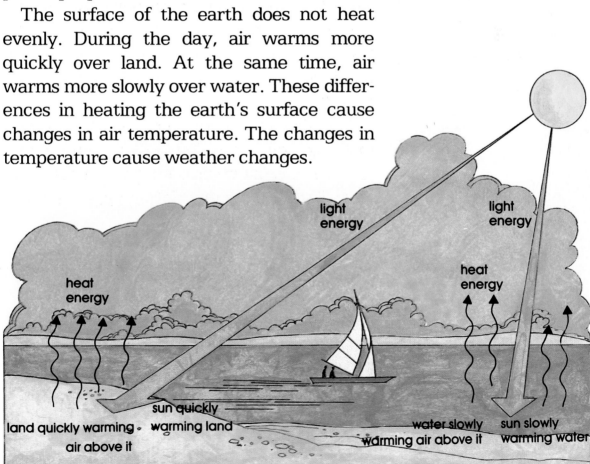

light energy

light energy

heat energy

heat energy

land quickly warming air above it

sun quickly warming land

water slowly warming air above it

sun slowly warming water

Thermometer

Temperature is measured with a thermometer. Many thermometers are made of a glass tube with colored alcohol inside. When the air gets hotter, the level of the liquid in the tube rises. When the air cools, the liquid level falls.

Look at the picture of the thermometer. The scale on the left side of this thermometer measures temperature in degrees Celsius. What temperature does this thermometer show? What kind of clothing would you wear if this was the temperature outside?

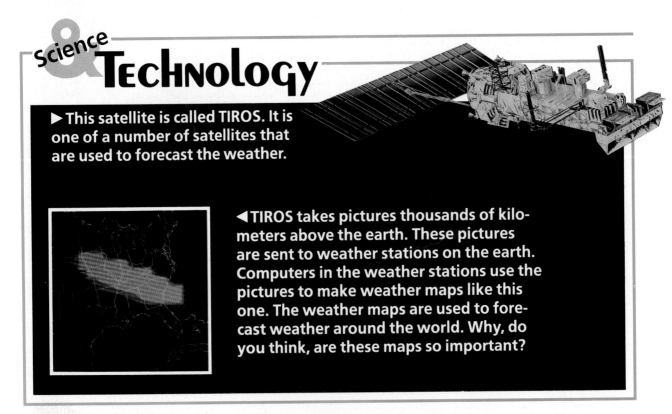

Science & TECHNOLOGY

▶ This satellite is called TIROS. It is one of a number of satellites that are used to forecast the weather.

◀ TIROS takes pictures thousands of kilometers above the earth. These pictures are sent to weather stations on the earth. Computers in the weather stations use the pictures to make weather maps like this one. The weather maps are used to forecast weather around the world. Why, do you think, are these maps so important?

TEMPERATURES FOR OCTOBER 16

Time	Temperature
4 A.M.	6°C
8 A.M.	8°C
12 NOON	16°C
4 P.M.	14°C
8 P.M.	11°C
12 P.M.	9°C

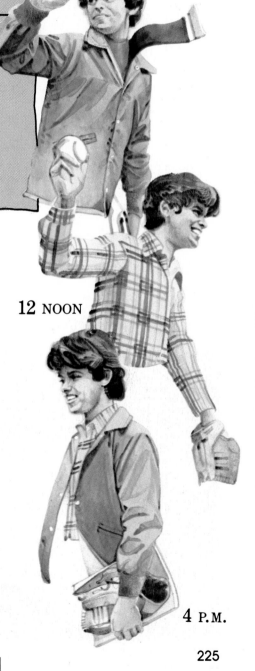

8 A.M.

12 NOON

4 P.M.

The temperature of the air is always changing. Within a single day, temperatures may differ from hour to hour. By using a thermometer you can keep a record of these changes. Look at this daily temperature chart. On what day were these temperatures recorded? At what time of the day was it the warmest? The coldest? What was the air temperature at 8 A.M.? What do you think caused these differences in temperature?

Air temperature is a very important part of the weather. If the temperature of the air never changed, the weather would always be the same. A change in temperature causes changes in air pressure, wind, and the amount of moisture in the air.

For Lesson Questions, turn to page 340.

Air Pressure

How does air press on the earth?

Have you ever felt your ears "pop" when you rode in a car driving up a mountain road? If you have, you felt a change in **air pressure.** You might also have felt this change while riding in an elevator or flying in an airplane.

It might be difficult to think of air having pressure at all, but it does. All the air in the atmosphere pushes down on everything on earth. When you climb a mountain, you are going higher into the atmosphere. There is less air above you, so there is less air pressure.

Low-pressure area

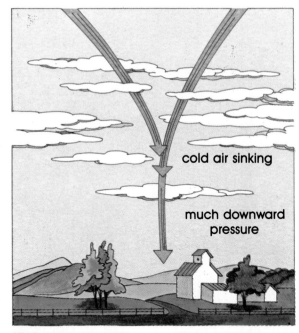

High-pressure area

The air pressure at the surface of the earth does not stay the same. When a part of the earth is heated, the air above it gets warmer. The warm air begins to rise. As it rises, it does not press downward as much on the earth's surface. This results in less pressure on the earth. This warm rising air forms a **low-pressure area.** It is called a *low* on a weather map.

The rising warm air cools slowly. As the air cools, it becomes heavier. In time it sinks to the earth's surface. The sinking air puts more pressure on the earth. This cool air forms a **high-pressure area.** It is called this because there is more downward pressure by air. It is called a *high* on the weather map.

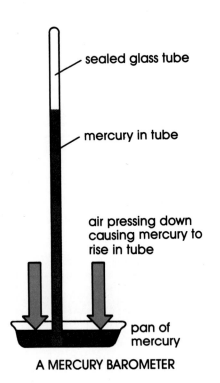

sealed glass tube

mercury in tube

air pressing down
causing mercury to
rise in tube

pan of
mercury

A MERCURY BAROMETER

Changes in air pressure can be measured with a **barometer** (bə rom'ə tər). In the drawing you can see a mercury barometer. A mercury barometer consists of a glass tube that has one end sealed. There is very little air in the closed end of the tube. The tube is partly filled with mercury. Its open end sits in a pan of mercury. Air pushes down on the mercury in the pan. This pushes the mercury up the tube. When air pressure increases, more air pushes on the pan of mercury. This causes the mercury level to rise in the tube. When air pressure decreases, less air pushes on the pan of mercury. This causes the mercury level to fall. By measuring the height of the mercury in the tube, you can measure the air pressure.

SKILLS: Communicating, Interpreting data

Finding Out

How can you measure air pressure?

Make a barometer with a wide-mouth jar, a large balloon, rubber bands, a drinking straw, and glue. Cut a large piece from the balloon. Stretch it over the mouth of the jar. Use one or two rubber bands to hold the balloon in place. Glue the straw to the lid for a pointer.

Tape a piece of paper to the wall. Place your barometer next to the paper. Mark a line where the straw is pointing. Write down the day and the weather conditions. Do this every day for a week. Then see if you can use your barometer to predict the weather.

Another type of barometer consists of a metal box that has had some air removed. The box is attached to a pointer on a dial. Air pressure pushes on the sides of the box. This pressure causes the pointer to move to a higher number on the dial. When air pressure decreases, the pointer moves back to a lower number.

A barometer can help you to predict the weather. A slowly rising pressure may mean fair weather. A steady pressure means the weather will stay the same. A slowly falling pressure indicates stormy weather. The barometer shown below has a description of the weather on its dial. What type of weather is the pointer indicating?

For Lesson Questions, turn to page 340.

Barometer

Wind Speed and Direction

How does wind move?

It has often been said that the wind brings us our weather. Wind is the movement of air. As air moves, it brings warmth, cold, rain, or snow. Differences of temperature and pressure cause air to move.

During the day, the surface of the earth heats up. It heats up faster in some areas than it does in others. Beaches, highways, and buildings heat up quickly. Forests, grassy fields, and bodies of water heat up slowly. When warm air rises, cooler air moves in to take its place. For example, the warm air over a road rises. Cooler air over a nearby field moves under the rising warm air. The cooler air then starts to heat up quickly. What happens to this air as it becomes warmer?

warm air rising

cooler air moving down

Wind vane

Knowing the speed and direction of the wind can be a great help in predicting the weather. Have you ever seen a wind vane on the roof of a house? Wind vanes show the direction of the wind. The arrow of the vane points into the wind. When wind is blowing from the south, it is called a south wind. What would you call a wind blowing from west to east? Sometimes the arrow of the vane points between two directions. When the arrow points between the north and the west, it is called a northwest wind. Look at the wind vane in the picture. From what direction is the wind blowing?

Anemometer

An instrument that measures how fast the wind is moving is an **anemometer** (an ə-mom'ə tər). Look at the picture of the anemometer. The wind causes the cups to spin. The speed of the spinning cups is recorded in kilometers per hour. Before anemometers were used, people judged wind speed by how wind moved the objects around them. A scale showing different wind speeds is shown below. The scale is called the Beaufort scale. Use this scale to tell what the wind speed is outside your school today.

BEAUFORT WIND SCALE

	Description of wind	Type of wind	Wind speed (km/h)		Description of wind	Type of wind	Wind speed (km/h)
	Smoke rising straight up	Calm	0.0– 0.7		Loose paper blown	Moderate breeze	20.0–28.5
	Smoke drifting	Light air	0.8– 5.4		Small trees swaying	Fresh breeze	29.0–38.5
	Wind felt on face; wind vane moving	Light breeze	5.5–12.0		Umbrella difficult to control	Strong wind	39.0–50.0
	Flags blown straight out	Gentle breeze	12.1–19.5		Difficult to walk	Stiff wind	50.5–61.5

For Lesson Questions, turn to page 340.

How does an anemometer measure wind speed?

Materials 4 small paper cups / tape / 4 plastic drinking straws / stapler / straight pin with a large head / pencil with a new eraser / crayon

Procedure

A. To make an anemometer, staple one end of a plastic drinking straw to the side of a paper cup near its open end. Repeat this with three other straws and cups. Make sure that all the straws are stapled to the same side of the cup.

B. Set two of the cups on their sides so that the straws are on top. Arrange the two cups so the ends of the straws are alongside each other, as shown. Tape the two straws together. Repeat this with the two other cups and straws. Use a crayon to mark the bottom of one cup.

C. Lay the two pairs of straws across each other to form a cross. Tape the two pairs of straws together.

D. Carefully push a straight pin through the center of the cross and into the top of a new pencil eraser. Blow on the anemometer to make it spin. Each time the marked cup passes, one full spin has been made.

E. Take your anemometer outside. Count how many times it spins in 1 minute.

   1. How many times does it spin in 1 minute?

Conclusion

How does an anemometer measure wind speed?

Using science ideas

How does measuring wind speed help us to predict weather?

Water in the Air

How do clouds form?

Have you ever wondered why water is found in so many places? As you can see in the drawing, water from oceans, lakes, and rivers gets heated by the sun. As the water heats up, some of it escapes into the air as gas. This gas is called **water vapor.**

When the air has a large amount of water vapor, tiny droplets start to form. Countless numbers of these droplets make up clouds. As the air in a cloud cools, the tiny droplets come closer together. Small droplets come together to form bigger droplets. These fall to the ground as rain, sleet, or snow. When water falls to the ground, it is called **precipitation** (pri sip ə tā′shən). This water moves to oceans, lakes, and rivers.

precipitation

droplets forming clouds

water vapor entering air

sun heating water

Activity

How does the weather change during the week?

Materials thermometer

Procedure

A. Make a chart like the one shown.

B. Write down today's date in the first column.

C. Use a thermometer to measure the temperature outside. Write this number in the second column.

D. Describe today's cloud cover in the third column. If there are no clouds, write *Clear.* If the sky is completely filled with clouds, write *Cloudy.* If some sky can be seen through the clouds, write *Partly cloudy.*

Day	Temp.	Cloud cover	Wind speed	Description of weather

E. Using the wind chart on page 232, determine the wind speed. Write the wind speed in the fourth column.

F. Describe today's weather in the fifth column. You might use words such as *Fair, Raining, Snowing, Windy, Cold,* or *Hot.*

G. Repeat steps **B** through **F** at the same time every day for 1 week.

Results

1. What day had the highest temperature? What day had the lowest?

2. How many days were clear? How many were partly cloudy? How many were cloudy?

3. What was the wind speed on the windiest day? What was it on the calmest day?

Conclusion

In general, how did the weather change during the week?

235

Precipitation is measured with an instrument called a rain gauge such as the one shown here. During a rainstorm, rain falls into the tube. Rainfall is measured in inches (in.). How many inches of water have collected in this rain gauge?

Snow can also be collected in a rain gauge. Scientists have found that 10 in. of snow has the same amount of water as 1 in. of rain.

Most of the moisture in the atmosphere cannot be seen. Even when the sky is cloudless, the air still holds water. Warm air can hold more water vapor than cold air. The amount of water the air holds is called **humidity** (hyü mid'ə tē). This picture shows a hot summer day. On days such as this, the air may have a lot of water vapor in it. The weather is said to be humid. How do people feel on a hot humid day?

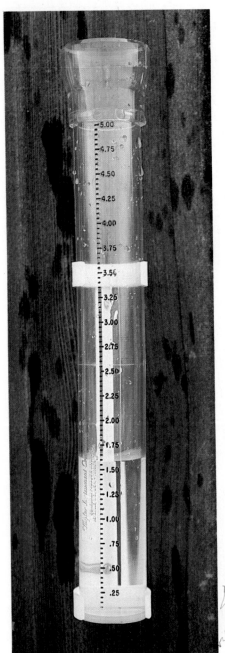

Rain gauge

An instrument used to measure humidity is a **hygrometer** (hī grom'ə tər). The hygrometer shown here consists of two thermometers. The bulb of the thermometer on the right is covered with a wet cloth. The temperature on this thermometer is lower than the temperature on the other thermometer. Humidity is measured by comparing the two temperatures and using a chart.

For Lesson Questions, turn to page 340.

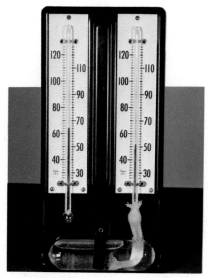

Hygrometer

Ideas to Remember

▶ Weather is the condition of the air in one place at one time. Weather changes occur in the troposphere.

▶ Temperature, wind speed and direction, air pressure, and moisture can be measured to predict the weather.

▶ Air temperature is measured with a thermometer.

▶ A barometer can measure air pressure to predict the weather.

▶ A wind vane shows wind direction; an anemometer measures wind speed.

▶ Water that falls to earth is called precipitation.

▶ Humidity is the amount of water the air holds. It is measured by a hygrometer.

Reviewing the Chapter

SCIENCE WORDS

A. Write the letter of the term that best matches the definition. Not all the terms will be used.

1. An instrument that measures air pressure
2. An area of warm rising air
3. Any water that falls to the ground
4. The air surrounding the earth
5. Water in the air
6. An instrument that measures wind speed
7. The condition of the air around us

    a. atmosphere
    b. anemometer
    c. weather
    d. low-pressure area
    e. barometer
    f. high-pressure area
    g. precipitation
    h. humidity

B. Copy the sentences below. Use science terms from the chapter to complete each sentence.

1. An instrument that measures humidity is a/an ____.
2. The force of the air pushing down on everything on earth is called ____.
3. An area of cooled heavy air is called a/an ____.
4. Water that escapes into the air as a gas is called ____.

UNDERSTANDING IDEAS

A. Tell which of the following sentences are true and which are false.

1. Weather is always changing.
2. By observing temperature, wind speed and direction, air pressure, and moisture, you can predict changes in the weather.
3. The earth's surface is heated evenly.
4. The temperature of the air always stays the same.
5. Warm air can hold more moisture than cold air can.

238

B. Describe the troposphere. Tell why it is so important.

C. Identify each of the following instruments. Explain how each instrument is used.

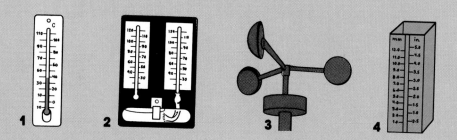

USING IDEAS

Set up a weather station outside your home. Use the barometer you made on page 228, the anemometer you made on page 233, and a thermometer. Keep a daily record of the weather for a month.

THINKING LIKE A SCIENTIST

You may be able to answer some of these questions just by thinking about them. To answer other questions, you may have to do some research.

1. A balloon filled with air at the earth's surface would expand and burst in the upper atmosphere. Why would this happen?
2. You have learned that the liquid part of a thermometer is colored alcohol. Why is alcohol used in thermometers instead of water?
3. Use the information you have learned in this chapter to explain how a hot-air balloon works. What makes the balloon rise? What does the person in the balloon have to do to lower the balloon to the ground?
4. How could you determine the wind direction without using a weather vane? Describe at least three ways.

CHAPTER 12
The Solar System

Do you ever look at the night sky? Do you wonder what other worlds are like? Long before the first trip into space, artists were painting pictures of these worlds. These pictures showed how the artists thought another planet, a moon, or a star might look.

Chesley Bonestell

▲ Look at Ludek Pesek's painting. Take a mental journey to Venus. You are on a planet wrapped in a heavy, smothering haze. Dark mounds of searing embers crouch before a smoldering field. Gases hiss. Thunder rumbles. Distant clouds of acid tower like billowing dust from the crashing of a giant skyscraper.

LUDEK PESEK   (1919–   )

CHESLEY BONESTELL   (1888–1986)

◄ For many years, artists have admired the work of Chesley Bonestell. Here is how he thought the surface of Mercury might look. He painted big cliffs jutting high above pitted, sun-cracked plains. According to Bonestell, what color is Mercury's sky? Did this painter think people might someday visit the surface of Mercury?

240a

PAMELA LEE (1949–   )

▲ Pamela Lee is another space artist. She wanted to show how large the planet Jupiter would look from its moon Io. She wanted to show that there are volcanoes on this moon. What, do you think, are the yellow "rivers" she shows? What is the large round object in her painting?

▶ Being a space scientist helps William Hartman with his space art. In painting this scene, he pretended to be in one of planet Saturn's rings. Imagine yourself on one of these ice stones. Up and down you bob around Saturn.

240b

Pretend that you are a space artist. Draw a planet named NoWayJay. Remember these facts.

Planet NoWayJay has water. It has almost no air or other gases as does Earth. NoWayJay is farther from its sun than is Earth from our sun. It is colder on NoWayJay than it is at Earth's North Pole. NoWayJay has three moons. Two of the moons are the same size. The largest moon is much farther from the planet than are the other moons. Huge rings of tiny ice chunks circle the planet. NoWayJay's volcanoes are no longer active.

With the help of several space artists, you've toured part of the solar system. Open the pages of this chapter to complete your tour. Bon voyage!

**WILLIAM K. HARTMANN
(1939–   )**

The Sun and Its Family

Which planets are inner planets and which are outer planets?

1 sun

333,000 earths

People have always wondered what the sun was. Some thought the sun was a ball of fire. Others thought it was some sort of god slowly riding across the sky.

Today scientists know that the sun is a huge ball of hot churning gases. They have learned that it is a million times larger than the earth. They know that it has hundreds of thousands of times more mass than the earth. They also know that the sun gives off huge amounts of energy. A small part of this energy reaches the earth about 8 minutes after it leaves the sun.

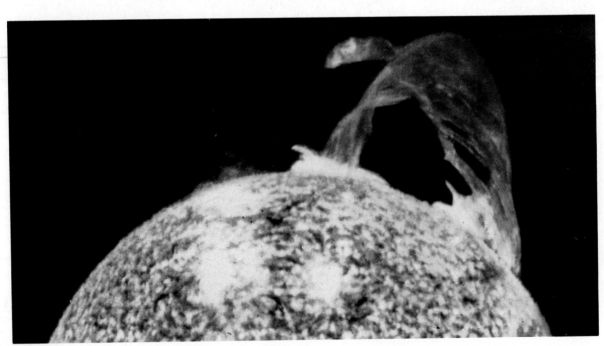

Hot gases exploding from the sun

Nine planets revolve, or travel around, the sun. The time it takes for a planet to revolve around the sun is called a year. An Earth year is 365 days long. The farther a planet is from the sun, the longer its year is. A year on the planet closest to the sun is 88 Earth days long. A year on the planet farthest from the sun is 247 Earth years long.

Each planet also rotates, or spins on its axis. The time it takes for a planet to rotate once is called a day. An Earth day is 24 hours long. A day on the planet with the shortest day is less than 10 Earth hours long. A day on the planet with the longest day is about 176 Earth days long.

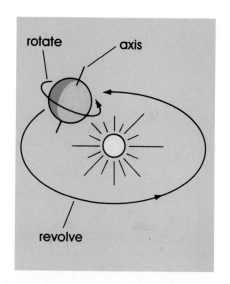

SKILL: Making a model

What does an ellipse look like?

The path that planets follow as they revolve around the sun is called an ellipse (i lips'). To draw an ellipse, tape some paper to a bulletin board. The paper should be about 60 cm long and 45 cm wide. Insert two pushpins near the center of the paper. The pushpins should be 14 cm apart. Tie the end of a string together to make a loop. The loop should be 30 cm long. Place the loop around both pins.

Hold a crayon against the inside of the loop. Use the crayon to pull the loop tight. Guide the crayon around the inside of the loop until you reach the point at which you started. The shape you have drawn is an ellipse.

Finding Out

243

The nine planets can be divided into two groups. The four planets closest to the sun can be called the **inner planets.** Mercury (mėr′kyər ē), Venus (vē′nəs), Earth, and Mars are the inner planets. The five planets farthest from the sun can be called the **outer planets.** Jupiter (jü′pə tər), Saturn (sat′ərn), Uranus (yür′ə nəs), Neptune (nep′tün), and Pluto (plü′tō) are the outer planets.

Look at the drawing of the solar system. What ways can you see that the inner planets are different from the outer planets?

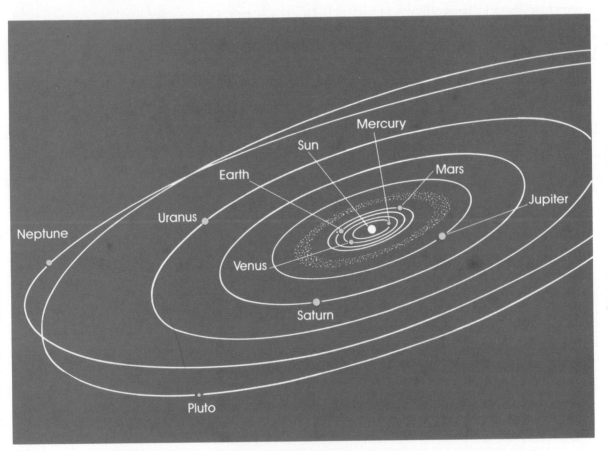

244

For Lesson Questions, turn to page 342.

Activity

What does a model of the solar system look like?

Materials   tape / meterstick / paper models of the planets and the sun

Procedure
A. Get paper models of the planets and the sun from your teacher. Tape the model of the sun to the wall at one end of a hallway.

B. Measure 58 mm from this sun. Tape the model of Mercury at this point.
  1. If Mercury is this far from the sun in this model, at what point in the hallway do you think Pluto will be?

C. Measure 50 mm from Mercury. Tape the model of Venus at this point. Tape the model of Earth 42 mm from Venus. Tape the model of Mars 78 mm from Earth.

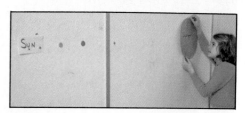

D. Measure 55.1 cm from Mars. Tape the model of Jupiter at this point. Tape the model of Saturn 65.1 cm from Jupiter. Tape the model of Uranus 144 cm from Saturn. Tape the model of Neptune 163 cm from Uranus. Tape the model of Pluto 140 cm from Neptune.
  2. How close is Pluto to where you thought it would be?

Conclusion
1. How would you describe the location of the planets in your model of the solar system?
2. How do the distances between the inner planets compare to the distances between the outer planets?

The Inner Planets

How are the inner planets different from each other?

Which planet in the solar system is closest to the sun and moves the fastest? This planet is **Mercury.** It takes Mercury about 88 Earth days to travel once around the sun. In the daytime the temperature on Mercury may reach 425°C. But at night the temperature may fall as low as −183°C.

Mercury is a little larger than our moon. The drawing below shows the surface of Mercury. What makes this surface very much like the surface of our moon?

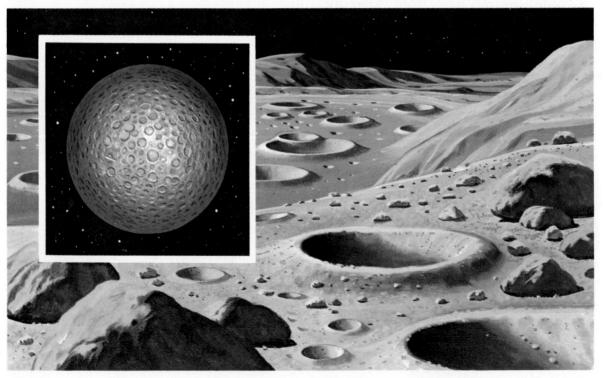

Mercury

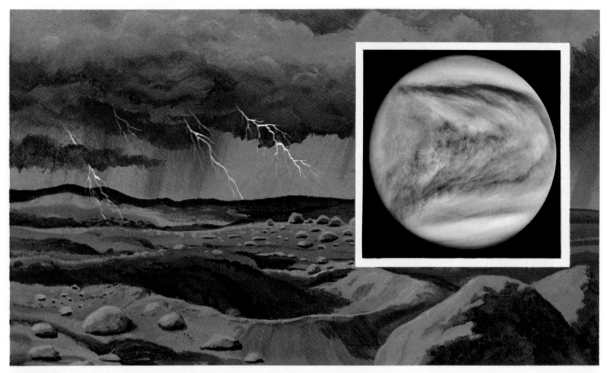

Venus

The second planet from the sun is **Venus.** Venus is about the same size as Earth. It is also the closest planet to Earth. Like Earth, Venus has an atmosphere. But the atmosphere of Venus is very dense. The upper atmosphere has layers of thick clouds. The lower atmosphere is mainly carbon dioxide gas. The dense atmosphere helps to keep the temperature on the surface at about 450°C. The atmosphere presses down with a force that is 90 times greater than air pressure on Earth.

Venus only rotates twice for every trip around the sun. So every year on Venus is about two days long!

Earth

Our planet, **Earth,** is the third planet from the sun. From space, our planet looks like a blue ball covered by swirling clouds. The atmosphere of Earth is made mainly of nitrogen, oxygen, and carbon dioxide. Water covers about three fourths of the surface of our planet. The temperature at the surface rarely goes below −30°C or above 43°C.

Unlike Mercury or Venus, Earth has a moon. The moon revolves around Earth about once every 27 days. The moon is about one-fourth the size of Earth. Besides having a moon, in what other ways is Earth different from Mercury and Venus?

The fourth planet from the sun is **Mars.** For hundreds of years people thought life could be found on Mars. Large lines that could be seen on the planet were thought to be canals. When the planet was explored, however, no signs of life were found.

Mars and Earth are alike in many ways. When it is summer on Mars, daytime temperatures can reach 27°C. Both planets rotate at about the same rate. Also, small amounts of frozen water can be found on Mars. Unlike Earth, Mars has two moons. Both of these moons are much smaller than our moon. In this picture, Mars appears red. The color is caused by a rustlike dust on the surface. This dust is blown around by winds on Mars. Mars was named after the Roman god of war. Can you guess why?

Mars

You can use the following table to compare the inner planets. You can also use the drawings below the table to compare the sizes of the inner planets. Which planet is the smallest? Which has the longest day? Which has the shortest year? How much farther from the sun is Mars than Mercury? How much longer is a year on Earth than a year on Venus?

THE INNER PLANETS

Planet	Average distance from sun (in millions of km)	Diameter (in km)	Length of year (in Earth time)	Length of day (in Earth time)	Number of known moons
Mercury	58	4,880	88 days	176 days	0
Venus	108	12,100	225 days	116.7 days	0
Earth	150	12,756	365 days	24 hours	1
Mars	228	6,784	687 days	24.6 hours	2

Mercury

Venus

Earth

Mars

For Lesson Questions, turn to page 342.

The Outer Planets

Beyond Mars lies the fifth planet, **Jupiter.** Jupiter is the largest planet in the solar system. About 1,000 Earths could fill the inside of this giant planet. Jupiter is so large that it has its own family of moons. At least 16 moons revolve around Jupiter. One of Jupiter's moons has active volcanoes on it. Ice can be found on another. One of Jupiter's moons can be seen in front of the planet in the larger picture below.

Unlike any of the inner planets, Jupiter is made almost completely of gases. Huge storms move through these gases. The largest of these storms forms the Great Red Spot, which you can see in the smaller picture below. This one storm is as big as three Earths! Jupiter also has a ring that is thought to be made of rocky materials.

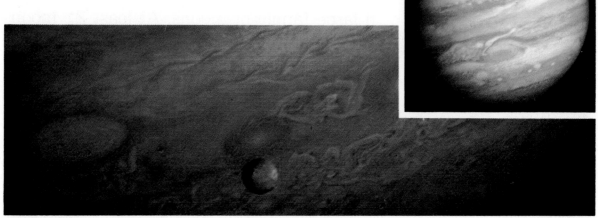

Jupiter

251

Saturn

The sixth planet from the sun is **Saturn.** Saturn is the second largest planet in the solar system. Like Jupiter, Saturn is made mainly of gases. And like Jupiter, Saturn has a large family of moons. At least 21 moons revolve around Saturn.

Saturn is best known for its beautiful rings. These rings can easily be seen from Earth with a telescope. Scientists have learned that Saturn's six large rings are made up of hundreds of smaller rings. Each smaller ring seems to be made of millions of frozen particles.

The seventh planet, **Uranus,** takes 84 Earth years to travel around the sun. While making this trip, Uranus rotates on its side. If people lived at the north pole of Uranus, they would have a night that would last 42 Earth years! This night would be followed by a day just as long. Can you imagine what a day that is 42 years long would be like?

Like Jupiter and Saturn, Uranus is made mainly of gas. Scientists think the atmosphere is made of hydrogen and helium. Uranus also has about eleven rings and about fifteen moons.

The smallest of the gaseous planets is **Neptune.** Neptune is about the same size and color as Uranus. But unlike Uranus, Neptune does not rotate on its side.

Neptune has two moons. The smaller of the two moons takes 1 Earth year to make a trip around Neptune. The larger moon is much closer to Neptune. This moon takes only 6 Earth days to revolve once. This larger moon makes the trip backwards!

Uranus

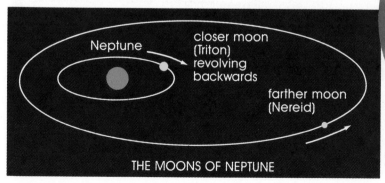

Neptune

closer moon
(Triton)
revolving
backwards

farther moon
(Nereid)

THE MOONS OF NEPTUNE

Neptune

253

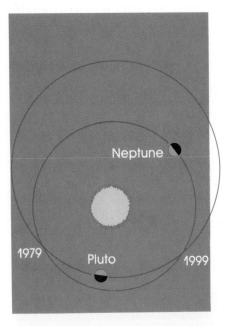

Until 1999, **Pluto** is the eighth planet. As you can see in the drawings, Pluto's orbit makes it the ninth planet from the sun for most of its year. Pluto takes longer than any other planet to revolve around the sun. Each trip takes 247 Earth years. From Pluto the sun looks like a bright star. The sun cannot warm this distant planet much. The temperature on Pluto stays around −230°C.

Unlike the other outer planets, Pluto is solid. Pluto is also the smallest planet in the solar system. It is about one-quarter the size of Earth. Pluto has one moon.

Pluto

THE OUTER PLANETS

Planet	Average distance from sun (in millions of km)	Diameter (in km)	Length of year (in Earth time)	Length of day (in Earth time)	Number of known moons
Jupiter	778	143,200	11.9 years	9.9 hours	16
Saturn	1,425	120,000	29.5 years	10.4 hours	21
Uranus	2,867	51,400	84 years	17.2 hours	15
Neptune	4,497	49,500	164.1 years	17.8 hours	2
Pluto	5,900	3,000	247 years	6.4 days	1

This table and drawing describe the outer planets. Which of these planets is the largest? Which is the smallest? Compare the outer planets with the inner planets on page 250. How much longer is the day on Mercury than the day on Pluto?

For Lesson Questions, turn to page 342.

255

Activity

What are conditions like on the other planets?

Procedure

A. Pretend that you are an astronaut preparing to explore the solar system. You have been given the chart below so that you can prepare for your trip.

1. On which planets could you land your spacecraft?
2. On which planets would you find the atmosphere different from Earth?
3. For which planets would you need to bring protection from heat?
4. On which planets would you find the gravity to be less than that on Earth?

B. Now pretend that you are in your spacecraft on the way to Mars.

5. What things would you need in your spacecraft to survive on Mars?

Conclusion

In general, what are conditions like on the other planets?

OFFICIAL PLANET DATA

PLANET	AVERAGE TEMPERATURE	WHAT PLANET IS MAINLY MADE OF	AMOUNT OF GRAVITY COMPARED TO EARTH	GASES FOUND IN ATMOSPHERE
MERCURY	425 C	ROCK	LESS	VERY FEW, IF ANY, GASES
VENUS	450 C	ROCK	LESS	CARBON DIOXIDE
EARTH	15 C	ROCK	XXXX	NITROGEN, OXYGEN, WATER
MARS	12 C	ROCK	LESS	CARBON DIOXIDE, WATER
JUPITER	−130 C	GAS	GREATER	HYDROGEN, METHANE
SATURN	−180 C	GAS	LESS	HYDROGEN, METHANE
URANUS	−215 C	GAS	LESS	HYDROGEN, METHANE
NEPTUNE	−200 C	GAS	GREATER	HYDROGEN, METHANE
PLUTO	−250 C	ROCK	LESS	VERY FEW, IF ANY, GASES

Other Members of the Solar System

What are asteroids, meteors, and comets?

Besides the sun, the planets, and the moons, there are many other members of our solar system. One group of objects are called comets (kom'its). A **comet** is a mass of ice, frozen gases, and dust. Like planets, comets revolve around the sun. But unlike planets, the orbit of a comet may be long and narrow. This orbit can bring a comet very close to the sun. Some comets pass by the sun every few years. Others may pass by only once every 100 years or more.

As a comet approaches the sun, its gases begin to heat up. As the gases heat up, they produce a long tail. The tail may be millions of kilometers long. It usually points away from the sun.

tail

head

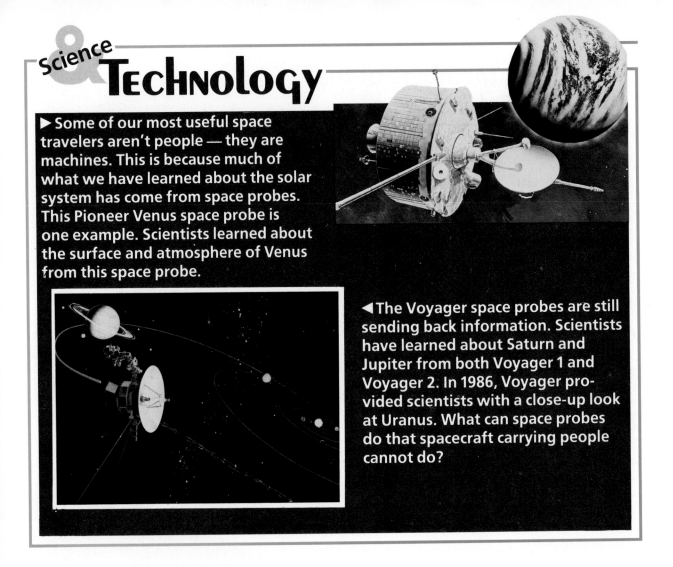

Science & Technology

▶ Some of our most useful space travelers aren't people — they are machines. This is because much of what we have learned about the solar system has come from space probes. This Pioneer Venus space probe is one example. Scientists learned about the surface and atmosphere of Venus from this space probe.

◀ The Voyager space probes are still sending back information. Scientists have learned about Saturn and Jupiter from both Voyager 1 and Voyager 2. In 1986, Voyager provided scientists with a close-up look at Uranus. What can space probes do that spacecraft carrying people cannot do?

A second group of objects are called asteroids (as'tə roidz). **Asteroids** are pieces of rock that orbit the sun between Mars and Jupiter. Some asteroids are small lumps of rock. Others are very large. The largest known asteroid is about 3,400 km across. It is a little smaller than the moon. Most asteroids take about 5 years to orbit the sun.

Besides asteroids, there are other pieces of rock in space. When one of these rocks is pulled into our atmosphere, it is called a **meteor** (mē'tē ər). Have you ever seen a "shooting star"? A shooting star is not a star. It is a meteor burning as it passes through the atmosphere. Sometimes a meteor strikes the ground. A meteor that strikes the ground is called a **meteorite** (mē'tē ə rīt). Very few meteorites are ever found. This is because most meteors completely burn up in the atmosphere.

A meteorite

For Lesson Questions, turn to page 342.

Ideas to Remember

▶ Our solar system is made up of a sun, nine planets, and moons. It also has countless smaller objects including comets and asteroids.

▶ The four inner planets are Mercury, Venus, Earth, and Mars.

▶ The five outer planets are Jupiter, Saturn, Uranus, Neptune, and Pluto.

▶ A belt of rocks called asteroids separates the inner planets from the outer planets.

▶ Comets are masses of ice, frozen gases, and dust that revolve around the sun.

Reviewing the Chapter

SCIENCE WORDS

A. Use these terms to answer the questions.

asteroid   meteor   comet   meteorite

1. I am a piece of rock from space that has been pulled into Earth's atmosphere. What am I?

2. I am a piece of rock that orbits the sun between Mars and Jupiter. What am I?

3. I am a piece of rock from space that falls through the earth's atmosphere and strikes the ground. What am I?

4. I am a mass of frozen gas and dust. I have a head and a long tail. What am I?

B. Use all the terms below to complete the sentences.

Mars   inner planets   Neptune   Pluto
Uranus   outer planets   Jupiter   Saturn
Earth   Mercury   Venus

The solar system is made of nine planets. Our planet, __1__, is one of the four planets closest to the sun. This group of planets can be called the __2__. The other three planets in this group are __3__, __4__, and __5__. The five planets farthest from the sun can be called the __6__. Until 1999 the farthest of these planets is __7__. The other planets in this group are __8__, __9__, __10__, and __11__.

UNDERSTANDING IDEAS

A. What is an asteroid? Where are asteroids found? How is an asteroid different from a comet?

B. Write the letter of the planet that best matches the description. Not all the planets will be used.

1. It has daytime temperatures of 425°C. It takes 88 Earth days to revolve around the sun once.

2. It has one moon. Its surface is mainly covered with water.

3. It has two moons. Small amounts of frozen water can be found on its surface.

4. It has at least 21 moons and 6 large beautiful rings.

   a. Jupiter
   b. Neptune
   c. Mars
   d. Mercury
   e. Saturn
   f. Earth

C. Identify each of the following.

1   2   3   4

USING IDEAS

Pretend you are an astronaut. You have discovered a tenth planet. Describe your trip to the planet and your experiences on it. Draw a picture of the surface of the planet.

THINKING LIKE A SCIENTIST

You may be able to answer some of these questions just by thinking about them. To answer other questions, you may have to do some research.

1. Today it may seem silly to imagine that the sun and planets revolve around the earth. Yet, centuries ago great scientists made this mistake. Why wasn't it obvious to them that the sun was in the center of the nine planets?

2. How would Earth be different if it did not rotate on its axis?

Science in Careers

Earth science involves the study of the solid, liquid, and gaseous parts of the earth. There are many careers for people in earth science.

Geology is the study of the solid earth. Different geologists study different aspects of the earth. A **paleontologist** is a geologist who studies fossils. A **petroleum geologist** studies where oil is found. **Mineralogists** study minerals. A **volcanologist** is a geologist who studies volcanoes.

Oceanography is the study of the oceans. **Physical oceanographers** study ocean currents, tides, and waves. They also study underwater sound. **Chemical oceanographers** study the chemistry of salt water. **Biological oceanographers** study the living things in the sea. **Geological oceanographers** use echo sounders to map the ocean floor.

Meteorologist

Meteorologists are scientists who study the atmosphere. They make measurements that help them predict weather. Many predictions are made with the help of computers.

Geologist

LINDA A. MORABITO
(1953–   )

Linda Morabito is a navigation engineer. She is one of a team that helped to steer the space probe Voyager 1 past Jupiter.

On March 9, 1979, Morabito made an important discovery. She was checking a picture that Voyager 1 had taken of Io, one of Jupiter's moons. She used a computer to brighten the picture on a screen. Suddenly she spotted a large umbrella-shaped cloud on the edge of Io. This was the very first time that an active volcano had been seen anyplace but on Earth.

Volcano on Io

Developing Skills

WORD SKILLS

Many English words have word parts that come from other languages. This table lists some of these word parts. Use the table to help you write a definition for each of the words listed. You can do this by breaking each word into parts. For example, the word atmosphere is made of the parts atmo- and sphere. Check your definitions by looking in a dictionary.

Word part	Meaning
atmo-	vapor, steam
geo-	earth
hydro-	water
litho-	stone
tele-	over a long distance
topo-	place
sphere	globe
-graphy	writing
-logy	science of
-scope	for seeing

1. atmosphere
2. geology
3. hydrosphere
4. lithosphere
5. telescope
6. topography

READING A PICTOGRAPH

A pictograph uses symbols to show information. The pictograph on the next page uses a cup of water to show the amount of water used in a typical American house every day. Use this pictograph to answer the following questions.

1. How much water is used every day for bathing?
2. How much water is used every day for drinking and cooking?
3. How much water is used every day for washing clothes?
4. How much water is used for activities outside the home?
5. Which of the activities shown use more than 75 L of water every day?
6. Which activity uses more water—washing clothes or washing dishes?
7. Is more water used in activities inside the home or in activities outside the home?

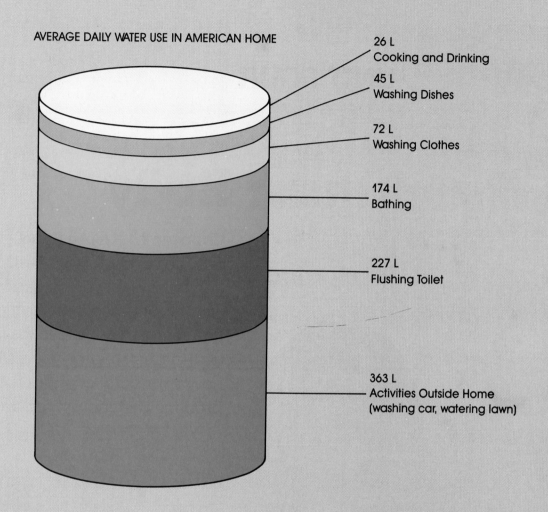

AVERAGE DAILY WATER USE IN AMERICAN HOME

26 L
Cooking and Drinking

45 L
Washing Dishes

72 L
Washing Clothes

174 L
Bathing

227 L
Flushing Toilet

363 L
Activities Outside Home
(washing car, watering lawn)

USING THINKING SKILLS

More than three fourths of the earth is covered by water. Even so, there is very little water on the earth that is suitable for drinking. Many cities have had periods when their water supplies have been very low. These cities have had to limit the amount of water people use.

Think about this as you answer these questions.
1. Should people be made to limit the amount of water they use? Explain your answer.
2. In what ways can you and your family save water?

265

UNIT FOUR

Learning About the Human Body

Chapter 13—Using Food

Eating a breakfast like this is a good idea. Before you can work or play, you need energy. You get energy from the foods you eat. In this chapter you will learn how your body changes food to produce the energy you need.

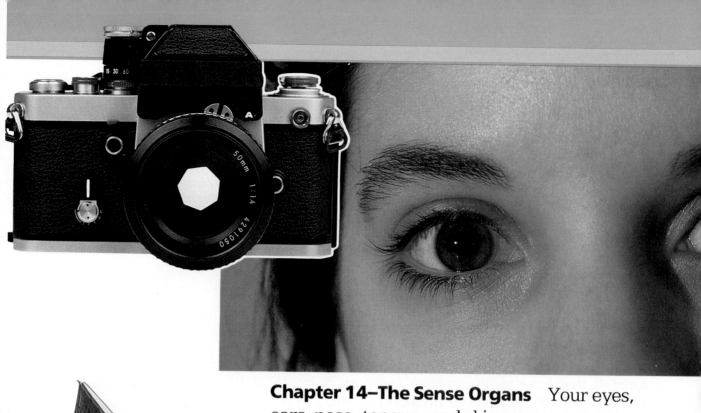

Chapter 14—The Sense Organs Your eyes, ears, nose, tongue, and skin are sense organs. They help to keep you aware of what is going on around you. Perhaps your eyes and ears help you the most. How can the machines in the pictures be compared to your eyes and ears?

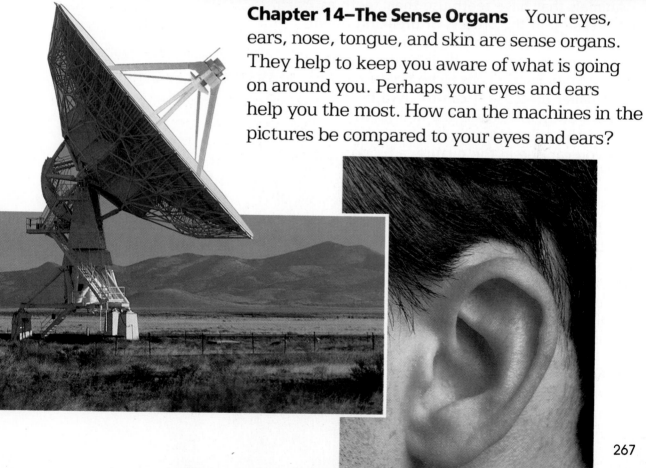

CHAPTER 13
Using Food

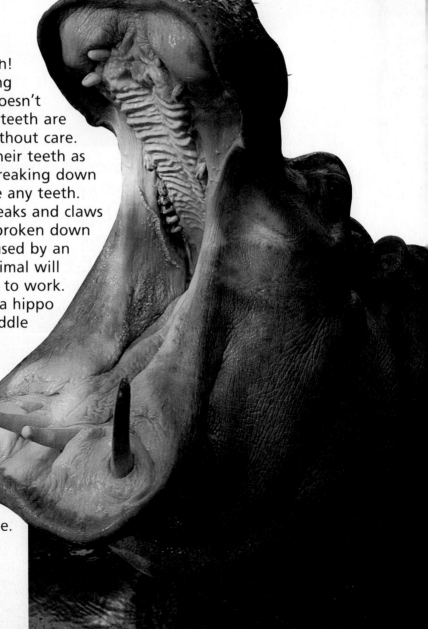

Open wide. Let's see those pearly white hippopotamus teeth! You're doing a great job brushing and flossing. Actually, a hippo doesn't need to clean its teeth. Its large teeth are made of ivory and stay white without care.

Animals that have teeth use their teeth as the first step in the process of breaking down food. Other animals do not have any teeth. These animals might use their beaks and claws to tear food. Food needs to be broken down into smaller pieces so it can be used by an animal's body. Otherwise the animal will not get the energy that it needs to work.

As you can see in the picture, a hippo has long, curved teeth in the middle of its mouth. The hippo uses these teeth to grind about 59 kilograms of vegetables a day. The hippo's teeth grow all the time. But they never get too long because the hippo's jaws grind against each other and wear away. The side teeth are even longer and look tusklike. These are used to fight enemies.

268

The red-tailed hawk has a hooked beak and hooked claws. This hawk eats mice, rabbits, insects, and snakes. Because it eats so many mice, the red-tailed hawk keeps the number of mice from becoming too large.

A tiger uses its sharp claws and cutting teeth when hunting prey. Usually, a tiger hunts at night. It charges its prey and pulls it down. The tiger's teeth hold the prey and tear off chunks of meat. Eating 23 kilograms of meat in a night is normal for a tiger.

What a smile the chimp has! With these teeth the chimp can bite and chew fruit, leaves, palm nuts, seeds, and stems.

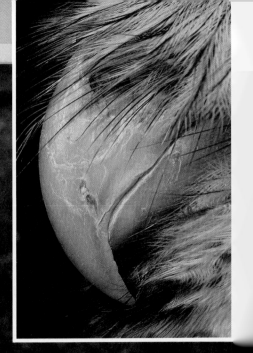

The American alligator has large jaws with many sharp teeth. The alligator eats different kinds of small animals, such as fish, frogs, and turtles. A very large alligator might attack a dog or a pig. The alligator drags its prey underwater, drowning the victim. Then it tears the victim to pieces with its teeth and jaws. The barred owl eats mostly mice and other small rodents. This owl swoops down silently and grabs its prey with one foot. Then the barred owl flies back to its perch and tears its prey to pieces. Any parts that are not digested, such as bones or hair, are spit out in the form of pellets.

Teeth are used to begin the breakdown of food. What happens if food is not chewed properly? You will need 1 teaspoon of ground hamburger, a 2.5 cm cube of stew beef, 1 teaspoon of meat tenderizer, and 2 paper plates. Put each type of meat on a separate paper plate. Sprinkle the meat with tenderizer. Observe and record what happens every 30 minutes. From this activity, what can you say about how teeth help to prepare food for the body to use?

The killer whale has between 40 and 48 teeth. This whale eats salmon, other large fish, and sometimes seals and walruses.

In your lifetime you will eat about 10,500 kilograms of food. Your body cannot use this food until it is broken down. In this chapter you will learn about the parts of the body that work together to break down food.

From Cells to Systems

What are cells, tissues, organs, and systems?

What are the smallest parts of your body? Are your hands the smallest parts? Are your fingers? How about your knuckles? No, none of these parts are the smallest. The smallest parts of your body are called **cells.** The body is made of millions of cells. Most of these cells are so small that you need a microscope to see them. Even the largest cell in the body is only about the size of a pinpoint. Look at the cells shown in the pictures on these pages. In these pictures the cells are hundreds of times larger than they are in the body.

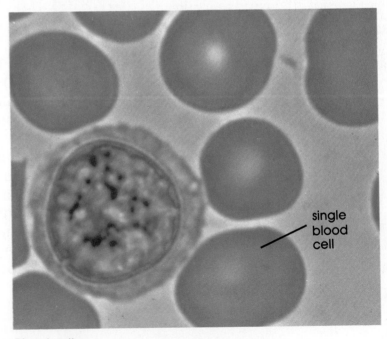

single
blood
cell

Blood cells

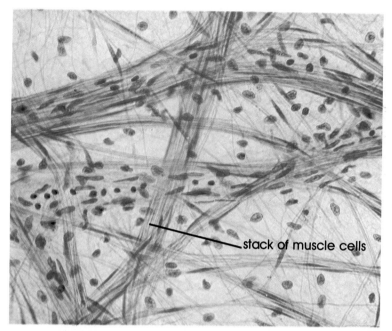

stack of muscle cells

Muscle cells

The body is made of different types of cells. Blood is made of blood cells, while muscles are made of muscle cells. As you can see in the pictures, different types of cells have different shapes and sizes. Blood cells are round, while muscle cells are long and thin.

Groups of cells work together to do certain jobs in the body. These groups of cells are called **tissues** (tish′üz). Muscle tissue is made of muscle cells. These cells work together to help move parts of the body. Bone tissue is made of bone cells. These cells work together to support parts of the body. What types of cells make up skin tissue? What do these cells work together to do?

Just as groups of cells work together to form tissues, groups of tissues also work together in the body. These groups of tissues form **organs** (ôr′gəns). Organs have special jobs in the body. Your heart is an organ that is made mainly of muscle tissue. The heart pumps blood throughout the body. Your brain is an organ that is made mainly of nervous tissue. The brain controls most of the body. What are some other organs in your body?

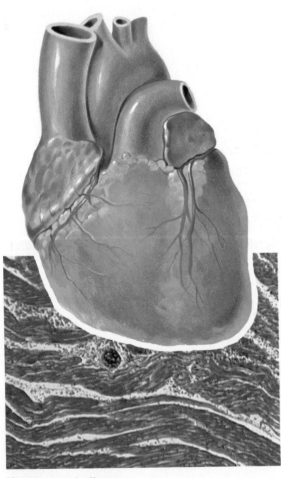

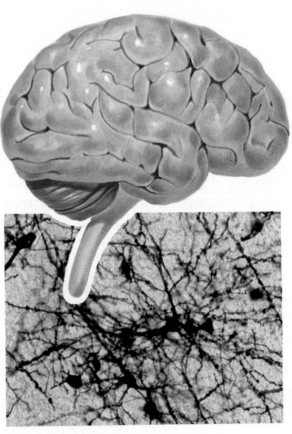

Heart muscle tissue

Brain nervous tissue

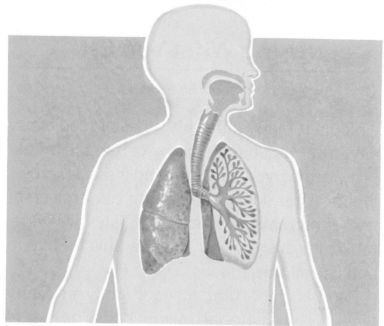

Respiratory system

So far, you have learned that your body is made of cells, tissues, and organs. Did you know that groups of cells, tissues, and organs also work together? These groups make up **systems** (sis′təms).

Your body has many important systems. The respiratory (res′pər ə tôr ē) system brings oxygen into the body and releases carbon dioxide from the body. Two parts of this system are the lungs and the windpipe. They are made of many types of tissues and cells.

Another important body system is the digestive (də jes′tiv) system. This system breaks down food so that it can be used by the body. You will learn more about this important body system in the rest of this chapter.

For Lesson Questions, turn to page 344.

Using What You Eat

What is digestion?

You eat many different types of food every day. You may have eggs or cereal for breakfast. Maybe you eat soup and a sandwich for lunch. After school you might eat a piece of fruit. You may eat chicken or fish with vegetables for dinner. Your body is able to take in and use all these foods.

Food is important to your body in many ways. The materials your body needs to grow come from the food you eat. Your body uses food to repair and replace worn-out and damaged parts. Food also provides the energy needed by the cells. Without this energy, the parts of the body could not do their jobs.

The food you eat is not in a form that can be used by your cells. Every piece of food you eat is too big to fit into a cell. Also, one piece of food may contain materials that are needed by different groups of cells. So food must be changed. Changing food into a form your cells can use is called digestion. Digestion takes place in the **digestive system.**

Digestion begins in the mouth, where food is broken into small pieces. These small pieces of food travel down a tube into the stomach. There the food is broken into tiny chemical particles. The chemical particles pass into the intestines (in tes'tans), where digestion is completed. Now the food is in a form that can pass from the intestines into the bloodstream. The blood then carries the digested food to your cells.

food broken into small pieces in mouth

food traveling down tube into stomach

food broken into tiny chemical particles in stomach

digested food passing from intestines into bloodstream

For Lesson Questions, turn to page 344.

Digestion in the Mouth

How is food digested in the mouth?

Your teeth are important to the way you look. They are also a very important part of your digestive system. Teeth help to carry out the first step of digestion.

Did you know that you have different kinds of teeth? The teeth in the front of your mouth are called **incisors** (in sī′zərs). Incisors are thin and flat. They have sharp edges that help to cut and bite food. Next to the incisors are pointed teeth called **canines** (kā′nīns). The sharp points of these teeth help to bite and tear food.

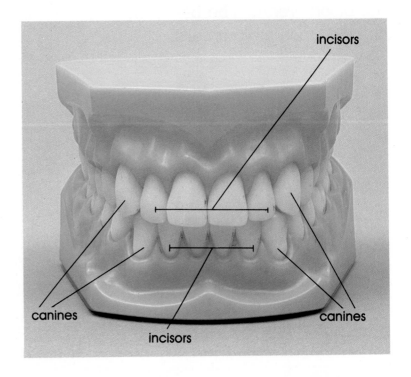

incisors

canines

incisors

canines

Next to the canine teeth are teeth with flat tops. These teeth are called **premolars** (prē mō′lərs). Premolars help to crush food into smaller pieces. The teeth at the back of your mouth are **molars** (mō′lərs). Molars have large flat tops that help to crush and grind food into smaller pieces. Look at these pictures. Then look in a mirror. Try to identify your teeth.

Digestion begins as soon as food enters your mouth. You bite and tear pieces of food with your incisors and canines. You grind food into smaller pieces with your premolars and molars. The longer you chew a piece of food, the smaller the pieces become.

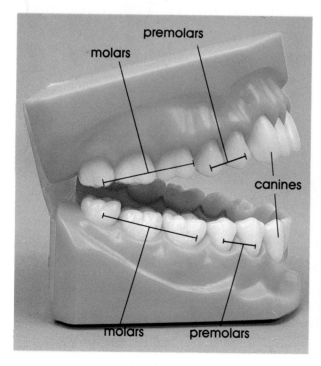

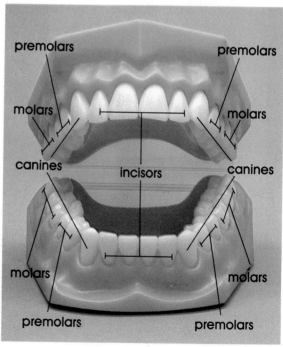

As you can see in the drawings, digestion in the mouth involves more than teeth. As you chew food, a juice called saliva (sə lī′və) is released. **Saliva** helps to make food wet and soft. Soft, wet food is easy to swallow. Saliva also helps to break down chemicals in food.

The whole time you are chewing your food, your **tongue** is moving the food around in your mouth. Your tongue helps to mix the food with saliva. When you swallow, your tongue pushes the food into the back of your mouth.

By the time you swallow, one step of digestion is complete. Your teeth, tongue, and saliva have made large pieces of food smaller, softer, and wetter. They have made it easier for the food to travel through the rest of the digestive system.

For Lesson Questions, turn to page 344.

biting food

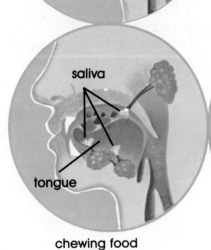

chewing food

release of saliva

tongue mixing food with saliva

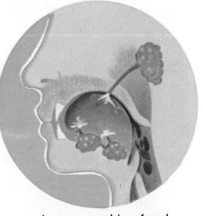

tongue pushing food to back of mouth

food swallowed

278

What happens to food in your mouth?

Materials   cracker / slice of bread / clock

Procedure

A. Take a few bites of a cracker. While looking at a clock, chew the cracker for one minute before you swallow it. Notice how the taste of the cracker changes as it mixes with saliva while you chew it.

1. What did the cracker taste like when you started chewing it?
2. How did the cracker taste after one minute?
3. Besides changing the taste, how else did saliva change the cracker as you chewed it?

B. Take a few bites of a slice of bread. Chew the bread for one minute.

4. What did the bread taste like when you started chewing it?
5. How did the bread taste after one minute?
6. Besides changing the taste, how else did saliva change the bread as you chewed it?

Conclusion

1. What happens to the taste of foods such as crackers and bread when they are mixed with saliva in the mouth?
2. What else happens to the food in the mouth?

Using science ideas

Repeat step **A** using other foods, such as fruits, meats, and vegetables.

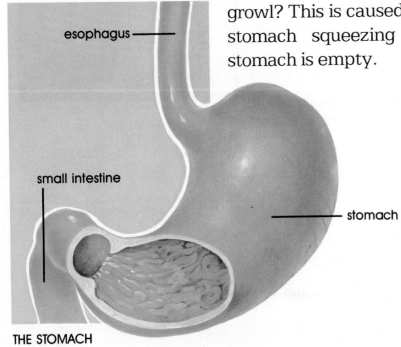

mouth

esophagus

muscles pushing food

food

stomach

THE ESOPHAGUS

esophagus

small intestine

stomach

THE STOMACH

The Digestive Path

What happens to food after it is swallowed?

After food is swallowed, it enters a long hollow tube called the **esophagus** (ē sof′ə-gəs). The esophagus is made of strong muscles that push the food into the stomach. These muscles can push food even if you are standing on your head.

The **stomach** is a hollow organ that is shaped like the letter *J.* It is made mainly of muscles. Food in the stomach is mixed with juices. The juices come from cells in the wall of the stomach. They help to further digest the food. The muscles of the stomach squeeze together and mix the food and juices. Have you ever heard your stomach growl? This is caused by the muscles in your stomach squeezing together when your stomach is empty.

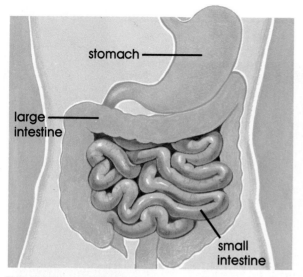
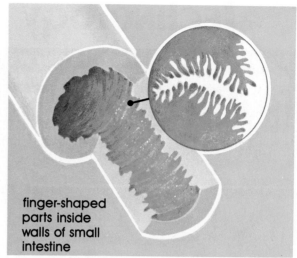

stomach

large intestine

small intestine

finger-shaped parts inside walls of small intestine

THE SMALL INTESTINE

When food leaves the stomach, it is a thick liquid. The thick liquid moves into the small intestine. The **small intestine** is an organ that is shaped like a long tube. It is about four times longer than your height. Muscles in the walls of the small intestine squeeze the food. This mixes the food with more juices. Some of these juices come from the small intestine itself. Other juices come from organs that are connected to the small intestine.

As you can see in the drawing, the inside of the small intestine has parts that look like fingers. These finger-shaped parts contain many small tubes filled with blood. The food, which is now a liquid, leaves the small intestine and enters the bloodstream here. The blood carries the digested food to cells throughout the body.

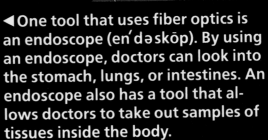

▶ Until recently, surgery was the only way a doctor could examine a problem within the body. Today, thanks to fiber optics, surgery is no longer always necessary. A fiber optic is a glass fiber that is as thin as a hair. Light is carried down such a fiber, as shown here.

◀ One tool that uses fiber optics is an endoscope (en′də skōp). By using an endoscope, doctors can look into the stomach, lungs, or intestines. An endoscope also has a tool that allows doctors to take out samples of tissues inside the body.

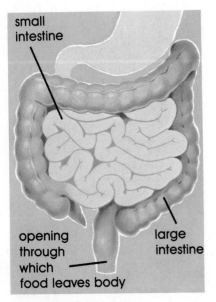

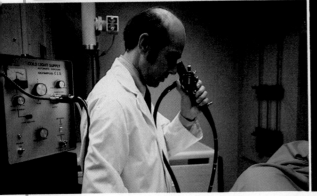

small intestine

opening through which food leaves body

large intestine

THE LARGE INTESTINE

Most of the food that the body uses enters the bloodstream through the small intestine. Food that does not enter the bloodstream moves into the large intestine. The **large intestine** is an organ that is shaped like a wide tube. Water is removed from the food in this organ. Like the small intestine, the large intestine has finger-shaped parts. Water taken out of the food enters the bloodstream through these parts. Unused food leaves the body through an opening at the end of the large intestine. This completes digestion. Look at the table on page 283. It shows the steps in digestion.

For Lesson Questions, turn to page 344.

THE DIGESTIVE SYSTEM		
	Body part	Part in digestion
	Mouth	• Teeth bite, chew, grind food • Saliva softens and wets food, breaks down some chemicals
	Esophagus	• Connects mouth with stomach
	Stomach	• Mixes food with juices that help break down food
	Small intestine	• Squeezes food • Mixes food with juices • Removes useful parts of food and releases them into bloodstream
	Large intestine	• Removes water from food and releases it into bloodstream

SKILL: Measuring

Finding Out

How long is a digestive path?

To get an idea of how long a digestive path is, you need a ball of string, a meterstick, and a pair of scissors. Measure 8 cm of string. This is about how deep your mouth is. Your esophagus is about 43 cm long. Measure another 43 cm of string. Your stomach is about 20 cm long. Measure another 20 cm of string. Your small intestine is much longer. It is about 6.4 m long. Measure another 6.4 m of string. Your large intestine is about 1.5 m long. Measure another 1.5 m of string. Cut the string at this point. Now measure the whole piece of string. How long is this digestive path?

Activity

What foods contain starch?

Materials iodine solution / starch solution / dropper / bread / other pieces of food

Procedure

A. One of the many chemicals your digestive system breaks down is starch. You can test a piece of food to see if it contains starch by using iodine. Get a container of iodine solution and another container of starch solution from your teacher. **Caution:** *Do not taste anything used in this activity.*

   1. What color is the iodine solution?
   2. What color is the starch solution?

B. Use a dropper to put a few drops of the iodine solution into the starch solution.

   3. What color does the starch solution become?

C. Put a few drops of the iodine solution on a piece of bread. If the bread becomes the same color as the starch did, then the bread contains starch.

   4. What color did the bread become?
   5. Does the bread contain starch?

D. Make a chart with headings like the one shown. Test other foods supplied by your teacher for starch. Complete the chart.

Results
What happens to foods that contain starch when iodine is put on them?

Conclusion
Which of the foods you tested contained starch?

Food	Color food turns when iodine is added	Does food contain starch?

Digestive System Problems

**How can you take care of
your digestive system?**

Has anyone ever told you that you should not exercise right after you eat? Do you know why? The muscles in your digestive system use energy. If you exercise while these muscles are working, you take away some of the energy they need. This can cause stomach cramps. Stomach cramps can be painful. You could drown if you get them while you are swimming. Because of this, you should not do any active exercise right after you eat.

Like most people, you have probably had a stomachache. Stomachaches are a common problem of the digestive system. A stomachache can be very painful. It can be caused by eating too much food. It can also be caused by eating food that is very spicy. Stomachaches usually go away after a short time. They can be prevented by taking care of the digestive system.

One way you can take care of your digestive system is to eat the proper kinds of foods. You should not eat too many fatty or fried foods. You should not eat too many foods that are very spicy. What you should eat are plenty of fruits and vegetables. These foods contain a material called fiber. Many doctors think that foods with fiber help to keep the digestive system healthy.

Fruits and vegetables

For Lesson Questions, turn to page 344.

Ideas to Remember

► Your body is made up of cells, tissues, organs, and systems.

► The digestive system changes food into a form the cells in the body can use.

► Food travels from the mouth to the stomach through the esophagus. From the stomach, food travels to the small intestine, and then to the large intestine.

► Stomachaches and stomach cramps are common digestive system problems.

► One way you can take care of your digestive system is to eat the proper kinds of foods.

Reviewing the Chapter

A. Use all the terms below to complete the sentences.

saliva   incisors   stomach   large intestine   small intestine
canines   esophagus   tongue   premolars   molars

The digestion of food begins in the mouth. Teeth called __1__ and __2__ bite and tear food. The __3__ and __4__ grind the food. At the same time a juice called __5__ helps make the food wet and soft. Before swallowing, the __6__ pushes the food into the back of the mouth. After the food is swallowed, it first enters a long tube called the __7__. The food then moves first into the __8__, and then into the __9__, and finally into the __10__.

B. Identify each of the following.

1. I am a group of cells, tissues, and organs. What am I?

2. I am the smallest parts of the body. What am I?

3. I am a group of tissues that work together. What am I?

4. I am a body system that changes food into a form that the cells can use. What am I?

5. I am a group of cells. What am I?

A. Identify each of these parts of the digestive system. Explain how each part helps in digestion.

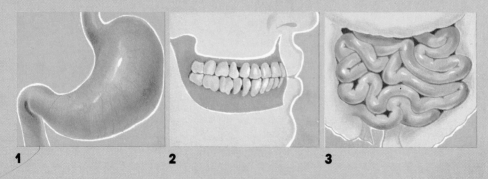

1   2   3

B. Tell which of the following sentences are true and which are false.

1. Muscle cells work together to help move parts of the body.
2. Skin tissue and bone tissue are made of the same kind of cells.
3. Groups of cells work together to do certain jobs.
4. Bone tissue is made of blood cells.
5. The brain is made mainly of nervous tissue.

C. Explain what problems you might have with your digestive system. Describe the proper care for your digestive system.

USING IDEAS

You may have heard the saying "You are what you eat." Use reference books to find out what foods are good for you. Plan a 3-day menu that contains these foods.

THINKING LIKE A SCIENTIST

You may be able to answer some of these questions just by thinking about them. To answer other questions, you may have to do some research.

1. Imagine that the food you eat is digested in the stomach and passed to the small intestine. Here the food is further digested. What would happen if the digested food could not enter the bloodstream? Describe some ways that this would affect you.

2. Long-distance runners will eat large amounts of high-energy foods for several days before a big race. Then for several hours before the race, they will not eat. Why do you think they do this?

CHAPTER 14
The Sense Organs

Have you ever spun around and around on a ride at a fair or carnival? As you spun, you may have felt strange. It may have seemed as if your stomach were moving up and down. Think about how you felt when you got off the ride. It is likely that you felt dizzy. You may even have had a hard time walking.

Different sense organs in your body are affected when you spin around. When your brain gets signals from these organs, you feel dizzy.

When they traveled in space, some of the astronauts felt dizzy. Some felt sick to their stomach. Having these feelings during a space flight can be a sign of space sickness. Space sickness usually occurred during the first few days of a space flight. Not everyone who traveled in space got space sickness. And those who did were not greatly affected by it. But as longer and longer space missions are planned, curing space sickness has become more important.

What causes space sickness? The answer is still not known. It is thought that being weightless is a major cause. Things and people are weightless in space. Astronauts must work, eat, and sleep in a weightless state. This takes some getting used to.

How people see things when they are weightless may be another cause of space sickness. In space, there is no up and no down! Suppose you are floating around weightless. What you see as up and down changes as you move in different ways. This odd, changing way of seeing things may produce a dizzy feeling. Now come back to the earth. Why do you feel dizzy after spinning on a carnival ride? The reason is that your sense of balance is upset.

A special organ inside each of your ears helps you keep your balance when you turn your head. This special organ is made up of three canals lined with tiny hairs. There is a liquid inside the canals. When you turn your head, the liquid moves. The moving liquid presses against the hairs. This action causes a message to be sent to your brain. The message is that your head is turning. When you stop turning, the liquid presses against the hairs in a different way. Your brain gets

▲ Canals in ears.

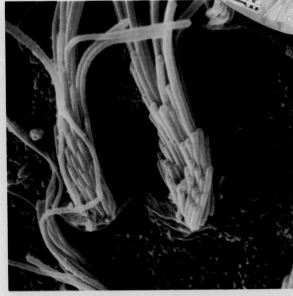

a new message—that you have stopped turning your head.

Suppose you spin around many times. When you stop spinning, the liquid in your ears may keep moving for a few moments. You know that your body is no longer spinning. But your brain is getting another message. For your brain, the things around you still seem to be spinning. The result is that you feel dizzy.

▲ Hairs in canals.

290b

You have learned why you may feel dizzy after being on a carnival ride. Feeling dizzy is a result of the kind of message that the brain gets from the special organ in each ear. You can see how this organ works by doing a simple activity.

Put water in a jar or drinking glass so that it is half full. Get a powdered material, such as flour, talcum powder, or chalk dust. Sprinkle a spoonful of the powder onto the surface of the water.

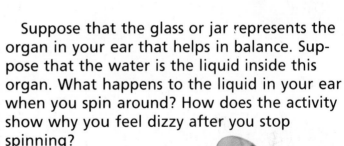

Lift the jar or glass and slowly move it in a circle. Notice what happens to the powder. Gently put the jar or glass down, but keep watching the powder. What happens to the powder? Why does this happen?

Suppose that the glass or jar represents the organ in your ear that helps in balance. Suppose that the water is the liquid inside this organ. What happens to the liquid in your ear when you spin around? How does the activity show why you feel dizzy after you stop spinning?

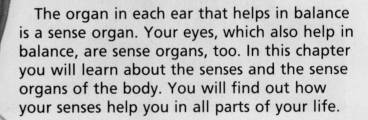

The organ in each ear that helps in balance is a sense organ. Your eyes, which also help in balance, are sense organs, too. In this chapter you will learn about the senses and the sense organs of the body. You will find out how your senses help you in all parts of your life.

Sense Organs and the Brain

How do sense organs and the brain work together?

Can you name the five senses? The five senses are seeing, hearing, tasting, smelling, and touching. Each of these senses depends on special organs in the body. These organs are called **sense organs.** The eyes, ears, tongue, nose, and skin are the sense organs. What sense organs are the people in these pictures using?

Your sense organs do not work alone. You do not see with just your eyes or hear with just your ears. Your sense organs are connected to your brain. How do the sense organs send information to your brain?

The brain is made of billions of nerve cells that are closely packed together. Other nerve cells lead from the brain to all parts of the body. These nerve cells join together to form nerves. The nerves send signals to and from the brain. The endings of some nerves are in your sense organs.

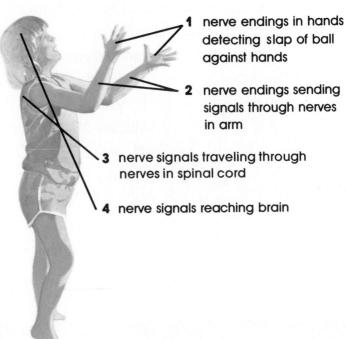

1 nerve endings in hands detecting slap of ball against hands

2 nerve endings sending signals through nerves in arm

3 nerve signals traveling through nerves in spinal cord

4 nerve signals reaching brain

In the drawing you can see how nerve signals are sent when the girl catches the ball. Trace this path with your finger as you read. First, nerve endings in the hands detect the slap of the ball against the hands. The nerve endings send signals through the nerves in the arm to nerves in the spinal cord. The signals travel through the spinal cord to the brain. When they reach the brain, the girl is aware of catching the ball.

Signals can move very quickly along nerves. Some signals can travel over 90 m in 1 second. Why would it be so important for these signals to travel quickly if you touched a hot stove?

For Lesson Questions, turn to page 346.

The Eye and Sight

How does the eye work?

Did you ever stop to think how useful the sense of sight is? With the sense of sight, you can see things that are tiny, like an insect on a flower. You can also see large objects, such as trees and buildings. You can read this page when it is close to you. You can also see stars that are billions of kilometers away. You can notice the color of a sunset or the movement of a cat in tall grass. How are you able to see so many different things?

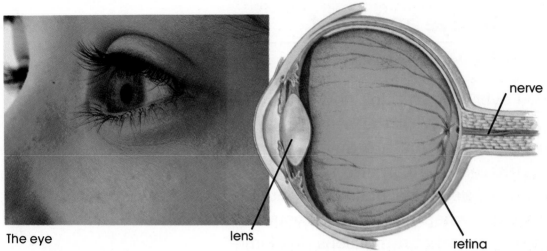

The eye

lens

nerve

retina

The eye contains special cells that can detect light. When light hits an object, some of the light bounces off the object. You see the object because some of this light enters your eyes.

As you can see in the drawing, light entering the eye goes through a lens. The **lens** is a clear part of the eye. It is made of living cells. The lens bends light. The bent light forms a tiny picture on the back wall of the eye.

The back wall of the eye is called the **retina** (ret′ə nə). The retina has millions of cells in it. These cells are close to nerve endings. When light from an object hits the cells, the nerve endings pick up signals. These signals are passed along a nerve that leads to the brain. The brain then sends signals that "tell" parts of the body how to react toward what the eye saw. How would your body react to a juicy hamburger?

The lenses in the eyes of some people do not bend light correctly. Clear pictures do not always form on the retinas of their eyes. Sometimes a person can clearly see only things that are near. Such a person is said to be nearsighted. A farsighted person can clearly see only things that are far away. Some people who are nearsighted or farsighted wear eyeglasses. Eyeglasses are made of glass or plastic. They help the eye to bend light correctly. This helps the person to see things clearly.

SKILL: Observing

Finding Out

How can you tell if you are color-blind?

The retina of the eye is made up of different types of cells. Some of these cells can detect colors. Sometimes people are born without certain kinds of these cells. These people are said to be color-blind. Some color-blind people cannot see green colors. Others cannot see red colors.

You can find out if you are color-blind by looking at these drawings. If you see a 29 in the top circle and a 26 in the bottom circle, you are not color-blind. If you see only a 6 in the bottom circle, you are red-blind. If you see only a 2 in the bottom circle, you are green-blind. If you see a 70 in the top circle and nothing in the other circle, you are red-and green-blind. If you cannot see any numbers in either circle, you are totally color-blind. If you are not color-blind, maybe someone in your family is. Give this test to other members of your family.

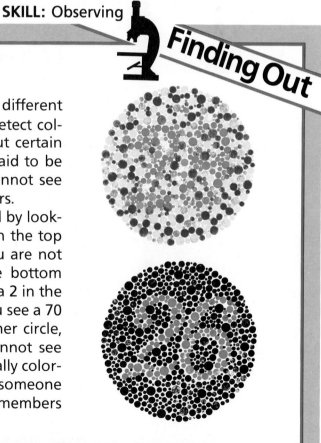

Eye protection

Eye protection

People often take their eyes for granted. But it is easy to injure your eyes if you are not careful. Some household cleaners can sting or burn your eyes. While playing sports you can poke your eyes with balls, sticks, and rackets. Another way your eyes can be hurt is by looking right at the sun.

Having eyes checked by a doctor

You can help to prevent lifelong damage by taking care of your eyes if anything happens to them. You should not rub your eyes if dirt gets in them. Tears usually wash dirt out of your eyes. Specks of dirt that do not wash out should be removed by a doctor. If any harmful liquid gets in them, you should rinse your eyes with warm water for several minutes. Above all, you should have your eyes checked regularly by a doctor. In this way you will be taking good care of one of your most important senses.

For Lesson Questions, turn to page 346.

The Ears and Hearing

How does the ear work?

Have you ever known about something happening far away without seeing it happen? Maybe you first knew about a parade by the sounds of music. You might have known a frog was nearby when you heard its croak. Hearing is another important sense that tells you about the world.

You can hear when sound waves reach the ear. Sound waves cause particles of air to vibrate, or move back and forth. The ear picks up sound waves.

As you can see in the drawing, the part of the body that most people call the ear is just the **outer ear.** The outer ear catches sound waves and guides them into the **ear canal.** The vibrating air in the ear canal causes the eardrum to vibrate. The **eardrum** is a thin tissue at the end of the ear canal. The eardrum is close to three small bones that make up the **middle ear.** When the eardrum vibrates, so do the three bones. They pass the vibrations to the **inner ear.**

In the inner ear is a long coiled tube that looks like a snail's shell. The tube is filled with a liquid. When the liquid vibrates, it moves the tiny hairlike nerve endings that are found in the tube. The nerve endings send signals to the brain.

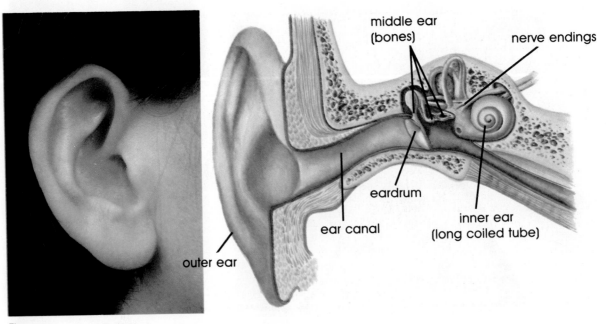

middle ear
(bones)

nerve endings

eardrum

ear canal

inner ear
(long coiled tube)

outer ear

The ear

Some sounds can be harmful to a person's ears. Sudden loud noises can tear the eardrum or damage the nerve endings of the inner ear. They can cause loss of hearing. Constant noise can also be harmful. Factory workers often spend many hours around loud machines. The noise can make them lose some of their hearing.

You can help take care of your ears by staying away from noisy places. If you must be in a noisy place, you should protect your ears the way the person in the picture is. Also, you should never stick anything in your ears. Your doctor can show you the correct way to clean your ears. Your doctor can also check your ears to make sure you are hearing properly.

For Lesson Questions, turn to page 346.

Ear protection

Activity

When can you best tell the direction from which a sound is coming?

Where clock was held	Pointed correctly	
	Yes	No

Materials paper towel / ticking clock

Procedure

A. Make a chart like the one shown. Mark your chart as you do each test.

B. Work with a partner. Have your partner use a paper towel as a blindfold. The blindfold can be held in place with one hand.

C. Hold a ticking clock about 15 cm away from the left side of your partner's head. Then ask your partner to point to where he or she thinks the sound is coming from.

D. Hold the clock in different positions on the left side and then on the right side of your partner's head. Have your partner point each time.

E. Hold the clock behind your partner's head. Have your partner point to where he or she thinks the sound is coming from. Move the clock over the top of the head from back to front so that the clock is always the same distance between the right ear and the left ear. Have your partner point.

Results

Could your partner tell where the sound was coming from when the clock was on the left side of the head? On the right side of the head? Between the right ear and the left ear?

Conclusion

When can you best tell the direction from which a sound is coming?

The Tongue and the Nose

How are you able to taste and smell?

Remember the last time you had a bad cold? Your food probably didn't seem to have much flavor. Most people think they use only their tongue to taste food. But the odors your nose picks up also help to give food its flavor. This is why it is difficult for a person with a stuffy nose to taste food.

Have you ever taken a close look at your tongue? It is covered with tiny bumps. Each bump has several **taste buds** in it. Each taste bud is made up of cells that are connected to nerve endings. The taste of food is picked up by these nerve cells.

The tongue can only detect four different tastes. It can tell whether something is sweet, sour, salty, or bitter. As you can see in the drawing, taste buds in different areas of the tongue detect different tastes. On what part of your tongue could you taste a piece of cake?

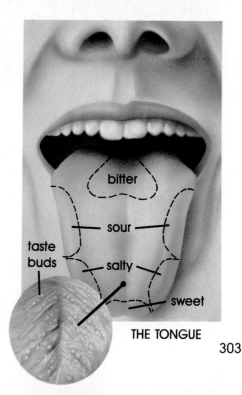

THE TONGUE

303

In the back of the inside of the nose are thousands of nerve endings. You can see where they are in the drawing. When you breathe normally, very little air goes into this part of the nose. But what happens when you sniff air? Sniffing causes air to rush up into the back of the nose. There the nerve endings pick up odors in the air. The nerve endings send signals to the brain. Have you ever sniffed a flower? Signals your brain gets from sniffing a flower let you know how good the flower smells.

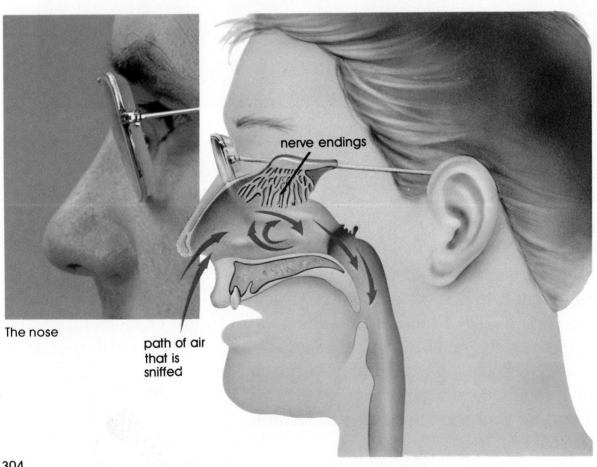

The nose

nerve endings

path of air that is sniffed

304

For Lesson Questions, turn to page 346.

The Skin

What are some of the things your skin can detect?

Your fifth sense organ, the skin, can detect many different things. Some of these things are shown here. Your skin can detect a mosquito on your arm. It can tell warm from cold. If someone squeezes your hand, your skin can detect pressure. The skin also lets you feel pain. How can the skin do all these things?

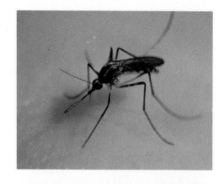

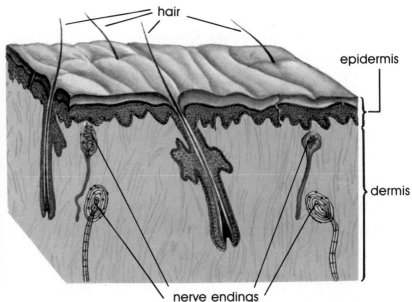

hair

epidermis

dermis

nerve endings

The skin

Look at the drawing. As you can see, the top layer of the skin is the **epidermis** (ep ə-dėr′mis). The epidermis has a thin water-proof covering made of dead cells. Below the epidermis is a thicker layer, called the **dermis** (dėr′mis).

There are many different types of nerve endings in the skin. Some of the nerve endings are used when you touch something. Other nerve endings detect pain, pressure, and changes in temperature. You might not think that having a sense organ that detects pain is important. But the skin is very important. Feeling pain is the way your body warns you that something is wrong. Can you imagine not being able to know that you cut your foot? What could happen if you could not feel this kind of pain?

Besides being a sense organ, the skin also protects you. It keeps out germs and helps to keep your body warm. It also protects you from the sun.

To care for your skin, you should keep it clean. You should also properly treat cuts. A cut should be washed and covered with a bandage. Taking care of your skin is one way you can stay healthy.

Science & TECHNOLOGY

▶ One of the newest ways to save a person's eyesight is to use lasers. A person with a disease called glaucoma (glô kō′mə) has too much fluid in the eyeball. Lasers can be used to make tiny holes in the eyeball, letting out some of the fluid.

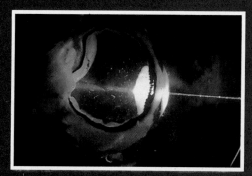

◀ There are many ways to help people who cannot hear properly. One of the newest ways is to use special glasses to "see" speech. A microphone in the frames of the glasses receives sounds. The glasses contain a microcomputer that analyzes these sounds. The computer changes the sounds into symbols. Can you see the tiny lines on the right lens? This is where the symbols appear on the glasses. What problems might occur with reading sounds? What problems might be overcome?

For Lesson Questions, turn to page 346.

Activity

Is the sense of touch the same in all parts of the body?

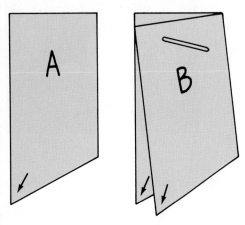

Materials paper towel / piece of cardboard with one point, marked *A* / piece of cardboard with two points, marked *B*

Procedure

A. Make a chart like the one shown. Write *yes* or *no* as each test is done.

B. Your teacher will give you two pieces of cardboard, one marked *A* and the other marked *B*.

C. You are going to use the pieces of cardboard to touch your partner on different parts of the body. You will touch your partner's fingertip, palm of the hand, back of the hand, and arm. Do not tell your partner which piece of cardboard you are using. Mix them up. But make sure you touch each place on your partner with each piece of cardboard.

D. Each time you touch your partner, ask: *Do you feel one point or two points?*

Part of body	One point	Two points

Results

On which parts of the body was your partner able to feel two points?

Conclusion

Is the sense of touch the same in all parts of the body? Explain your answer.

Ideas to Remember

▶ The eyes, ears, tongue, nose, and skin are the sense organs. Each of the sense organs is connected to the brain by nerves.

▶ Light that bounces off objects enters the eye and passes through the lens. A picture of the object forms on the back wall of the eye, called the retina.

▶ Sound waves enter the outer ear and pass into the ear canal. They cause the eardrum to vibrate, which causes the bones of the middle ear to vibrate. These bones pass the vibrations on to the inner ear.

▶ Both the nose and the tongue are used to taste foods.

▶ The skin can detect pain, pressure, and changes in temperature.

Reviewing the Chapter

A. Write the letter of the term that best matches the definition. Not all the terms will be used.

1. The tiny bumps on the tongue that are made up of cells connected to nerve endings
2. The top layer of skin
3. The back wall of the eye
4. The eyes, ears, tongue, nose, and skin
5. The part of the eye that bends light

    a. taste buds
    b. lens
    c. retina
    d. outer ear
    e. dermis
    f. sense organs
    g. epidermis

B. Use all the terms below to complete the sentences.

eardum   middle ear
ear canal   inner ear
outer ear

In order to hear, the __1__ must catch sound waves. The sound waves are guided into the __2__, and at its end they reach a thin tissue. This tissue is called the __3__. As this tissue vibrates, it causes the three bones that make up the __4__ to vibrate, too. These bones pass the vibrations along to the __5__. Signals are sent to the brain. Then you are aware of sound.

A. Explain how the sense organs send information to the brain.

B. Explain how to care for your eyes and ears.

C. Identify each of the following sense organs. Write the correct term for each number in the diagram. Tell how the sense organs work.

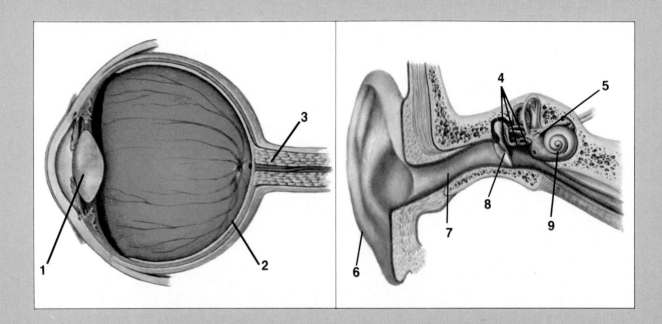

1. Pretend you are a scientist who has made a robot. Write a report explaining how you made the robot's sense organs. Discuss some of the experiences your robot has had.

2. Use reference books to find out what people who are blind can do to overcome their loss of sight.

THINKING LIKE A SCIENTIST

You may be able to answer some of these questions just by thinking about them. To answer other questions, you may have to do some research.

1. Scientists use models to help them explain how things work. How is the human brain like a library and a telephone switchboard?

2. Explain why people who have colds cannot taste the foods they eat.

Science in Careers

There are a number of careers for people interested in helping other people stay healthy. One group of these careers involves food. **Dietitians** are people who plan meals for other people. Many dietitians work in hospitals and schools. **Chefs** are people who prepare food. The food prepared by a chef must be tasty and must look good.

Medical laboratory worker

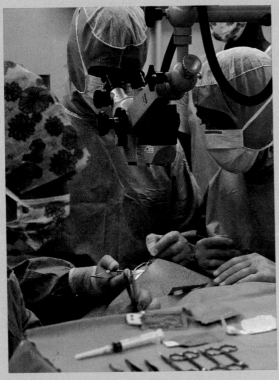

Doctors

Another group of careers in the health field involves medicine. There are many careers in medicine. **Dentists** treat people who have problems with their teeth. **Dental assistants** help the dentists. **Nurses** and **doctors** care for people who are sick or hurt. **Medical laboratory workers** do tests for doctors. These tests help the doctor find out what is wrong with someone.

People in Science

ADELLE DAVIS
(1904–1974)

Adelle Davis was born and raised on a farm in central Indiana. As a youngster she was active in the 4-H Club. Davis went to college at Purdue University, where she studied nutrition. Nutrition is the study of how food is used by the body. For most of her life, Davis tried to educate Americans about nutrition. She felt that Americans ate too many foods containing salt and sugar. Davis also felt that a proper diet should include fresh fruits and vegetables.

Developing Skills

Many English words have word parts that come from other languages. This table lists word parts that come from other languages and gives their meanings. Use the table to help you write a definition for each of the words listed.

1. auditory

2. carbohydrate

3. endoderm

4. monocle

5. stereoscopic

6. stereophonic

Word Part	Meaning
audio-	hearing
carbo-	relating to carbon
endo-	inner
hydro-	water
mono-	one
phon-	sound
stereo-	three-dimensional
-ar	resembling
-ate	having to do with
-derm	skin
-ic	one that produces
-ocul, -ocle	eye
-scope	for seeing
-tory	relating to

Some maps contain a great amount of information. This map compares the amount of Calories people in different countries get each day. The map shows countries in North America and South America. Use the map to answer the following questions.

1. In which of these countries do people get more Calories than they need each day–the United States, Venezuela, Mexico, and Ecuador?

2. In which of these countries do people get fewer Calories than they need each day–Canada, Honduras, and Argentina?

3. In which of these countries do people get about the number of Calories they need each day–Peru, Paraguay, Bolivia, and Canada?

4. Do people in Colombia get more or less than the amount of Calories they need each day?

5. Do people in Chile get more, less, or about the amount of Calories they need each day?

CALORIE INTAKE IN DIFFERENT COUNTRIES

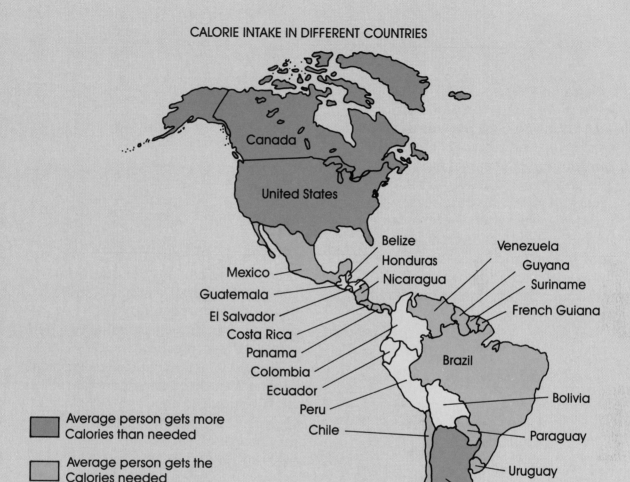

Average person gets more
Calories than needed

Average person gets the
Calories needed

Average person gets fewer
Calories than needed

USING THINKING SKILLS

When people do not get enough nutrition or Calories, they are said to have malnutrition (mal nü trish'ən). Malnutrition is common throughout the world. Keep this in mind as you answer these questions.

1. What can be done to help end malnutrition?

2. What can *you* do to help end malnutrition?

Study Guide

Reading your book will help you learn more about the world around you. Your book will provide answers to many questions you may have about living things, the earth, space, matter, and energy.

On the following pages you will find questions from each lesson in your book. These questions will help test your understanding of the terms and ideas you read about. You will also find information about metric measurement.

There are three sections for each chapter. You can answer questions in the first section, "Lesson Questions," by using the information you read in each chapter. Careful reading will help answer these questions.

The second section is called "Problem Solving." These questions are more challenging. The answer may not be found just by reading the lesson. You may have to think harder.

The third section is called "Skills." In this section you will be asked to read tables and graphs.

Units of Measurement 318

Chapter 1 **Animals That Live Together** 320

Chapter 2 **The World of Plants** 322

Chapter 3 **Food Chains and Food Webs** 324

Chapter 4 **How Living Things Survive** 326

Chapter 5 **Measuring Matter** 328

Chapter 6 **Energy and Machines** 330

Chapter 7 **Heat Energy** 332

Chapter 8 **Electricity and Magnetism** 334

Chapter 9 **Rocks and Minerals** 336

Chapter 10 **The Earth's Oceans** 338

Chapter 11 **Measuring Weather** 340

Chapter 12 **The Solar System** 342

Chapter 13 **Using Food** 344

Chapter 14 **The Sense Organs** 346

Units of Measurement

Two systems of measurement are used in the United States, the metric system and the English system. Feet, yards, pounds, ounces, and quarts are English units. Meters, kilometers, kilograms, grams, and liters are metric units. Only metric measurements are used in science. The following tables list some metric and English units. The tables show what each unit is approximately equal to in the other system. The metric mass/English weight relationships hold true for objects on the earth.

MEASUREMENT	METRIC UNITS (symbol)	EQUAL TO IN ENGLISH UNITS (symbol)
Length	1 millimeter (mm)	0.04 inch (in.)
	1 centimeter (cm)	0.4 inch (in.)
	1 meter (m)	39.4 inches (in.) or
		1.1 yards (yd)
	1 kilometer (km)	0.6 mile (mi)
Mass (weight)	1 gram (g)	0.035 ounce (oz)
	1 kilogram (kg)	2.2 pounds (lb)
Volume	1 liter (L)	1.06 quarts (qt)

MEASUREMENT	ENGLISH UNITS (symbol)	EQUAL TO IN METRIC UNITS (symbol)
Length	1 inch (in.)	2.5 centimeters (cm) or
		25 millimeters (mm)
	1 foot (ft)	30.5 centimeters (cm)
	1 yard (yd)	0.91 meter (m)
	1 mile (mi)	1.6 kilometers (km)
Weight (mass)	1 ounce (oz)	28.4 grams (g)
	1 pound (lb)	0.45 kilogram (kg)
Volume	1 quart (qt)	0.95 liter (L)

Chapter 1

Animals That Live Together

LESSON QUESTIONS

An Animal Town (pp. 4–8)
1. Name some kinds of animal populations.
2. How can prairie dogs tell members of their family group from other prairie dogs?

Insect Colonies (pp. 9–12)
1. Which insects live in colonies?
2. Explain the importance of the queen, the workers, and the drones in a bee colony.

Schools of Fish (pp. 13–15)
1. Where are schools of fish found?
2. Why do fish swim in schools?

Animal Herds (pp. 16–18)
1. Name some animals that live in herds.
2. Why do caribou form herds only at certain times of the year?

Other Animals That Live Together (pp. 19–21)
1. Why is a flea a parasite?
2. What is a host?
3. How do a zebra and an oxpecker help each other?

PROBLEM SOLVING

Use after page 9.
Sometimes a population of bees becomes too large for a hive. Then a new queen develops. The old queen and thousands of workers swarm out of the hive to find a new home. Sometimes this swarm lands on cars or houses. Beekeepers then try to capture the swarm and remove it to a new hive. What must beekeepers know about bees to capture the swarm?

Use after page 15.
How might the schooling behavior of fish help people who fish for a living? How might schooling be a problem?

Use after page 18.
Not long ago, large herds of bison roamed the plains of America. Hunting has made the bison an endangered animal. How did living in herds contribute to the decrease in the bison population? If the same-sized herds were returned to the plains today, what new problems would they have?

Use after page 21.
Birds often perch on the backs of animals such as warthogs, giraffes, and antelopes. These animals make no attempt to get rid of the birds. What hypothesis would explain this behavior?

Reading a Map

Look at this map. It gives information about where black-tailed and white-tailed prairie dogs can be found. As you can see, black-tailed prairie dogs and white-tailed prairie dogs are usually found in different places. Use the map to answer the following questions.

1. Can white-tailed prairie dogs be found in Idaho?
2. Can black-tailed prairie dogs be found in Alberta?
3. A friend tells you that she saw a prairie dog town in North Dakota. What kind of prairie dog did she see?
4. In which states and provinces can both kinds of prairie dogs be found?

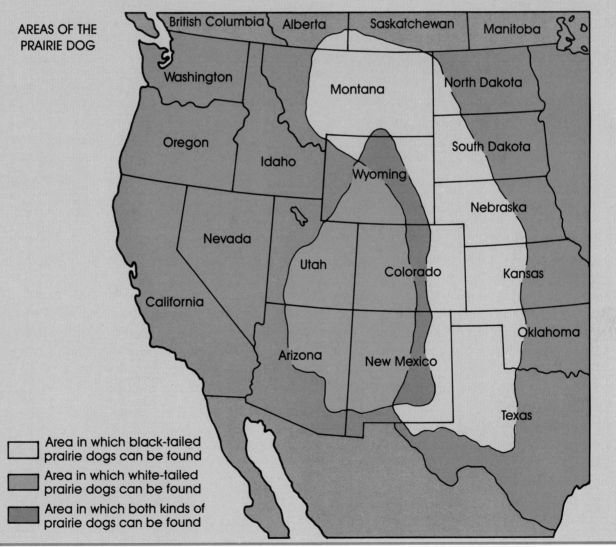

AREAS OF THE PRAIRIE DOG

Area in which black-tailed prairie dogs can be found
Area in which white-tailed prairie dogs can be found
Area in which both kinds of prairie dogs can be found

Chapter 2

The World of Plants

LESSON QUESTIONS

Grouping Plants (pp. 26–28)

1. How do some scientists classify plants?
2. How are the two main groups of plants different from each other?

Flowering Seed Plants (pp. 29–32)

1. What basic parts are found in most flowers?
2. How are monocots different from dicots? Give an example of each.

Cone-Bearing Seed Plants (pp. 33–35)

1. Describe the differences between flowering plants and conifers.
2. What are two ways you can identify cone-bearing plants?

Nonseed Plants (pp. 36–43)

1. Explain why ferns produce spores.
2. How do fungi get their food?
3. How are algae similar to mosses and different from ferns?

PROBLEM SOLVING

Use after page 28.

Suppose that a space probe sends back reports of plants on a planet in another solar system. What would be the three most important pieces of information you would like to have about the plants? Write three questions about the new plants.

Use after page 32.

In animals the most important body parts are protected from injury by special structures, such as the skull, ribs, and hipbone. Which parts of a flowering plant are most important? Why? How are these parts protected?

Use after page 35.

Many plants produce seeds in flowers. In many of these plants, the flowers change to a fruit. The seeds are found inside the fruit. The seeds of cones that produce trees are found inside the scales of the cones. What advantage do you think seeds produced in fruit have over seeds produced in cones?

Reading a Diagram

Diagrams can contain information about many different things. This diagram compares the sizes of various trees. Each drawing shows the largest example of the particular type of tree. Use the diagram to answer these questions.

1. Which of these trees is the largest?

2. Which is the smallest?
3. How much larger is the largest California redwood than the largest hemlock?
4. How many times larger than a 2-m-tall adult is the largest ponderosa pine?
5. How much smaller is the largest beech than the largest Douglas fir?

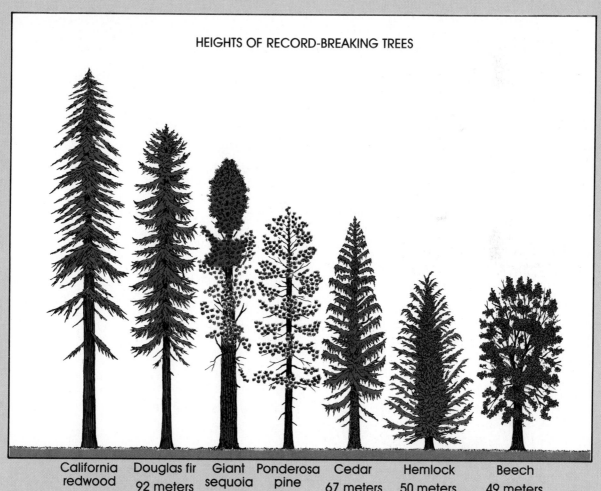

HEIGHTS OF RECORD-BREAKING TREES

California redwood 112 meters | Douglas fir 92 meters | Giant sequoia 83 meters | Ponderosa pine 68 meters | Cedar 67 meters | Hemlock 50 meters | Beech 49 meters

Chapter 3

Food Chains and Food Webs

LESSON QUESTIONS

Living Things Need Energy (pp. 48–49)

1. How do green plants get their energy?
2. What is the main difference between a producer and a consumer?

Animals and Their Food (pp. 50–53)

1. What kinds of food are eaten by herbivores? By carnivores?
2. Why is a bear a good example of an omnivore?
3. Are the animals shown below herbivores or carnivores? Explain your answer.

Food Chains (pp. 54–57)

1. Of what importance are green plants in a food chain?
2. Copy these items. Arrange them so that they form a food chain.
   bull snake   seeds
   deer mouse   red-tailed hawk

Food Webs (pp. 58–60)

1. What is a food web?
2. How is a food web like a spider web?
3. How are food chains and food webs related to each other?

PROBLEM SOLVING

Use after page 53.
Would you expect to find more herbivores, carnivores, or omnivores living at the icy poles of the earth? Explain your answer.

Use after page 53.
Herbivores, carnivores, and omnivores differ in their eating habits. Which one has the best chance of survival? Explain your answer.

Use after page 57.
Look at the food chain on page 55. What would happen to the food chain if a disease killed all the deer mice?

Reading a Bar Graph

A bar graph can be used to compare information. These bar graphs show different members of the same food chain. The first bar graph shows how many of each kind of animal were found in a forest one year. The second bar graph shows how many of each kind of animal were found one year later. Use these bar graphs to answer the following questions.

1. Which type of animal was found in the greatest number the first year? The second year?
2. Which animal was found in the least number the first year? The second year?
3. How many more mice than snakes were found the first year?
4. What happened to the number of mice from the first year to the second year?

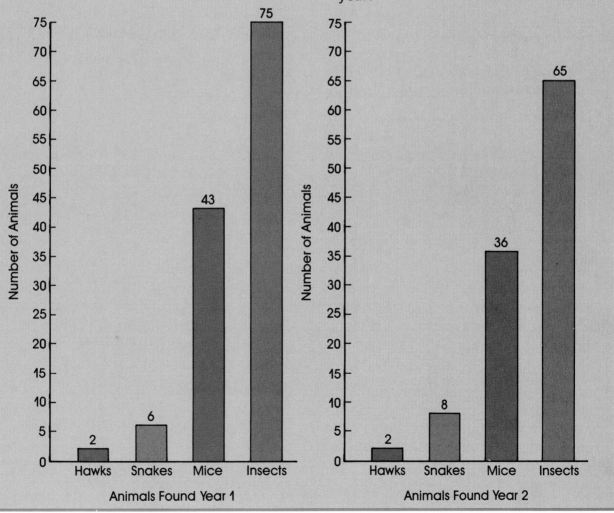

Chapter 4

How Living Things Survive

LESSON QUESTIONS

Why Living Things Are Different (pp. 66–67)

1. Give some examples of how living things are different from each other.
2. Why are adaptations important to living things?

Trees Change with the Seasons (pp. 68–70)

1. Explain how maple trees survive without their leaves during the winter.
2. Why is it that pine trees do not lose their leaves during the winter?

Plant Adaptations (pp. 71–74)

1. How are some small plants able to get sunlight even though they are near tall plants?
2. Describe the adaptation that helps a creosote plant get water.
3. Explain how cactus plants store water.

Animal Adaptations (pp. 75–79)

1. How are giraffes and zebras able to survive in the same place?
2. Explain how the beaks of eagles and woodpeckers differ. How does each kind of beak help that bird survive?

Winter Adaptations of Animals (pp. 80–83)

1. Why is it hard for some animals to survive during the winter?
2. What are two adaptations that help animals survive winter? Name an animal that uses each adaptation.

PROBLEM SOLVING

Use after page 70.
The giant sequoia is a tree with needles. The needles spray a fine mist of water over the tree. How might this adaptation help the tree survive?

Use after page 74.
Some plants, such as tulips and crocuses, close their petals at night. Scientists are not certain why this happens in some kinds of flowers but not in others. What hypothesis might explain this adaptation?

Use after page 79.
A duck-billed platypus is not a bird. Yet it has a duck-like bill and webbed feet. Based on this description, tell where the platypus lives and what it eats.

Use after page 83.
Suppose you did not know if bats that live in cold climates hibernate. What information about bats would you need to know to form a hypothesis about what bats do in winter?

Reading a Pictograph

A pictograph uses drawings or symbols to compare things. This pictograph shows the number of offspring that different animals have each time they lay eggs or give birth. Use this pictograph to answer the following questions.

1. Which of these animals has the most offspring?

2. Which of these animals has the fewest offspring?

3. How many more offspring does a crayfish have than an ostrich does?

4. From this pictograph, can you determine any connection between the size of an animal and the number of offspring it has? What, if anything, is this connection? How could you find out if this connection was true for all animals?

5. What advantages might there be to having many offspring? What advantages might there be to having few offspring? From this pictograph, can you find any connection between the type of place in which an animal lives and how many offspring it has? How could you find out if this connection was true for all animals?

NUMBER OF OFFSPRING

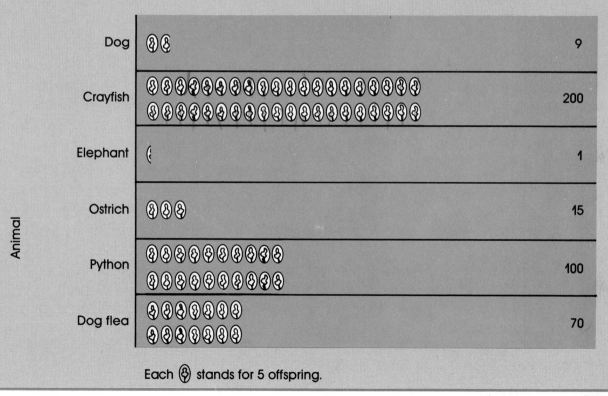

Animal		Number
Dog		9
Crayfish		200
Elephant		1
Ostrich		15
Python		100
Dog flea		70

Each 🥚 stands for 5 offspring.

Chapter 5

Measuring Matter

LESSON QUESTIONS

The Properties of Matter (pp. 94–95)
1. What is matter?
2. What are some properties of matter?

The Length of Matter (pp. 96–98)
1. Which unit of measure would be best to measure each of the following distances?
   a. your height
   b. the length of a pencil
   c. the distance from your home to school

Mass of Matter (pp. 99–102)
1. Which units are used to measure the mass of matter?

2. How would you use a balance to measure the mass of a paper clip?

Volume (pp. 103–106)
1. What is volume?
2. What is a good way to measure the volume of an odd-shaped solid?

Density (pp. 107–109)
1. If you were to compare an iron nail with a pencil, which would have the greater density?
2. Explain why most kinds of solid matter have greater density than most liquids do.

PROBLEM SOLVING

Use after page 95.
Most science books use metric units of measurement. In everyday situations many people still use customary units of measure. Teachers encourage students not to constantly convert from one system to the other. Why is this idea helpful in learning how to measure matter?

Use after page 95.
Choose an object in the classroom. Name the properties that cannot be measured.

Use after page 98.
Sometimes, exact measurement of length is not important. At these times, we can estimate length. Describe two situations when measuring accurately would not be necessary.

Use after page 106.
Estimating volume can be a useful problem-solving skill. Describe an emergency or problem situation in which estimating volume would be helpful.

Use after page 109.
Why do swimmers release air from their lungs as they dive to the bottom of a pool? Why does holding a deep breath help you float? Give your answers in terms of the density of the swimmer's body.

Reading a Map Scale

The scale of a map helps you to measure distances on the map. The scale tells you how far one place is from another. The scale on some maps is written in a form such as "One centimeter equals five kilometers." To use this type of scale, you would measure the distance between any two points on the map. Suppose this distance was 3 cm. Since every centimeter on the map equals five kilometers, you would multiply the distance you measured by five. In this case, you would multiply 3 cm by five, which would give you 15. This tells you that two points that are 3 cm apart on the map are 15 km apart on the earth.

Use the map scale on this map of Rocky Mountain National Park to answer the following questions.

1. What is the scale of this map?
2. How far is it across the park from top to bottom?
3. How far is it from Estes Park to Grand Lake?
4. How far is it from Mt. Adams to Longs Peak?
5. How far is it from Park Headquarters to Specimen Mountain?

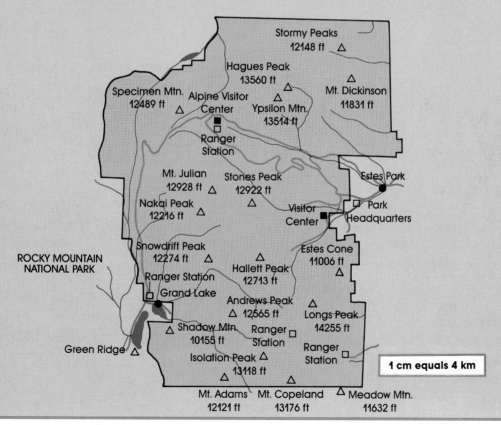

Chapter 6

Energy and Machines

LESSON QUESTIONS

Forms of Energy (pp. 114–116)
1. Why is energy needed?
2. What kind of energy do both food and gasoline contain?
3. Explain how one form of energy is changed to another form when wood is burned.

Two Kinds of Energy (pp. 117–119)
1. What is the difference between kinetic and potential energy?
2. How is a battery an example of both kinetic and potential energy?

Simple Machines and Energy (pp. 120–125)
1. How does a car jack make work easier?
2. What is friction? When is it necessary to reduce friction?

Compound Machines and Energy (pp. 126–129)
1. Explain why a wheelbarrow is a compound machine.
2. What kind of energy does a wheelbarrow use?

PROBLEM SOLVING

Use after page 116.
Imagine that you are watching workers build a tall building. Describe six situations where energy is either stored or being used. Name the kind of energy in each situation.

Use after page 119.
Describe a situation in which potential energy changes to electrical energy, then to kinetic energy, and back to potential energy.

Use after page 125.
Why is it easier to take a winding road up a steep mountain than to climb straight up?

Use after page 129.
Design a new amusement park ride that is a compound machine. Identify the simple machines that make up this new ride.

Reading a Diagram

Some diagrams can be used to explain how things work. This diagram shows how a car engine works. Use the diagram to answer these questions.

1. What happens during the intake stroke?

2. What is the fuel that an engine burns made of?

3. During what stroke is the fuel ignited?

4. What happens during the second stroke?

5. What happens to burned gases in a car engine?

AUTOMOBILE ENGINE

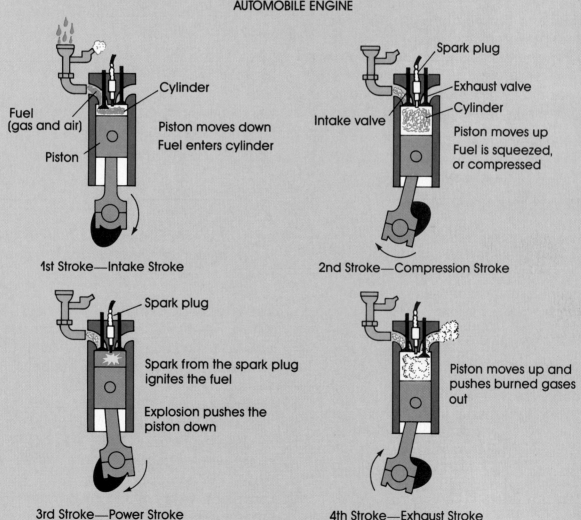

1st Stroke—Intake Stroke

Cylinder
Fuel (gas and air)
Piston
Piston moves down
Fuel enters cylinder

2nd Stroke—Compression Stroke

Spark plug
Exhaust valve
Cylinder
Intake valve
Piston moves up
Fuel is squeezed, or compressed

3rd Stroke—Power Stroke

Spark plug
Spark from the spark plug ignites the fuel
Explosion pushes the piston down

4th Stroke—Exhaust Stroke

Piston moves up and pushes burned gases out

Chapter 7

Heat Energy

LESSON QUESTIONS

Heat (pp. 134–135)

1. How does heat energy affect particles of matter?
2. What is a calorie?
3. What happens when you add calories to matter?

Heat and Temperature (pp. 136–138)

1. What is temperature?
2. The temperature of the liquids in a small pot and in a large pot are the same. Which of these pots of liquid contains more heat energy? Explain your answer.

How Heat Moves Through Solid Matter (pp. 139–142)

1. Explain why the handle of a pan in which food is being cooked gets hot.
2. Why is a thermos used to keep hot liquids hot?

How Heat Moves Through Liquids and Gases (pp. 143–144)

1. What is convection?
2. How are hot air and cool air different from each other?

Heat from Sunlight (pp. 145–147)

1. When does sunlight change to heat?
2. What is radiation?

PROBLEM SOLVING

Use after page 135.

How many different ways can you think of to cool a bowl of hot soup? How does each method reduce the amount of heat energy in the soup?

Use after page 138.

In cold climates, ice skating is a favorite pastime in winter. In most towns the police must determine when each pond is safe for skating. If the temperature is below 0°C, why would it be necessary to check each pond? If one pond is safe, wouldn't the other ponds be safe also?

Use after page 142.

Imagine that you are stranded in a blizzard. Why would digging a hole in the snow in which to keep warm be a good idea?

Use after page 144.

When water in a covered pot starts to boil, you can usually hear the lid rattle. Why, do you think, does this happen?

Use after page 147.

Pets are often accidentally killed by heat in closed cars during hot weather. Explain why the temperature inside a closed car can rise to over 50°C. How can people prevent temperature increases in parked cars?

Reading a Table

The temperature at which a material melts is called its melting point. The temperature at which a material boils is called its boiling point. Use the table to answer these questions about melting points and boiling points.

1. Which material has the highest boiling point?

2. Which material has the highest melting point?

3. Which material has the lowest boiling point?

4. Which material has the lowest melting point?

5. Which material has a higher boiling point—iron or tin?

6. How much higher is the melting point of gold than the melting point of silver?

MELTING POINTS AND BOILING POINTS		
Material	Melting point	Boiling point
Aluminum	660°C	2,467°C
Calcium	842°C	1,487°C
Carbon	3,550°C	4,827°C
Copper	1,083°C	2,595°C
Gold	1,063°C	2,966°C
Iron	1,535°C	3,000°C
Lead	327°C	1,744°C
Nickel	1,453°C	2,732°C
Silver	961°C	2,212°C
Tin	232°C	2,270°C
Zinc	419°C	907°C

Chapter 8
Electricity and Magnetism

LESSON QUESTIONS

Static Electricity (pp. 152–154)
1. What kind of electricity is caused by friction?
2. How are charged particles in matter affected when two objects are rubbed together?

Current Electricity (pp. 155–157)
1. How is current electricity produced?
2. What is a circuit? What are the parts of a circuit?
3. Explain the difference between a complete circuit and an incomplete circuit.

Making Electricity (pp. 158–159)
1. Explain how electricity is produced in a flashlight.

2. How is energy produced in a hydro-electric power plant?

Magnetism (pp. 160–163)
1. What would show the magnetic field of a magnet?
2. Explain the difference between the two poles of a magnet.
3. How are the particles in magnetized iron different from those in un-magnetized iron?

Electricity and Magnetism (pp. 164–165)
1. How is magnetism used to produce electricity?
2. What are some uses of electro-magnets?

PROBLEM SOLVING

Use after page 154.
Static electricity causes clothes coming out of a dryer to cling together. One inventor has solved this problem by inventing a spray for clothes. Clothes softeners used in the washer also eliminate static electricity. How do you think these products work?

Use after page 157.
A fuse is a strip of metal that can be placed into an electric circuit. When too much electricity passes through the strip, it gets hot and melts. This breaks the circuit. What problem does a fuse help to solve?

Use after page 159.
When people store battery-operated equipment, they should always remove the batteries. What might happen if batteries are left in unused equipment for a very long period of time?

Use after page 165.
The picture on page 164 shows an electromagnet being used in a scrapyard. Why, do you think, is an electromagnet used instead of a regular magnet?

334

Reading a Diagram

Diagrams can be used to show electric circuits. Symbols are used in these diagrams. These symbols stand for different parts of the circuits. Use the diagrams shown here to answer the following questions.

1. What is the symbol for a battery in these circuits?

2. Which of these circuits includes a bell?

3. What is happening in circuit **C**?

4. What is happening in circuit **D**?

5. Which of these circuits is incomplete?

6. Will the light bulb in circuit **A** be lit? Explain your answer.

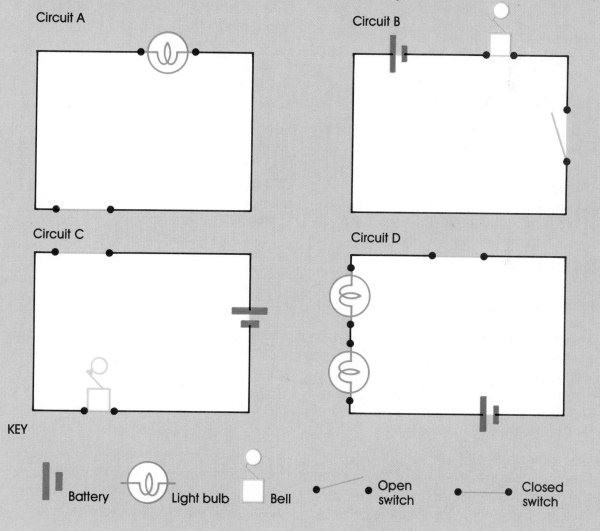

Circuit A

Circuit B

Circuit C

Circuit D

KEY

Battery   Light bulb   Bell   Open switch   Closed switch

Chapter 9

Rocks and Minerals

LESSON QUESTIONS

Inside the Earth (pp. 176–177)

1. Name the earth's layers. Describe the layer you live on.
2. Which layer of the earth is the thickest?
3. Which layer of the earth is the hottest?

Minerals (pp. 178–180)

1. How are different kinds of minerals identified?
2. What are some properties of minerals?
3. How do scientists know that diamond is the hardest mineral?

Melted Rock (pp. 181–184)

1. What is magma? Where is it formed?
2. Why is pumice an unusual kind of rock?

Rocks from Sediment (pp. 185–187)

1. What is sediment?
2. Describe how sediment is changed to sedimentary rock.
3. Name some kinds of sedimentary rock.

Plants and Animals from Long Ago (pp. 188–191)

1. In what kinds of rocks are fossils found?
2. How is a mold fossil different from a cast fossil?
3. Explain how trees are petrified.

Rocks That Change into Other Rocks (pp. 192–193)

1. How is metamorphic rock formed?
2. How is the metamorphic rock called marble different from the sedimentary rock called limestone?

PROBLEM SOLVING

Use after page 177.

Scientists can sometimes draw conclusions about things they have not seen. For example, no scientist has ever seen the inside of the earth. How do scientists know that the core is hot?

Use after page 184.

Pretend that you have just landed on the moon. You begin to explore the surface. You suspect volcanoes at one time erupted on the surface near your spaceship. You collect rocks and return to your spaceship. How can you tell if the rocks you have collected were formed by rapid or slow cooling of magma?

Use after page 187.

Astronauts brought back many rocks from the moon's surface. Would you expect to find sedimentary rocks in the collection? Why or why not?

Reading a Circle Graph

The earth's crust is made up of a number of different materials. These materials can be shown in a circle graph, such as the one below. This circle graph tells what percentage of the crust each material makes up. Use the circle graph to answer the following questions.

1. How much of the earth's crust is oxygen?

2. How much of the earth's crust is aluminum?

3. Which material makes up a greater part of the crust–iron or sodium?

4. How much more of the crust is silicon than is iron?

5. One of the materials listed under "All other materials" is carbon. Does carbon make up more or less than one percent of the crust? How do you know?

MATERIALS IN THE EARTH'S CRUST

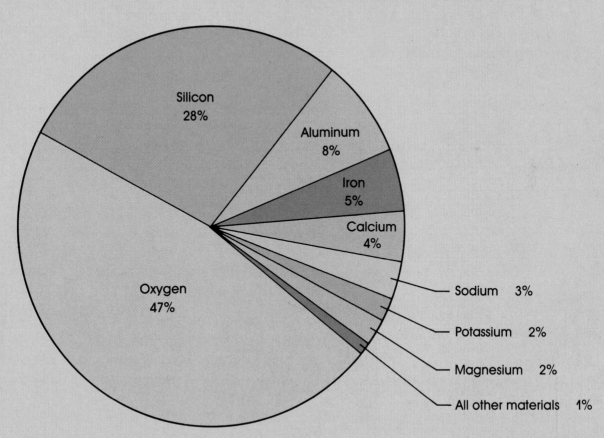

Silicon 28%
Aluminum 8%
Iron 5%
Calcium 4%
Oxygen 47%
Sodium 3%
Potassium 2%
Magnesium 2%
All other materials 1%

Chapter 10

The Earth's Oceans

LESSON QUESTIONS

A Look at the Oceans (pp. 198–199)
1. Explain how the water in the oceans became salty.
2. Why is it difficult to study the oceans?
3. How do scientists use *Alvin?*

The Ocean Floor (pp. 200–203)
1. Where is the continental shelf?
2. Describe the ocean floor plain.
3. Where is the Mariana Trench? How deep is it?

The Moving Ocean (pp. 204–208)
1. How are most waves formed?

2. Identify the parts of a wave.

The Ocean's Rivers (pp. 209–211)
1. In which direction do warm-water currents flow? In which direction do cold-water currents flow?
2. Describe the Gulf Stream.

Ocean Resources (pp. 212–214)
1. What are some ways that people use oceans?
2. How is seaweed used?
3. How are tides used to produce energy?

PROBLEM SOLVING

Use after page 199.
A line from a poem says "Water, water everywhere, but not a drop to drink." What do you think the poet is describing?

Use after page 203.
What kinds of living things would you expect to find in an ocean trench?

Use after page 208.
People often speak of undertows along the ocean shore. What do you think an undertow is, and what do you think causes it?

Use after page 214.
Pearls come from oysters that grow in the ocean. Pearls have no food value. They are not used for fuel. Are pearls one of the ocean's resources? Explain your reasoning.

Use after page 214.
You have learned that the ocean bottom contains valuable minerals. What are some of the problems involved with using these minerals?

Reading a Bar Graph

Some of the largest animals on the earth live in the ocean. This bar graph shows the lengths of some of the largest ocean animals ever found. Use the bar graph to answer the following questions.

1. What is the largest animal shown? How long is it?

2. What is the largest shark shown? How long is it?

3. Which is longer, the largest jellyfish ever found or the largest blue whale?

4. How much larger is the largest ribbon worm than the largest giant squid?

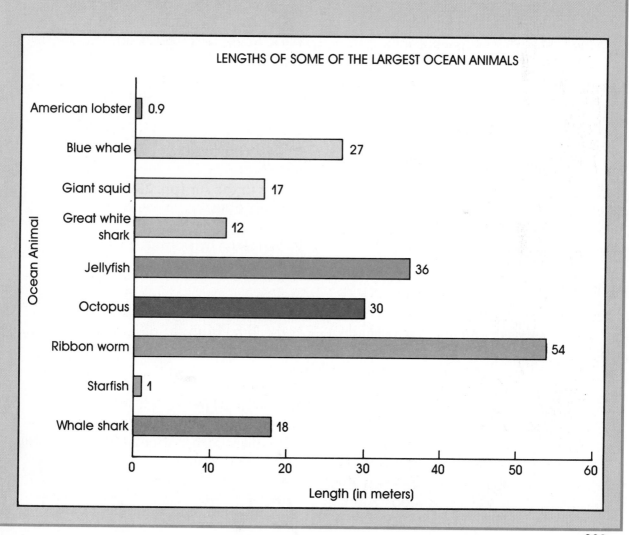

LENGTHS OF SOME OF THE LARGEST OCEAN ANIMALS

Ocean Animal	Length (in meters)
American lobster	0.9
Blue whale	27
Giant squid	17
Great white shark	12
Jellyfish	36
Octopus	30
Ribbon worm	54
Starfish	1
Whale shark	18

Chapter 11

Measuring Weather

LESSON QUESTIONS

Weather Around Us (pp. 220–222)
1. What is weather?
2. To answer the following questions, use the letters in the drawing.
   a. In which area is most of the air in the atmosphere found?
   b. In which area is the air colder?

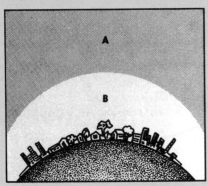

Changes in Air Temperature (pp. 223–225)
1. Why doesn't the surface of the earth heat evenly?

2. How do changes in air temperature affect weather?

Air Pressure (pp. 226–229)
1. How might a change in air pressure affect you?
2. Explain how a mercury barometer shows changes in air pressure.

Wind Speed and Direction (pp. 230–233)
1. Explain how wind is produced by differences in temperature.
2. How does an anemometer work?
3. What information is given in the Beaufort scale?

Water in the Air (pp. 234–237)
1. How does water vapor get into the air?
2. What is a hygrometer used for?

PROBLEM SOLVING

Use after page 225.
If warm air rises and cool air falls, why are the tops of mountains so cold?

Use after page 233.
When a hurricane passes over a city, people notice something strange about the speed and direction of the wind. At first the wind speed increases and comes from one direction. Then the wind speed decreases and stops. After a short time the high winds suddenly return, but from a different direction. Form a hypothesis about what is happening.

Use after page 237.
Sweat evaporating from your skin cools your body. On a humid day you feel warmer because sweat does not evaporate as quickly as on a dry day. Explain why.

Reading a Pictograph

For thousands of years, people have tried to fly. This pictograph shows how high people have flown at different times in history. Use it to answer the following questions.

1. What is the highest a spacecraft flew in 1970?

2. What is the highest an airplane flew in 1930?

3. Which is higher—the height to which a hydrogen balloon flew in 1933 or to which an airplane flew in 1930?

4. How much higher did an airplane fly in 1930 than in 1923?

5. How much higher did a jet fly in 1961 than in 1954?

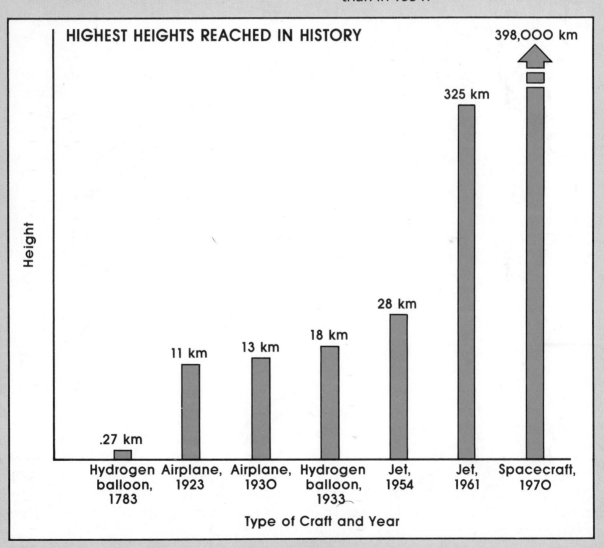

HIGHEST HEIGHTS REACHED IN HISTORY

398,000 km

325 km

28 km

18 km

13 km

11 km

.27 km

Height

Hydrogen balloon, 1783 | Airplane, 1923 | Airplane, 1930 | Hydrogen balloon, 1933 | Jet, 1954 | Jet, 1961 | Spacecraft, 1970

Type of Craft and Year

Chapter 12

The Solar System

LESSON QUESTIONS

The Sun and Its Family (pp. 242–245)

1. What is the difference between the rotation and the revolution of a planet?
2. Name the inner planets and the outer planets.

The Inner Planets (pp. 246–250)

1. Which planet is closest to the sun? Describe it.
2. How is Venus like Earth?
3. How long does it take the moon to revolve around Earth?
4. How is Mars like Earth?

The Outer Planets (pp. 251–256)

1. Which planet is the largest?
2. How many moons does Saturn have?
3. Describe the rotation of Uranus.
4. How long does it take Pluto to revolve around the sun?

Other Members of the Solar System (pp. 257–259)

1. Describe the orbit of a comet.
2. Explain how an asteroid is different from a meteor.

PROBLEM SOLVING

Use after page 250.

Which of the inner planets, do you think, would most likely support life? Give reasons for your answer.

Use after page 256.

Look at the table on page 255. What can you say about the relationship of planet size and day length? How does the speed of Jupiter's rotation compare with that of Earth? How does the distance of these planets from the sun compare with their size?

Use after page 256.

Imagine that Earth had 21 moons revolving around it, as Saturn does. Would the moons all be in the same phase at the same time? Explain your reasoning.

Use after page 259.

Sometimes, astronomers are able to predict a comet's exact orbit as it enters the solar system. This is because the planets Jupiter and Saturn can change a comet's course slightly. Form a hypothesis to explain how this might happen.

Use after page 259.

Pieces of rock, such as meteors, float through space for millions of years without changing. Yet when they enter our atmosphere, they burn up. Why does this happen?

Reading a Diagram

This diagram shows some of the largest moons in the solar system. It shows the diameter of each moon and the planet it revolves around. Use the diagram to answer the following questions.

1. Which is the largest moon shown? Which planet does it revolve around?

2. Which of the moons shown revolve around Jupiter?
3. Which of the moons shown is the largest of Saturn's moons?
4. Which of the moons are larger than the earth's moon?
5. How much bigger is Callisto than Rhea?

DIAMETERS OF THE LARGEST MOONS IN THE SOLAR SYSTEM

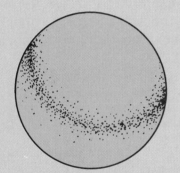

Ganymede
5276 km
(Jupiter)

Titan
5140 km
(Saturn)

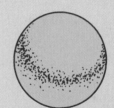

Callisto
4820 km
(Jupiter)

Triton
4800 km
(Neptune)

Io
3620 km
(Jupiter)

Moon
3476 km
(Earth)

Europa
3126 km
(Jupiter)

Rhea
1530 km
(Saturn)

Iapetus
1440 km
(Saturn)

Chapter 13

Using Food

LESSON QUESTIONS

From Cells to Systems (pp. 270–273)
1. What are the smallest parts of your body?
2. How are blood cells different from muscle cells?
3. What is an organ? Name two body organs.

Using What You Eat (pp. 274–275)
1. Why do you need food?
2. What happens to food during digestion?

Digestion in the Mouth (pp. 276–279)
1. Tell what each kind of tooth does.
   - a. incisor
   - b. canine
   - c. premolar
   - d. molar

2. Why is saliva important in digesting food?

The Digestive Path (pp. 280–284)
1. Where does food go after it is swallowed?
2. Describe the stomach.

Digestive System Problems (pp. 285–286)
1. Why isn't it a good idea to jump rope or swim right after eating a big meal?
2. What may cause a stomachache?
3. Which foods contain fiber?

PROBLEM SOLVING

Use after page 275.
People who are sick or recovering from operations are given only liquids and soft foods to eat. Why, do you think, are they given these kinds of foods?

Use after page 279.
Write the name of an important type of tooth or teeth used in eating each of the foods below. Which foods could be eaten without teeth?

raw carrots	applesauce
steak	french fries
gelatin	hot dog
popcorn	apple

Use after page 284.
Doctors recommend that people on a diet eat slowly. The doctors claim that after about 20 minutes these people will be less hungry. Use the facts you have learned about the digestive system to support this claim.

Reading a Bar Graph

Look at this bar graph. A bar graph can be used to compare information. This bar graph compares the number of Calories used up each hour that certain activities are performed. Use the bar graph to answer the following questions.

1. Which of the activities shown uses up the most Calories in 1 hour?

2. Which of the activities shown uses up the fewest Calories in 1 hour?
3. Which activity uses up more Calories in 1 hour, jogging or jumping rope?
4. Which activity uses up more Calories in 1 hour, walking or jogging?
5. How many more Calories are used up in playing baseball for 1 hour than in walking for 1 hour?

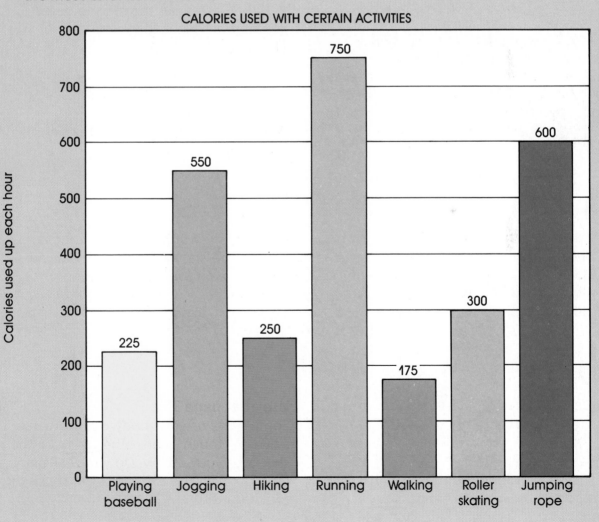

CALORIES USED WITH CERTAIN ACTIVITIES

Chapter 14

The Sense Organs

LESSON QUESTIONS

Sense Organs and the Brain (pp. 292–294)

1. What are the five sense organs? What are the five senses?
2. Explain how a nerve signal travels from your hand to your brain when you catch a ball.

The Eye and Sight (pp. 295–298)

1. Describe the parts of the eye.
2. How can people whose eye lenses do not bend light correctly be helped?
3. Describe three ways you can care for your eyes.

The Ear and Hearing (pp. 299–301)

1. Describe how the ear works.
2. Describe how you can care for your ears.

The Tongue and the Nose (pp. 302–304)

1. Describe the taste buds.
2. What tastes can the tongue detect?
3. Describe what happens when you sniff a flower.

The Skin (pp. 305–308)

1. Describe the parts of the skin.
2. How does skin protect you?
3. Describe how to care for the skin.

PROBLEM SOLVING

Use after page 298.
Staring at the sun can cause blindness. But it is painful to stare at the sun, so this cause of blindness is rare. During an eclipse of the sun, brightness is decreased. It is not painful to stare at the sun during an eclipse, but the sun still causes blindness. What part of the eye do you think is damaged by staring at the sun? Form a hypothesis to explain what might cause the blindness.

Use after page 298.
The small opening through which light enters the eye can change size. Which drawing shows the eye in bright light? Which one shows the eye in darkness? Give a reason for your choices.

A   B

Use after page 308.
Some parts of your body are more sensitive to touch than others. Pinch the skin over your elbow. Do you feel sharp pain? Explain the differences in sense of touch for different parts of the body.

SKILLS

Reading a Bar Graph

Sound can be measured in units called decibels (dB). This bar graph compares the loudness of different sounds. Use the bar graph to answer the following questions.

1. What is the loudest sound shown?
2. What is the softest sound shown?
3. What is louder–a jackhammer or heavy traffic?
4. How much louder is a rock band than light traffic?
5. Sounds that are greater than 130 dB are painful to humans. Which of the sounds shown here would be painful?

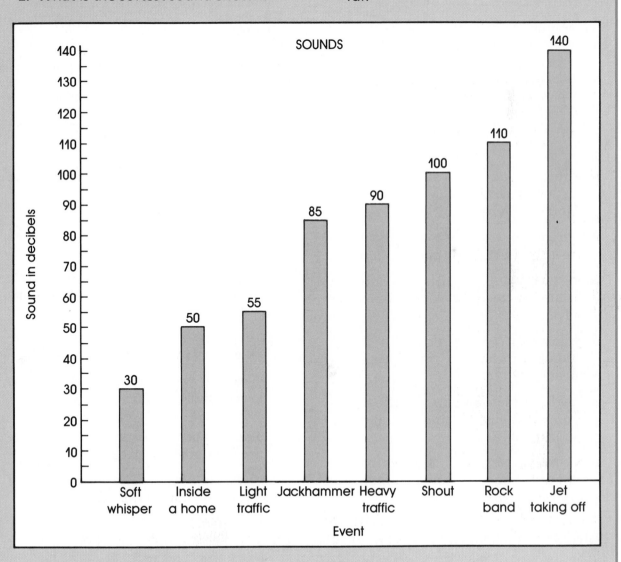

SOUNDS

Glossary

Key to Pronunciation

a apple, bat	i if, pig	sh she, wish	ə stands for:
ā ate, page	ī idea, fine	th think, moth	a in asleep
ã air, care	ng ring, sink	ᴛʜ the, bathe	e in garden
ä father, star	o ox, top	u uncle, sun	i in pencil
ch chest, such	ō owe, no	u̇ pull, foot	o in button
e egg, bed	ô orbit, saw	ü glue, boot	u in circus
ē even, me	oi oil, joy	zh usual, vision	
ėr earn, bird	ou out, mouse		

This Key to Pronunciation is adapted from *Scott, Foresman Intermediate Dictionary,* by E. L. Thorndike and Clarence L. Barnhart. Copyright © 1983 by Scott, Foresman and Company. Reprinted by permission.

adaptation (ad ap tā′shən) A body part or an activity that helps a living thing to survive. *p. 67*

air pressure The downward push of the air in the atmosphere. *p. 226*

algae A group of nonseed plants that do not have true roots, stems, or leaves. *p. 37*

anemometer (an ə mom′ə tər) An instrument used to measure wind speed. *p. 232*

animal population (pop yə lā′shən) A group of the same kind of animal living in an area. *p. 4*

asteroid (as′tə roid) A piece of rock that orbits the sun between Mars and Jupiter. *p. 258*

atmosphere (at′mə sfir) The air that surrounds the earth. *p. 222*

balance A tool for measuring mass. *p. 100*

barometer (bə rom′ə tər) An instrument used to measure changes in air pressure. *p. 228*

battery An object that changes chemical energy into electricity. *p. 158*

breaker A wave that falls as it comes close to shore. *p. 205*

calorie (kal′ər ē) A unit used to measure heat energy. *p. 135*

canines (kā′nīns) The pointed teeth next to the incisors. *p. 276*

carnivore (kär′nə vôr) An animal that eats only other animals. *p. 51*

cast fossil A rock with the exact shape of a plant or animal from long ago. *p. 189*

cell The smallest part of the body. *p. 270*

centimeter (sen′tə mē tər) A unit used to measure length. *p. 96*

circuit (ser′kit) The path along which negative charges move. *p. 155*

comet (kom′it) A mass of ice, frozen gases, and dust orbiting the sun. *p. 257*

community (kə myü′nə tē) All the plants and animals that live in an area. *p. 59*

complete circuit A circuit whose path is not broken. *p. 156*

compound machine A machine made of two or more simple machines. *p. 126*

conduction (kən duk′shən) The movement of heat energy through a solid. *p. 140*

conductor (kən duk′tər) Any material through which energy moves easily. *p. 141*

conifer (kō′nə fər) A seed plant that has cones. *p. 33*

consumer (kən sü′mər) A name given to animals, because they must eat food to get energy. *p. 49*

continental (kon tə nen′təl) **shelf** The underwater edge of a continent. *p. 200*

continental slope A steep drop in the ocean floor after the continental shelf. *p. 201*

convection (kən vek′shən) The movement of heat energy through a liquid or a gas. *p. 143*

core The inner layer of the earth. *p. 176*

crest The top part of a wave. *p. 205*

crust An outer layer of rock that covers the whole earth. *p. 176*

current (ker′ənt) A large moving river of water in an ocean. *p. 209*

current electricity A kind of electricity produced when negative charges move along a path. *p. 155*

degree Celsius (di grē′ sel′sē əs) A unit used to measure temperature. *p. 137*

density (den′sə tē) The mass in a certain volume. *p. 107*

dermis (dėr′mis) The inner layer of the skin. *p. 306*

dicot (dī′kot)   A plant whose seeds have two sections. *p. 30*

digestive system   The system used to break down food in the body. *p. 275*

drone   A male bee in a honeybee colony. *p. 11*

dry cell battery   A battery made of a zinc case, a carbon rod, and a chemical paste. *p. 158*

ear canal   The part of the ear between the outer ear and the eardrum. *p. 300*

eardrum   A thin tissue at the end of the ear canal. *p. 300*

Earth   The third planet from the sun. *p. 248*

energy   The ability to do work. *p. 114*

epidermis (ep ə dėr′mis)   The top layer of the skin. *p. 306*

esophagus (ē sof′ə gəs)   A tube that carries food to the stomach. *p. 280*

ferns   A group of nonseed plants that have roots, stems, and leaves. *p. 36*

food chain   The path by which energy passes from one living thing to another. *p. 55*

food web   Something that shows how all the animals in a community get energy. *p. 59*

fossil (fos′əl)   A trace of a plant or animal found in a sedimentary rock. *p. 180*

friction (frik′shən)   A force that slows down or stops motion. *p. 125*

fungi   A group of nonseed plants that cannot make their own food. *p. 37*

generator (jen′ə rā tər)   A machine that uses a magnet to make electricity. *p. 159*

graduate (graj′ü it)   A tool used to measure the volume of liquids. *p. 104*

gram   A unit used to measure mass. *p. 101*

herbivore (her′bə vôr)   An animal that eats only plants. *p. 50*

herd   A group of animals that live together, such as cattle, elephants, and whales. *p. 16*

hibernation (hī bər nā′shən)   A long period of deep sleep used by some animals to survive the winter. *p. 83*

high tide   The rise in the level of ocean water. *p. 207*

high−pressure area   An area of cool sinking air. *p. 227*

host   A living thing that a parasite lives on or in. *p. 19*

humidity (hyü mid′ə tē) Water in the air. *p. 236*

hygrometer (hī grom′ə tər) An instrument used to measure humidity. *p. 237*

igneous (ig′nē əs) **rock** A kind of rock formed from magma. *p. 181*

incisors (in sī′zərs) The teeth in the front of your mouth. *p. 276*

inclined plane A simple machine made of a slanted surface. *p. 123*

incomplete circuit A circuit whose path is broken. *p. 156*

inner ear The part of the ear shaped like a long coiled tube. *p. 300*

inner planets The four planets closest to the sun. *p. 244*

insect colony (kol′ə nē) A group of insects that live together. *p. 9*

insulator (in′sə lā tər) Any material through which energy does not move easily. *p. 141*

Jupiter (jü′pə tər) The fifth planet from the sun. *p. 251*

kilogram (kil′ə gram) A unit of mass equal to 1,000 g. *p. 101*

kilometer (kil′ə mē tər) A unit of length equal to 1,000 m. *p. 98*

kinetic (ki net′ik) **energy** The energy of motion. *p. 117*

large intestine A short tube through which water removed from food enters the body. *p. 282*

length A measured distance. *p. 96*

lens Part of the eye that bends light onto the retina. *p. 296*

lever A simple machine made of a bar or rod that turns on a point. *p. 120*

liter A unit of volume equal to 1,000 mL. *p. 105*

low tide The fall in the level of ocean water. *p. 207*

low-pressure area An area of warm rising air. *p. 227*

magnet An object that attracts metals such as iron and steel. *p. 160*

magnetic field The space around a magnet in which a magnetic force can be found. *p. 160*

mantle (man′təl) The middle layer of the earth. *p. 176*

Mars The fourth planet from the sun. *p. 249*

mass The amount of matter in an object. *p. 99*

matter Anything that has mass and takes up space. *p. 94*

Mercury (mer´kyər ē) The planet closest to the sun. *p. 246*

metamorphic (met ə môr´fik) **rock** A kind of rock formed when other kinds of rocks are changed by great heat and pressure. *p. 192*

meteor (mē´tē ər) A rock from space that has been pulled into the earth's atmosphere. *p. 259*

meteorite (mē´tē ə rīt) A meteor that strikes the ground. *p. 259*

meter A unit of length equal to 100 cm. *p. 98*

middle ear The part of the ear made up of three small bones. *p. 300*

migration (mī grā´shən) An adaptation of traveling great distances to survive the winter. *p. 80*

milliliter (mil´ə lē tər) A unit used to measure the volume of liquids. *p. 104*

mineral (min´ər əl) A pure, solid material found in the earth's crust. *p. 178*

molars (mō´lərs) The teeth with large flat tops found at the back of the mouth. *p. 277*

mold fossil An empty space in a sedimentary rock where a plant or animal used to be. *p. 188*

monocot (mon´ə kot) A plant whose seeds have one section. *p. 30*

moss A kind of nonseed plant that does not have true roots, stems, or leaves. *p. 37*

Neptune (nep´tün) The eighth planet from the sun. *p. 253*

nodule (noj´ül) A rock, which contains minerals, that is found on the ocean floor. *p. 213*

omnivore (om´nə vôr) An animal that eats both plants and other animals. *p. 52*

organ (ôr´gən) A group of tissues that works together in the body. *p. 272*

outer ear The part of the ear outside the head. *p. 300*

outer planets The five planets farthest from the sun. *p. 244*

parasite (par´ə sīt) An organism that lives on or in another organism and gets food from it. *p. 19*

plain The bottom of the ocean floor. *p. 202*

Pluto (plü´tō) The most distant planet from the sun. *p. 253*

pole The end of a magnet. *p. 161*

potential (pə ten´shel) **energy** Stored energy. *p. 118*

prairie (prâr′ē) **dog town**   An area where prairie dogs live. *p. 5*

precipitation (pri sip ə tā′shən) Water from the atmosphere that falls to the ground. *p. 234*

predator (pred′ə ter) An animal that hunts other animals for food. *p. 52*

premolars (prē mō′lərs)   The teeth with flat tops that are found between the canines and the molars. *p. 277*

prey (prā) An animal that is hunted for food by another animal. *p. 52*

producer (prə dü′sər) A name given to green plants, because they can make their own food. *p. 48*

property (prop′ər tē) Something that describes matter. *p. 95*

pulley   A simple machine made of a grooved wheel and a rope, chain, or belt. *p. 124*

queen   The bee that lays all the eggs in a honeybee colony. *p. 11*

radiation (rā dē ā′shən)   The movement of heat energy in waves. *p. 145*

resource (ri sôrs′) A useful material taken from the earth. *p. 212*

retina   The back wall of the eye. *p. 296*

saliva (sə lī′və) A juice released in the mouth. *p. 278*

Saturn (sat′ərn) The sixth planet from the sun. *p. 252*

school   A group of the same kind of fish that live together. *p. 13*

sedimentary (sed ə men′tər ē) **rock**   A rock formed from sediment. *p. 186*

sense organs   The parts of the body used for seeing, hearing, tasting, smelling, and touching. *p. 292*

simple machine   A machine made of very few parts. *p. 120*

small intestine (in tes′tən)   A long tube in the digestive system. Most of the food used by the body enters the bloodstream through the small intestine. *p. 281*

spores   The cells in nonseed plants used to reproduce. *p. 36*

static electricity   A kind of electricity made by friction. *p. 152*

stomach   A hollow organ that mixes food with digestive juices. *p. 280*

system   A group of cells, tissues, and organs that works together in the body. *p. 273*

taste buds   The cells in the tongue used for tasting. *p. 302*

temperature (tem′pər ə chər)   A measure of how fast the particles in matter move. *p. 136*

tendril (ten′drəl)   A thin coiled structure that helps a plant to climb. *p. 71*

tide   A change in the level of ocean water. *p. 206*

tissue (tish′ü)   A group of cells that works together to do certain jobs in the body. *p. 271*

tongue   An organ in the mouth that is part of the digestive system. *p. 278*

trench   A deep, narrow slit in the ocean floor. *p. 203*

trough (trôf)   The bottom part of a wave. *p. 205*

Uranus (yur′ə nəs)   The seventh planet from the sun. *p. 253*

Venus (vē′nəs)   The second planet from the sun. *p. 247*

volume (vol′yəm)   The amount of space an object takes up. *p. 103*

water vapor   Water as a gas. *p. 234*

weather   The condition of the air around us. *p. 220*

wet cell battery   A battery made of lead, water, and acid. *p. 159*

wheel and axle   A simple machine made of a wheel connected to an axle. *p. 123*

worker   A female bee that does most of the jobs in a honeybee colony. *p. 11*

Index

Adaptations, 66–83
  animal, 75–79
  plant, 71–74
  seasonal, 68–70, 80–83
Air pressure, 222, 225,
    226–229
Air temperature, 222,
    223–225
Alvin, 199–200
Anemometer, 232
Animal adaptations,
    75–79
  seasonal, 80–83
Animal populations, 4, 5,
    9, 15, 16
  flock, 2, 3, 15
  herd, 2, 3, 16–17
  pack, 2
  school, 2, 3, 13–15
  troop, 2
Animals
  as carnivores, 51
  as consumers, 49
  groups of, 2–17
  as herbivores, 50
  living together, 19–21
  as omnivores, 52–53
  as predators, 52

Asteroid, 258
Atmosphere, 222

Bacteria, 78
Balance, 100
Barometer, 228–229
Battery, 158
  dry cell, 158
  wet cell, 159
Beekeeper, 12
Bicycle, 127–128
Biological oceanographer,
    career as a, 262
Blood cells, 270–271
Bloodstream, in digestion,
    281–282
Brain, 272, 293
Breaker, 205

Calorie, 135
Calories, in food, 282
Canines, 276
Carnivore, 51

Cast fossil, 189
Cells, 270–271
  blood, 270–271
  muscle, 271
Centimeter, 96
Chef, career as a, 312
Chemical energy, 114, 116
  in batteries, 158–159
Chemical oceanographer,
    career as a, 262
Circuit, 155–157
  complete, 156
  incomplete, 156
  short, 157
Classification of plants, 24,
    26–43
  by flowers, 32
  by leaves, 34
  by reproduction, 27,
    36–42
Comet, 257
Community, 59
Complete circuit, 156
Compound machines,
    126–129
Conduction, 140–141
Conductors, 141
Conifers, 33–35

Conservationist, career as a, 86
Consumers, 49
Continental shelf, 200–201, 203
Continental slope, 201, 203
Convection, 143–144
Core, 177
Crest, of a wave, 205
Crust, 176
Crystals, 178–179, 181
Current electricity, 155–157
Currents, ocean, 209–210

Davis, Adelle, 313
Day, length of, 243
Degrees Celsius, 137, 224
Density, 107–109
Dental assistant, career as a, 312
Dentist, career as a, 312
Dermis, 306
Dicots, 30
  classification of, 31–32
Dietitian, career as a, 312
Digestion, 274–283
  in the mouth, 276–278
  path for, 280–283
Digestive system, 273, 275
  parts of, 274–283
  problems of, 285–286
Displacement, 105
Doctor, career as, 312

Drone, 10, 11
Dry cell battery, 158

Ear canal, 300
Eardrum, 300
Ears, 290, 292
  care of, 301
  and hearing, 299–300, 307
Earth, 248
  core, 177
  crust, 176
  mantle, 176, 182
  years and days on, 243
Earthquake, 205
Ecologist, career as an, 86
Electrical energy, 115, 116
Electrician, career as an, 168
Electricity, 150–165
  careers involving, 168
  current, 155–157
  and magnetism, 164–165
  making, 158–159
  static, 152–153
  from tidal power, 213
Electromagnet, 164
Energy, 114
  chemical, 114, 116
  electrical, 115, 116
  from food, 268, 274, 285
  forms of, 114–116
  heat, 115, 116, 132–165
  kinds of, 117–118

light, 115, 116
  mechanical, 115, 116
  from the ocean, 213
  sound, 115, 116
Engineer, career as an, 168
Epidermis, 306
Esophagus, 280
Eyes, 290, 292
  and sight, 295–297
  care of, 298
  laser surgery, 282

Farsightedness, 297
Ferns, 36
Fiber, 286
Fiber optics, 282
Flock, 2, 3, 15
Flowers, 29–32, 33
  groups of, 30–32
  parts of, 30
Food
  Calories in, 282
  careers involving, 312
  and digestion, 274–283
  eating proper, 286
  and energy, 268, 285
  from the ocean, 213
Food chains, 46, 54–56
Food webs, 46, 58–60
Force, 120
Forester, career as a, 86
Fossil fuels, 192
Fossils, 188–190

Friction, 125
  and static electricity,
    152
Fulcrum, 120
Fungi, 37, 38–39

Generator, 159
Geological oceanographer,
  career as a, 262
Geology, careers in, 262
Graduate, 104
Gram, 101
Gravity, 205, 207
Gulf Stream, 210

Halley's comet, 258
Hawaiian Islands, 202
Heart, 272
Heat, 134
Heat energy, 115, 116,
    132–165
  conduction of, 139–140
  convection of, 143–144
  radiation of, 145, 147
  and temperature,
    136–138
  unit of, 135
Heating mechanic, career
  as a, 168
Herbivore, 50
Herd, 2, 3, 16–17
Hibernation, 83
High tide, 206, 207
High-pressure area, 227

Hive, 9–10
Honeybees, 9–12
  colony of, 9–12
  dance of, 12
  drone, 10, 11
  queen, 10, 11
  worker, 10, 11
Host, 19
Humidity, 236–237
Hydroelectric power plant,
  159
Hygrometer, 237

Igneous rock, 181
Incisors, 276
Inclined plane, 123
Incomplete circuit, 156
Inner ear, 300
Inner planets, 246–250
Insect colony, 9
  ant, 10
  honeybee, 9–12
Insulators, 141
Intestine, 281–282
  large, 282
  small, 281

Jupiter, 251

Kilogram, 101
Kilometer, 98
Kinetic energy, 117–118

Large intestine, 282
Latimer, Lewis, 169
Lava, 182, 183, 196, 202
Leaves
  cactus, 74
  in conifers, 33, 34
  in flowering plants, 33
Length, 96–98
Lens, of the eye, 296, 297
Leopold, Aldo, 87
Lever, 120
Light energy, 115, 116
Lightning, 152
Liquids, measurement of,
  104
Liter, 105
Living things
  adaptations in, 66–83
  energy needs of, 48–49,
    54–55
  seasonal changes in,
    68–70, 80–83
  survival of, 64–85
Load, 120
Lodestone, 162
Low tide, 206, 207
Low-pressure area, 227

Machines
  compound, 126–129
  inclined plane, 123
  jack, 120–121
  pulley, 124
  simple, 120–125
  wheel and axle, 123

Magma, 181
Magnet, 160
   in generators, 159
Magnetic field, 160
Magnetism, 150, 160–162
   and electricity, 152–153
   of minerals, 179
Mantle, 176
Mariana Trench, 203
Mars, 249
Mass, 99–101
Matter, 94
   electric charges in, 152
   and heat, 135
   length of, 96–98
   mass of, 99–101
   measurement of,
      92–109
   properties of, 94–95
Measurement, 92–109
   of length, 96–98
   of mass, 99–101
   of volume, 103–105
   of time, 108
Mechanic, career as a,
   168
Mechanical energy, 115,
   116
Medical laboratory
      worker, career as a,
      312
Medicine, careers in, 312
Mercury (planet), 246
Metamorphic rock,
   192–193
Meteor, 259
Meteorite, 259

Meteorologist, career as a,
   262
Meter, 98
Metric ruler, 96
Microchips, 156
Mid-Atlantic Ridge, 202
Middle ear, 300
Migration, 80–81
Milliliter, 104
Mineralogist, career as a,
   262
Minerals, 178–180
   in the ocean, 212–213
   nodules, 212
   properties of, 179–180
Moisture, 222, 225, 234
Molars, 277
Mold fossil, 188
Monocots, 30
   classification of, 31–32
Moon, of Earth, 248
   and tides, 205, 207
Morabito, Linda, 263
Mosses, 37
Mount Vesuvius, 182
Mouth, 290
Muscle cells, 271

Natural gas, 213
Navigation engineer,
   career as a, 263
Nearsightedness, 297
Negative charge,
   152–153, 155
Neptune, 253
Nerve cells, 293–294

Nerve endings
   in the ear, 300, 301
   in the eye, 296
   in the hands, 294
   in the nose, 304
   in the skin, 306
   in the tongue, 302
Nerve signals, 294
Nodules, 213
Nonseed plants, 36–42
   algae, 37
   ferns, 36
   fungi, 38–39
   mosses, 37
Nose, 290, 292
   and sense of smell,
      302–304
Nurse, career as a, 312

Ocean floor, 200–203
Oceanographer, 199
Oceanography, careers in,
   262
Oceans, 196–215
   currents in, 209–210
   floor of, 200–203
   and gravity, 205–207
   life in, 201, 203
   movement of, 204–208
   resources of, 212–213
   saltiness of, 199
   tides in, 206, 207
   waves in, 204–205
Omnivore, 52
Operator (power plant),
   career as a, 168

Organs, 272
Outer ear, 300
Outer planets, 251–255
Ovary, 30, 33

Pack, 2
Paleontologist, career as a, 262
Parasite, 19
Petals, 30, 32
Petroleum geologist, career as a, 262
Physical oceanographer, career as a, 262
Pioneer spacecraft, 258
Pistil, 30
Plain, 202
Planets, 243, 244
    inner, 244, 246–250
    outer, 244, 251–255
Plant adaptations
    for protection, 74
    seasonal, 68–70
    for sunlight and water, 71–74
Plants
    classifying, 24, 26–43
    food production in, 48
    grouping, 25
    reproduction in, 27–42
Pluto, 254
Poles, of a magnet, 161
Pompeii, 182
Positive charge, 152–153
Potential energy, 118
Prairie dog town, 5–7

Precipitation, 234
Predators, 52
Premolars, 277
Prey, 52
Producers, 48
Properties of matter, 95
Pulley, 124

Queen bee, 10, 11

Radiation waves, 145
Rain gauge, 236
Rainfall, measurement of, 236
Reproduction in plants, 27
    with cones, 29, 33, 35
    with flowers, 29–32, 33
    by seeds, 27, 29–32
    without seeds, 27, 36–42
Resources, of the ocean, 212–213
Respiratory system, 272
Retina, 296, 297
Robots, 125, 203
Rocks, 174
    igneous, 181–183
    metamorphic, 192–193
    sedimentary, 185–187

Saliva, 278
Salt, in oceans, 199
Saturn, 252, 258
School, 2, 3, 13–15

Sedimentary rock, 185, 186
Seed-bearing plants, 27, 29–35
    with cones, 33–35
    flowering, 29–32
Seismograph, 182
Sense organs, 290–305
    and the brain, 293
    ears, 290, 292, 299–301, 307
    eyes, 290–298, 307
    nose, 290, 292, 302–304
    skin, 290, 292, 304–307
    tongue, 292, 302
"Shooting star," 259
Short circuit, 157
Simple machine, 120
Skin, 290, 292, 305–307
    as protection, 307
    as sense organ, 305–306
Small intestine, 281
Solar system, 240
    planets, 243
    sun, 242
Sound energy, 115, 116
Sound waves and hearing, 299–300
Spores, 36
Stamen, 30
Static electricity, 152
Stomach, 280
    problems with, 285–286
Sun, 242
Surtsey, 196
Systems, 273

Taste buds, 302
Teeth, 276–277
    canines, 276
    incisors, 276
    molars, 277
    premolars, 277
Temperature, 136–138
    air, 222
    measurement of, 137
Tendrils, 71
Thermometers, 136, 224
Tidal power, 213
Tide, 206, 207
Tide pools, 208
Tissues, 271
Tongue, 278, 292
    and taste, 302
Trench, 203

Troposphere, 222–223
Trough, of a wave, 205
Tsunami, 205

Uranus, 253

Venus, 247, 258
Volcano, 182, 196, 202
Volcanologist, career as a, 262
Volume, 103–105
Voyager spacecraft, 258

Water vapor, 234
Waves

breaker, 205
    crest of, 205
    radiation, 145
    trough of, 205
Weather, 218–259
Weather satellite, 224
Wet cell batteries, 159
Wheel and axle, 123
Wildlife biologist, career as a, 86
Wind, 230
    speed and direction, 222, 225, 230–232
Wind chill, 224
Worker bee, 10, 11

Year, length of, 243

Credits

Science Source/Photo Researchers, Inc.; *b.r.* Silver Burdett & Ginn. 79: Silver Burdett & Ginn. 80: Jon Hull/Bruce Coleman. 81: *t.* Gary Zahm/Bruce Coleman; *m., b.* E.R. Degginger. 82: *t.* © Gregory Scott/Photo Researchers, Inc.; *b.* © Charlie Ott/ Photo Researchers, Inc. 83: Warren Gurst/Tom Stack & Associates. 86: *l.* Frank Miller/Photo Researchers, Inc.; *r.* © M.P. Kahl/ Photo Researchers, Inc. 87: Gary Zahm/Bruce Coleman.

Unit Two 90: *l.* E.R. Degginger; *r.* Michael Tamborino/Leo deWys, Inc. 91: *l.* Brian Parker/Tom Stack & Associates; *r.* © Grapes-Michaud/Photo Researchers, Inc.

Chapter 5 Opener: Cezus/Click, Chicago; E.R. Degginger; © Peter D. Kaplan/Photo Researchers, Inc.; © Hank Morgan/ Science Source/Photo Researchers, Inc.; © Craig Aurness/West Light. 94–95: Silver Burdett & Ginn. 96: © 1987 Bill Weems/ Woodfin Camp & Associates. 97–98: Silver Burdett & Ginn. 99: *t.* IMAGERY; *b.* G. Rancinen/Sygma. 100: *t.l.* Robert Carr/ Bruce Coleman; *t.r., m.l., b.l.* Silver Burdett & Ginn. 101–102: Dan De Wilde for Silver Burdett & Ginn. 103–105: Silver Burdett & Ginn. 106: Dan De Wilde for Silver Burdett & Ginn. 107: Silver Burdett & Ginn. 108: *l.* Granger Collection; *t.r.* © Manfred Kage/Peter Arnold, Inc.; *b.r.* © National Bureau of Standards/U.S. Department of Commerce. 109: Silver Burdett & Ginn.

Chapter 6 Opener: Dept. of Mechanical Engineering, MIT. 114: *l.* Yoram Lehman/Peter Arnold, Inc.; *r.* © Tim Davis/Photo Researchers, Inc. 115: *t.* © Van Bucher/Photo Researchers, Inc.; *b.* Owen Franken/Stock, Boston. 116: *t.l.* Keith Michalek/ Taurus Photos; *b.l.* Silver Burdett & Ginn; *b.r.* © 1987 Focus/Woodfin Camp & Associates. 118: © Charles Harbutt/Archive Pictures, Inc. 119: Silver Burdett & Ginn. 120: IMAGERY. 122–123: Silver Burdett & Ginn. 124: *l.* IMAGERY; *r.* Silver Burdett & Ginn. 125: *l.* © Tom McHugh/Photo Researchers, Inc.; *r.* Yoav/Phototake. 126–129: Silver Burdett & Ginn.

Chapter 7 Opener: Silver Burdett & Ginn. 134: *t.* Dan De Wilde for Silver Burdett & Ginn; *m.* Larry Lawfer/The Picture Cube; *b.* IMAGERY. 136: Silver Burdett & Ginn. 137: *t.l.* Charles Schmidt/Taurus Photos; *t.r.* Fairfield/Taurus Photos. 137: Silver Burdett & Ginn. 139–140: Dan De Wilde for Silver Burdett & Ginn. 141–144: Silver Burdett & Ginn. 145: *t.* H. Gritsher/ Peter Arnold, Inc. 146: Dan De Wilde for Silver Burdett & Ginn. 147: IMAGERY.

Chapter 8 Opener: © Steve Northup/Black Star; © Tom McHugh/Science Source/Photo Researchers, Inc.; Robert McKenzie/Tom Stack & Associates. 152: *t.* Silver Burdett & Ginn; *b.* © 1987 Shelley Grossman/Woodfin Camp & Associates. 154–155: Silver Burdett & Ginn. 156: *t.l., m.l.* Phil Harrington/Peter Arnold, Inc.; *b.r.* courtesy IBM/E.R. Degginger. 157–158: Silver Burdett & Ginn. 160–163: Silver Burdett & Ginn. 164: E.R. Degginger. 165: Silver Burdett & Ginn. 168: *t.* Owen Franken/Stock, Boston; *b.* David Davidson/Tom Stack & Associates. 169: Silver Burdett & Ginn.

Unit Three 172–173: *t.* NASA; *m.* Grant Heilman Photography. 173: *t.r., inset* Tony Arruza/Bruce Coleman; *b.r.* Grant Heilman Photography.

Chapter 9 Opener: Emilee M. Mead; Silver Burdett & Ginn. 177: *t.l.* NASA; *b.l.* E.R. Degginger; *m.* © Jerry Irwin/Photo Researchers, Inc.; *t.r.* E.R. Degginger; *b.r.* Vince Streano/Bruce Coleman. 178–181: Silver Burdett & Ginn. 182: *t.* Silver Burdett & Ginn; *b.l.* J.D. Griggs/U.S. Geological Survey; *b.m.* R.W. Decker/U.S. Geological Survey; *t.r.* Peter Menzel/Stock, Boston. 183: Frank Siteman/Stock, Boston; *inset* Silver Burdett & Ginn. 184: Dan De Wilde for Silver Burdett & Ginn. 185: B.F. Molina/ Terraphotographics/BPS. 186: *t.* Wardene Weisser/Bruce Coleman; *b.* Dan De Wilde for Silver Burdett & Ginn. 187: Silver Burdett & Ginn. 188: E.R. Degginger/Bruce Coleman. 189: *t.* Breck Kent; *b.* Tom Stack & Associates. 191–192: Silver Burdett & Ginn. 193: Brian Parker/Tom Stack & Associates.

Chapter 10 Opener: Culver Pictures; © Hara; James M. King. 199: Rod Catanach/Woods Hole Oceanographic Institution. 201: Zig Leszczynski/Breck Kent. 230: *l.* Robert Ballard/Woods Hole Oceanographic Institution; *r.* Stefan Marse/Woods Hole Oceanographic Institution. 204: *t.* Tom Stack & Associates; *b.* Jonathan Wright/Bruce Coleman. 205: Silver Burdett & Ginn. 207: E.R. Degginger. 208: IMAGERY; *inset* E.R. Degginger. 211: Dan De Wilde for Silver Burdett & Ginn. 212: E.R. Degginger. 213: *t.* © 1987 Harry Gruyaert/Woodfin Camp & Associates; *b.* E.R. Degginger. 214: Dan De Wilde for Silver Burdett & Ginn.

Chapter 11 220: *t.l.* E.R. Degginger; *b.l.* Jonathan Barkan/The Picture Cube; *r.* Eric Carle/Shostal Associates, Inc. 221: *t.* Frank Siteman/The Picture Cube; *b.* A. Pierce Bonudo/Uniphoto. 224: *t.l.* Silver Burdett & Ginn; *b.l.* © Hank Morgan/Photo Researchers, Inc.; *b.r.* NASA. 226: Stuart Craig/Bruce Coleman. 228: Silver Burdett & Ginn. 229: Frederic Lewis. 231–232: IMAGERY. 233: Dan De Wilde for Silver Burdett & Ginn. 235–236: *l.* Silver Burdett & Ginn; *r.* E. Williamson/The Picture Cube. 237: Breck Kent.

Chapter 12 © Chesley Bonestell/Space Art International; © William K. Hartmann/Space Art International; © Pamela Lee/ Space Art International; © Ludek Pesek/Space Art International. 242: NASA. 243: Dan De Wilde for Silver Burdett & Ginn. 245: Silver Burdett & Ginn. 247: NASA. 248: E.R. Degginger; *inset* NASA. 249–259: NASA. 262: *t.* Michal Heron; *b.* Ken Lax/The Stock Shop. 263: NASA.